PHalarope Books

PHalarope books are designed specifically for the amateur naturalist. These volumes represent excellence in natural history publishing. Each book in the PHalarope series is based on a nature course or program at the college or adult education level or is sponsored by a museum or nature center. Each PHalarope book reflects the author's teaching ability as well as writing ability. Among the books:

At the Sea's Edge:
An Introduction to Coastal Oceanography
for the Amateur Naturalist
William T. Fox
illustrated by Clare Walker Leslie

Exploring Tropical Isles and Seas:
An Introduction for the Traveler and Amateur Naturalist
Frederic Martini

The Seaside Naturalist:
A Guide to Nature Study at the Seashore
Deborah A. Coulombe

Suburban Wildlife:
An Introduction to the Common Animals
of Your Back Yard and Local Park
Richard Headstrom

The Wildlife Observer's Guidebook
Charles E. Roth, Massachusetts Audubon Society

Sanford A. Moss

A SPECTRUM BOOK

Prentice-
Hall, Inc.,
Englewood
Cliffs,
New Jersey
07632

SHARKS

An Introduction
for the Amateur Naturalist

Library of Congress Cataloging in Publication Data

Moss, Sanford A.
    Sharks—an introduction for the amateur naturalist

    (PHalarope books)
    "A Spectrum Book."
    Includes bibliographical references and index.
    1. Sharks. I. Title.
QL638.9.M67 1984   597'.31   84-2047
ISBN 0-13-808312-6
ISBN 0-13-808304-5 (pbk.)

10 9 8 7 6 5 4 3 2 1

ISBN 0-13-808312-6

ISBN 0-13-808304-5 {PBK.}

Credits: Photographs 1-2, 3-3, 3-8, 4-11, 7-2, 8-11, 11-2, 11-4 by
Ronald A. Campbell; illustrations 4-1, 4-16, 5-6, 6-5, 7-1, 7-3, 7-5, 9-1,
9-2, 9-3, 9-6, 9-7 by Alfred J. Feeley.

Editorial/production supervision: Marlys Lehmann
Cover design: Hal Siegel
Cover illustration: Fredric Sweney
Manufacturing buyers: Doreen Cavallo/Frank Grieco

This book is available at a special discount when ordered in
bulk quantities. Contact Prentice-Hall, Inc., General
Publishing Division, Special Sales, Englewood Cliffs, N.J. 07632.

210866

Prentice-Hall International, Inc., *London*
Prentice-Hall of Australia Pty. Limited, *Sydney*
Prentice-Hall Canada Inc., *Toronto*
Prentice-Hall of India Private Limited, *New Delhi*
Prentice-Hall of Japan, Inc., *Tokyo*
Prentice-Hall of Southeast Asia Pte. Ltd., *Singapore*
Whitehall Books Limited, *Wellington, New Zealand*
Editora Prentice-Hall do Brasil Ltda., *Rio de Janeiro*

Contents

Foreword

Prior to World War II sharks were of little more than academic interest, and commercial fishermen in the United States regarded them as merely a nuisance. Shark attacks on bathers were relatively rare, as indeed they are today. With the deployment of troops in South Pacific waters shortly after Pearl Harbor, however, ships were torpedoed and planes were shot down and sailors and airmen found themselves in unfamiliar waters. Shark attacks on servicemen occasionally occurred and stories of such encounters had a profound effect on the morale of the survivors. The Department of Defense recognized that a shark repellent was badly needed to allay fears, and the search was on for an effective shark deterrent. In a remarkably short time, scientists at Woods Hole, Massachusetts, found that ammonium acetate (a product of decomposed shark flesh) repelled smooth dogfish. Believing the acetate ion was the responsible factor, it was replaced with the cheaper copper acetate and blended with a water soluble wax and nigrosine dye into a six-ounce packet enclosed in a plastic cover conspicuously labeled "Shark Chaser." This packet became part of the survival gear of U.S. air force and naval personnel and served effectively to reassure those who flew above or sailed on South Pacific seas.

In the years following World War II, it was reported with increasing frequency that Shark Chaser did not always work and that in some instances sharks even ate it. When the effectiveness of the packet was seriously questioned, a conference was convened in April 1958 in New Orleans to formulate basic research approaches that would lead to the development of more effective shark deterrents. The conference was sponsored by Tulane University and the American Institute of Biological Sciences (AIBS), with funding from the Office of Naval Research and Navy Bureau of Aeronautics.

The 34 scientists gathered in New Orleans from Australia, Japan, South Africa, and the United States decided in their first day of deliberations that all too little was known about the nature of the "enemy," and they were convinced that a basic knowledge of the biology and behavior of sharks was essential to an understanding of the shark-hazard problem and the development of more effective shark deterrents. The scientists recommended that basic investigations dealing with the taxonomy, physiology, anatomy, distribution, migrations, life history, behavior, ecology, and immunology of sharks be initiated.

To promote and coordinate these basic studies on a worldwide basis, the AIBS Shark Research Panel was established in June 1958, and in the succeeding 25 years more was learned about the biology and behavior of sharks than in the previous 250 years, thanks to the untiring efforts of scientists in many parts of the world. Sanford Moss was one of the dedicated scientists who became involved, as early as 1961, with studies of the biology and behavior of sharks and the development of shark deterrents while pursuing graduate work at Cornell University and the Lerner Marine Laboratory of Bimini, the Bahamas. In the succeeding years, after receiving his doctorate degree from Cornell, Dr. Moss contributed significantly to our understanding of feeding mechanisms and feeding behavior of sharks. His publications in professional journals and his participation in numerous symposia attest to the high regard his colleagues have for his work, much of which is engagingly presented in this volume.

A symposium, in which Dr. Moss participated, was recently held in New Orleans and dealt with current advances in our understanding of the biology and behavior of sharks. It was the consensus of participants that the shark is a highly successful vertebrate, admirably adapted to its environment, and one from which we may learn much about our own rich structural and functional heritage. I believe the present volume will serve to place the shark in perspective, for few are dangerous and many are beneficial. In the process of learning to cope with them, we will undoubtedly find that sharks contribute to a better understanding of humans and of some of the ailments that plague them.

Perry W. Gilbert, Professor Emeritus
Neurobiology and Behavior, Cornell University
Director Emeritus, Mote Marine Laboratory
Sarasota, Florida

Preface

It is a major purpose of this book to describe the biology of sharks and their allies, the skates and rays, placing particular emphasis on exciting new information about those adaptations that help to make them the marvelous creatures they are.

As a group of fascinating animals, sharks suffer from at least two misconceptions perpetuated by biologists and the public alike. The first is that these fish routinely carry out mayhem on any human bather so unfortunate as to unwittingly venture near them. The second misconception is that sharks represent a primitive vertebrate that somehow has survived in suspended animation for 350 million years of evolutionary history. In this sense sharks are looked on as living fossils—animals that are supposed to represent in living form what life might have been like hundreds of millions of years ago.

Although it is true that sharks have attacked and will attack swimmers, the incidence of such attacks is hardly commensurate with the publicity that attends them. As threats to human life, sharks are statistically greatly overshadowed by lightning, honeybees, or rabid pets. Latter-day biologists now recognize that sharks are marvelously adapted to do what they must. As predators that sit at the apex of the food pyramid, sharks cannot afford the luxury of great numbers of species or of large populations of single species. They have evolved adaptations that are shared only by what we usually consider "higher" vertebrates. They also have some adaptations absolutely unique to them.

Sharks, for example, have larger brains than any other group of "lower," "cold-blooded" vertebrates (indeed, a few sharks have constant, warm body temperatures). They have a unique system of coping with the osmotic stress of living in salt water, and they have a reproductive system more like that of humans than is found in any other group of submammalian animals. We now know that sharks are aware of exceedingly small electrical fields—fields so weak as to be nearly incomprehensible to us. They have feeding mechanisms that are unequaled by any other group of vertebrates in terms of diversity and capabilities. Sharks swim so efficiently that aerodynamic and hydrodynamic engineers are studying them to better design ships and rockets. To think that these fish are primitive is to ignore reality.

This, then, is a celebration, a celebration of the shark by way of a careful look into the intricacies and patterns of its biology.

In writing this book I depended heavily on the advice and counsel of a large number of friends and colleagues who also are enamored of elasmobranchs. Although the list is too long to include here, I would like to acknowledge the following who were especially helpful: Drs. Ron Campbell, John Lien, Roger Cressey, Peter Klimley, Ad Kalmign, Bob Griffith, and Bill Raschi. Barbara Edinger Moss read and thoughtfully criticized the entire manuscript. Sue Lacey, Jeanne Tartaro, Wes Pratt, Chuck Stillwell, Jim Feeley, and George Benz made valuable contributions. Special acknowledgment is made to my principal teachers—the men who first opened my eyes to the wonders of sharks, who facilitated my study of them, and who critically appraised that study. These are Drs. Daniel Merriman, Edward C. Raney, William N. McFarland, and especially Dr. Perry W. Gilbert.

For the reader who may be stimulated to read further about the aspects of sharks discussed in this book, Additional Readings are included at the conclusion of each chapter. These references are not exhaustive, but they provide an introduction to a specific literature. They include important review articles, standard books on the subject, and recent articles dealing with specific aspects of elasmobranch biology. Because most of the elasmobranch species mentioned in the book are referred to by their common names, a list of the appropriate scientific names is included as an appendix.

For Barbara,
without whom this book
would not have been written

1

Sharks—
The Negatives

The number of people who dislike sharks greatly outnumbers their fans. Sharks are considered villains for a number of reasons. The commercial fisherman finds nets and other gear damaged by sharks, loses part of his catch to them, and complains that they drive more valuable fish from the fishing grounds. Sport fishermen likewise believe that sharks present unfair competition; and oceanographers worry that these animals will cut valuable gear from deep mooring lines. Worst of all, however, is the knowledge that sharks can attack and kill humans swimming in the water. A human maimed or a life lost is a tragedy of the highest order, and there is economic damage done as well to resorts that have inadvertently hosted shark attacks. Sharks, then, are not considered by most people to be lovable creatures. What are the dimensions of the shark problem? And what can be done about it? These are the questions that are addressed in this chapter.

DAMAGE TO FISHING OPERATIONS

Elasmobranchs can have an adverse effect on fisheries in various ways. Most often this involves damage to the gear—usually nets—used to catch commercially important fishes. Large sharks entangled in fragile gill nets used by salmon and herring fisheries can completely rip them apart. Shrimp fishermen in the Gulf of Mexico encounter sharks that bite holes in the cod ends of their trawls, releasing valuable catches of shrimp. Special electrodes that are fastened to the trawls and that emit pulses of direct current are effective in preventing such damage. Sharks also seriously damage gear and catches in purse seine fisheries where large seines are set around entire schools of fish such as tuna, menhaden, or mackerel. The bottom of the seine is "pursed" under the school, which is then brailed or vacuumed into the hold of the fishing vessel. Sharks (and frequently, porpoises) feeding on schools of desirable fish are entrapped with them. The sharks are a problem because they can bite through the

3

seine, damaging this valuable net and releasing the catch. The porpoises pose a different kind of problem. Because they are protected by marine mammal laws, even their inadvertent capture can incur stiff fines to the captain and owner of the fishing vessel. There is, therefore, incentive to develop techniques that will frighten sharks and porpoises from the fishing gear without also causing the loss of the desired species.

Sharks also present problems to the operators of fixed fishing gear such as fish traps or weirs. A case in point involves the trap fishery for cod off Newfoundland. The trap is a "box" of netting with a mesh floor that can be raised to the surface to remove the catch. Cod are directed to the trap by long "leaders" of netting set across the paths these fish take in their migrations or daily feeding movements (Figure 1–1). A single cod trap is worth about $16,000, which is equal to the entire annual income of the group of fishermen who join together to buy and operate one. The trap fishery season for cod in Newfoundland is only six weeks long and is coincident with the appearance of basking sharks in those waters. If a basking shark of even average size—9 meters (30 feet) long, weighing more than 3 tons—blunders into a cod trap (and this happens from 50 to 130 times a summer), it is a disaster for the fishermen. Gear is destroyed, and scarce fishing time is lost while the nets are recovered and re-

Figure 1–1. The type of trap used to catch codfish off the coast of Newfoundland.

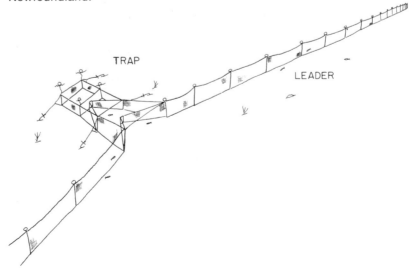

Figure 1–2. Basking sharks are enormous fish.

paired. In 1981, for example, these sharks destroyed about $40,000 of gear off Newfoundland. Even though a basking shark may be worth as much as $2000 for its meat, fins, and oil (Figure 1–2), this is not adequate compensation for the damage done.

Sharks are also disruptive to fisheries in which large fish are taken by hook and line. Sport fisheries for tuna and billfishes have long been bothered by sharks that attack hooked fish. Because mutilation by sharks disqualifies a record trophy, sport fishermen consider sharks anathema. The economic loss, however, is slight compared to the damage done by sharks to the catches of commercial longline fishermen.

At today's prices a single longline-caught giant tuna or swordfish can be worth over $1000. Frequently such catches are mutilated by sharks before they are landed. In some sets of longline gear over 50 percent of the fishes hooked are attacked. The damage amounts to millions of dollars annually on a worldwide basis and promotes unfriendly confrontations between sharks and fishermen.

Not all damage to commercial fishing interests is done by large sharks. When schools of small ones are abundant and unwanted, they can fill trawls and (so fishermen claim) frighten commercially important species from the fishing grounds. A trawl full of spiny dogfish is a discouraging sight to fishermen. Not only are they difficult to remove from the webbing of the net, but their sharp teeth and venomous spines make them hazardous to handle. In terms of damage to the gear and lost fishing time, this one species has a considerable impact on the ground fishery of the northwest Atlantic.

Populations of some elasmobranchs that are not presently commercially valuable may have important ecological interactions with exploited populations of bony fishes. Although difficult to assess quantitatively, the following may happen. The inshore ground fishery of the northwest Atlantic exploits several species of flounder, as well as cod and haddock. Little skates, winter skates, and thorny skates, which are seldom used, are also abundant in this area. When the contents of a trawl are dumped on the deck of a fishing vessel, the skates are culled and are usually returned to the ocean alive. The food fishes are kept. Because the preferred prey of the skates is coincident with those of the flounders, one effect of the fishery is to remove the teleost competitors of the skates. The long-term effect may be to concentrate an ever-increasing share of the total biomass in skates at the expense of the flounders, cod, and haddock. There is some evidence that this in fact has been happening on fishing grounds such as the Georges Banks. The economic price to the fisheries could prove to be large indeed.

OCEANOGRAPHIC STUDY COSTS

With the emergence of the modern study of oceanography has come yet another negative effect of elasmobranchs. Certain applications of oceanographic gear require that current meters, salinity and temperature sensors, hydrophones, and other instruments be tethered by synthetic fiber mooring cables at depths greater than 1000 meters. These instruments and the data recorded by them can then be recovered. The tensions placed on deep mooring cables are immense. Fishes, including sharks, have only to nick these taut lines to cause them to part. A particular menace to moored instruments are deepwater dogfishes of the genus *Isistius.* Damage to the cables, however, is not confined to sharks. Bony fishes, including triggerfishes, paralepids, and lancet fishes, are responsible for some of the damage. Such cables are at greatest risk during the first five days of deployment. During this period the rate of loss is as high as 10 to 20 per 1000 buoy days. After some passage of time this drops to about 6 per 1000 buoy days.

One idea about this pattern of loss is that bioluminescent animals such as jellyfishes become entangled in the cable. At first they create patches of luminescence that are attacked by the sharks and other fishes. Their teeth slice the cables, causing the failure. As time progresses, the cable ensnares more organisms until it become completely luminescent and thus attracts fewer hopeful predators. Suggestions have been made to counter this kind of gear damage—from painting the cables to make them luminescent to begin with, to searching for better and stronger cable materials. Among such materials are several new thermoplastics that may abate this problem.

DAMAGE TO VALUABLE WILDLIFE

In addition to damaging and competing with sport, commercial, and scientific interests, sharks have sometimes been blamed for the demise of natural resources valued by humans. In particular, sea turtles and marine mammals such as seals, porpoises, and sea otters are sometimes taken as food by large predaceous sharks—a practice that does not win them conservation awards. In Chapter 11 it is suggested that pelagic sharks regularly attack porpoises. In a study of shark–porpoise interactions, a captive bottlenose porpoise was trained at the Mote Marine Laboratory near Sarasota, Florida, to attack sharks. This training was initially carried out using dead sharks. When the switch to live sharks was made, the porpoise successfully drove away a sandbar shark. Unfortunately, funding was not available to continue this interesting program.

Other marine mammals occasionally attacked by large sharks include Hawaiian monk seals found in the northwest Hawaiian Islands. The shark most responsible for this predation is the tiger shark. The tiger also is noted for its attacks on sea turtles, including the endangered leatherback turtle.

The white shark is an important predator of seals and sea lions. Off the coast of southern Australia, frequented by the white shark, seals are a staple in its diet. The same is true along the coast of California, where white sharks consume elephant seals, harbor seals, and California sea lions. Of recent interest are reports that white sharks regularly attack sea otters in this region.

The return of the sea otter to California waters is a success story in the annals of wildlife management. This population of otters, however, has failed to continue to expand in recent years and has yet to reoccupy fully its former territory. The reasons for the slowdown in the growth rate of this population have not been pinpointed, but it is established that as many as 15 percent of dead sea otters found washed ashore are killed by white sharks. This fact prompted the suggestion that white shark populations off the California coast have grown in response to increases in marine mammal populations. This idea cannot be tested because no prior census of white sharks was conducted in these waters. It is difficult to see how animals with the low reproductive potential of white sharks could significantly increase their population density in such a short time. White sharks, particularly small specimens, were periodically reported in abundance in southern California well before the marine mammal protection act came into being in 1972.

The fact that white sharks feed on marine mammals leads to the suggestion that, having a seal-like or otterlike form as a "search image," these sharks are likely to attack human swimmers, who share that general form. This brings us to the question of attacks by sharks on humans.

SHARK ATTACKS ON HUMANS

Concern for the danger presented by sharks to humans has undergone dramatic shifts in the course of the last 50 or so years. Those people whose livelihoods depend on the sea, particularly in tropical waters, have always had a healthy respect for sharks. Eighteenth- and nineteenth-century seafaring fishermen also appreciated the danger represented by sharks, as witnessed by such famous paintings as Winslow Homer's "Gulf Stream" and John Singleton Copley's "Watson and the Shark" (Figure 1–3). In the early part of this century, however, some American naturalists, led by the redoubtable undersea explorer William Beebe, adopted a disdainful attitude toward the danger a few sharks represent. Beebe's pioneering underwater exploits took him to the tropical waters of the Caribbean and the eastern Pacific, where he failed to encounter aggressive sharks. Displaying his penchant for the well-turned phrase, Beebe declared in immensely popular books that sharks were "chinless cowards." His influence extended not only to the American public, but to his scientific peers at his home base, the American Museum of Natural History, as well. There ichthyologists, leaning on Beebe's experiences, expressed doubts about the ferocity of sharks.

All this seems curious today with our retrospective knowledge of the data concerning shark attacks. We know, for instance, that before 1930 (when Beebe was making his observations), there had been well over 200 documented unprovoked attacks on humans by

Figure 1–3. *Watson and the Shark*. John Singleton Copley, American, 1738–1815. Oil on canvas, 72 × 90¼ inches (182.9 × 229.2 centimeters). Gift of Mrs. George von Lengerke Meyer. (Courtesy, Museum of Fine Arts, Boston.)

sharks worldwide, and that at least 116 of these resulted in human fatalities.

Our newer understanding of the dimensions of the shark "problem" stemmed from two developments. The first involved the ship sinkings and airplane downings of World War II that resulted in indisputable evidence of shark attacks—attacks that caused troop morale problems so severe they had to be addressed by military leaders. The second development was the introduction and popularization of scuba (self-contained underwater breathing apparatus), which resulted in great numbers of divers exploring the realm of **9** large pelagic sharks.

These developments resulted in 1958 in the creation of the Shark Research Panel, a union of scientists chaired by Dr. Perry W. Gilbert and supported initially by the U.S. Office of Naval Research and the American Institute of Biological Sciences. The tasks coordinated by the Shark Research Panel included gathering documentation about shark attacks (both retrospectively and as they occurred), facilitating research and disseminating information on the basic biology of sharks, and setting up standards and procedures by which various antishark measures could be evaluated.

The success of this venture has been considerable. By 1963 data had been gathered and published that documented more than 1100 cases of shark attacks in the world. The continuing collection and updating of these data provide a significant perspective from which to assess the questions presented by shark attacks on humans. The work on antishark measures produced some workable shark deterrents and stimulated the search for more. The coordination of shark research by the panel resulted in a number of important conferences, several significant publications, and increased interest in the biology of sharks by working scientists. In a real sense our new understanding and appreciation of sharks is a product of the activities of the Shark Research Panel.

The data on shark attacks distinguish between "provoked" shark attacks—those resulting from deliberate attempts to molest or disturb sharks (grabbing by the tails or spearing them)—and "unprovoked" attacks. It is this latter category (where sharks, for no apparent reason other than the presence of human swimmers, seize the opportunity and attack someone in the water) that is of most concern to science and the public alike. What are the conditions under which such attacks occur? How frequently do they happen, and where? What kinds of sharks are involved? What are the important stimuli that provoke the attacks? These and other questions can be addressed through the data contained in the shark attack file.

Shark attacks are unlikely events. Given the millions of bathers and swimmers that venture into the world's oceans each year, probably fewer than 100 individuals actually are attacked by sharks in an average year. About 25 percent of the recorded attacks are fatal. As a source of mortality in the world, shark attacks are statistically inconsequential. Many more people die each year from slipping in bathtubs than die from shark attacks. Yet the specter of a shark attack looms large in the minds of most people. The vision of the uncontrolled and uncontrollable fury of a predatory shark is a terrible one indeed. It creates its own macabre sort of fascination, which acts to draw attention to sharks as elements of mayhem rather than the minor problem that they really are.

Shark attacks can occur at any time or place where swimmers venture into the water. It is true, however, that the frequency of attacks is proportional to the number or density of human swimmers. Because fewer swimmers prefer colder water temperatures, most shark attacks occur in warmer waters. This density dependence resulted in an earlier interpretation of the pattern of shark attacks that suggested such events were confined to water temperatures higher than about 68 °F (20 °C). Today we know this is not the case. White sharks in particular normally venture into colder waters, and attacks from this and other species have occurred in waters as cold as 50 °F.

The density effect results also in the observation that more shark attacks occur near shore (in shallow water) than offshore. Most bathers, in fact, swim from beaches rather than from boats. More attacks also occur in daytime rather than at night, when swimmers are generally absent from the water. Our understanding of the crepuscular and nocturnal feeding activity of many species of sharks predicts that the night should be a particularly dangerous time to swim. There is some evidence to suggest that more shark attacks occur in the late afternoon than at other times of the day. This is when the activity patterns of sharks and swimmers come closest to overlapping.

The mortality figures show that about 25 percent of the individuals attacked by sharks succumb to their injuries. The legs of swimmers are attacked most frequently, although many shark bites occur on the hands and arms, usually as the victim attempts to ward off the attacker. Because of the sharp teeth and huge biting forces of the jaws, shark bites lacerate deeply and occasionally dismember. The factors resulting in death stem from the dual problems of shock and massive hemorrhage of severed major blood vessels, creating unacceptably low blood pressure. The victims are usually not close to immediate medical care. Delays in bringing the person to shore, where procedures to reduce bleeding and to treat shock can be carried out, increase mortality.

The types of wounds suffered by shark attack victims are important sources of information about the identifications and behavior of the sharks responsible. Not all of the wounds are caused by feeding sharks. Often damage comes from the fins rather than from the jaws. The stiffly supported pectoral fins of a speeding shark, armed with sharp placoid scales, can severely gash a swimmer. Other injuries result from the "bumping" behavior of sharks, where they test prey by ramming it. These attacks can damage bathers and may be preparatory to more serious feeding attacks.

An analysis of the bites on shark attack victims shows that a high percentage of the wounds—as many as 60 percent—are caused only by the teeth of the upper jaw. Slashes of the upper jaw are typical of courting advances of some male sharks (Chapter 8). It would be useful to know if the attacking sharks that cause similar wounds on humans are males. If this were the case, then it could be surmised that many cases of shark attack are not the result of feeding forays, but rather courtship advances. This raises a question about the perception of a human victim by an attacking shark. What are the important stimuli that provoke sharks?

Our understanding of the feeding behavior of sharks suggests that the distant sensing of a human swimmer in the water is by olfaction and sound reception. An injured bather bleeding from a cut, or a scuba diver trailing speared and bleeding fish, presents a rich olfactory stimulus. The movements of swimmers and bathers inevitably result in pulsed, low-frequency sounds that are most attractive to predaceous sharks. Both attractants can prove irresistible to a hungry shark. Nor does a swimmer have to be injured to produce an olfactory corridor for a shark to follow. Most shark attack victims are not bleeding prior to their misfortunes. The human body constantly produces secretions (sweat, sebum, urine, tears, and substances from the mucous membranes of mouth, nose, urinary, and reproductive tracts), and one or more of these may contain chemicals highly attractive to sharks. If some shark attacks are courtship advances, perhaps certain secretions contain substances similar to shark sex attractants or pheromones. Our present knowledge, however, makes this idea pure speculation. We know little about shark sex attractants.

When a human swimmer and a shark draw closer to each other, the sensory tools used by the shark increase in number. Eventually vision comes into play. The cryptic coloration of most sharks means that a shark can see an intended victim better than the victim can see the shark. Color and contrast can play a role in shark attacks. In eastern Australia, for example, light-skinned bathers are attacked by sharks more frequently than those with dark skins. Tests on the color and brightness sensitivity of sharks demonstrate that lighter, brighter objects are attacked more often than dark, less bright ones. The highly visible survival yellow of life vests proved so attractive in tests that it was called "yum-yum yellow" by the experimenters.

Having made auditory, olfactory, and visual contact with a potential victim, an approaching shark next receives "near-field" sound, the vibrations that stimulate its lateral line system. A swimmer, aware of a nearby shark and responding by wildly thrashing in the water, greatly increases the amount of information sent out on this channel. If the shark has not yet decided to attack, these vibrations can tip the scale against the swimmer. Tests with captive, hungry sharks show they will strike at the source of commotion in the water, even in the absence of other stimuli.

The shark, within a few centimeters of its objective, encounters the electric fields generated by any living thing in water. A wounded animal, with its skin or integument ruptured, produces an enhanced electric field. This phenomenon explains the puzzling observation that, having attacked a swimmer, a shark may again attack the same individual despite the presence of other nearby swimmers or rescuers. The injured victim emits a more intense electric field. This could guide the shark to repeat its attacks.

The hierarchy of sensory perception concludes when a shark makes physical contact with its prey. If the shark has not yet made the ultimate decision to bite, the "bump" allows the shark to make it. Attacking sharks that are warded off by swimmers who hit them on their snouts are probably in this undecided category. An unyielding object may not be worth the effort for these rather unmotivated sharks.

Motivation, of course, is the key to understanding shark attacks on humans. Some dangerous sharks (like the white shark) normally feed infrequently. After the time from the last meal passes a critical point, the motivation to eat probably increases. Little is known about hunger in sharks except to suspect that, as in other vertebrates, hormone or neurotransmitter levels in critical parts of the brain are important. The motivation to feed can be enhanced by social facilitation. Feeding frenzies are expressions of this. A group of sharks investigating one or more swimmers becomes exceedingly dangerous if an initial attack occurs.

Hunger, however, does not play a role in attacks by gray reef sharks in the Pacific. These animals will, under certain circumstances, aggressively defend their individual space or home territories (Chapter 5). They seem to react primarily to the visual stimulus of the victim, and they signal the threat that they perceive by their own behavior and displays. A shark attacking from hunger should not be expected to communicate its intentions so clearly and unambiguously.

Whatever the cause of the attack—hunger, defense, or sex—it

is clear that few species of sharks attack humans. Fewer than 30 species (out of more than 800 kinds of elasmobranchs) are considered dangerous. Generally these are sharks that grow to large size, are predaceous eaters of fish and/or marine mammals, and frequent warmer coastal waters where swimmers are apt to be in the water.

DANGEROUS SHARKS

Those sharks that pose threats to swimmers and divers fit three categories: (1) sharks that are always a danger to swimmers; (2) sharks that on occasion are known to attack humans; and (3) sharks that because of their size and predatory behavior could be dangerous, but for which reliable attack records are rare.

Category 1, the most dangerous sharks, includes three principal species: white shark, tiger shark, and bull shark. Together these species account for the majority of attacks on humans. All grow to large size, frequent shallow waters, and have diets that normally include human-sized objects.

The white shark—the shark of *Jaws* fame—is responsible for more attacks than any other species. Although it is found in all seas, the white shark is best known for its attacks on humans in the cooler waters of southern Australia, the east coast of South Africa, the middle Atlantic coast of North America, and the American Pacific coast north of Point Conception, California. In this last region there have been 39 unprovoked shark attacks recorded since 1950, all known or presumed to have been caused by white sharks. Three fatalities were recorded. The presence of white sharks there and the frequency of their attacks on humans correlates with breeding populations of marine mammals, especially seals and sea lions. While many areas of coastal waters host these sharks as transients, there is evidence that some whites may take up more or less permanent residence near seal colonies.

Because of its enormous size (up to 7 meters in length, weighing over 3 tons), its serrated teeth, and a search image for prey of the size and shape of a human, the white shark presents a terrifying sight to a swimmer. Fortunately the survival record of humans attacked by white sharks in California is high (about 90 percent). Elephant seals, sea lions, and sea otters are often observed bearing wounds attributable to unsuccessful white shark attacks. This suggests that these sharks are either tentative or inefficient predators. Perhaps this species is best adapted as a scavenger of infrequently encountered dead whales rather than as an active predator on fish or mammals (see Chapter 4). Still, white sharks are the greatest single danger to human swimmers.

The second most dangerous elasmobranch is the tiger shark. This species is also large, growing to lengths approaching 6 meters and weights in excess of a ton, and is distributed in all tropical and subtropical seas. They have probably caused more attacks on humans in warm-water environments than any other shark. Like the white shark, the tiger ordinarily eats large food items, particularly sea turtles. A sea turtle lolling at the surface may present, to the tiger shark, an image similar to a human swimmer or surfer paddling a surfboard. Tiger sharks often enter shallow waters near beaches and in embayments and are attracted to sites of garbage and carrion disposal, as well as other regions of intensive human activity.

Tiger sharks have large mouths with heavy, serrated teeth (Figure 1–4) and jaws capable of exerting great biting pressure. While they appear leisurely and deliberate in their feeding attacks, once the teeth engage the prey, they are tenacious and difficult to dislodge. An attack by even a small tiger shark is serious.

The bull shark is the final member of the "Gang of Three" most dangerous sharks. Again, this species is widely distributed in warm coastal waters around the world. In summer it also works its way into temperate latitudes. Its habit of entering brackish and fresh waters makes it a threat to bathers in rivers and lakes. Bull shark at-

Figure 1–4. The serrated teeth of the tiger shark are useful in carving up large, tough prey.

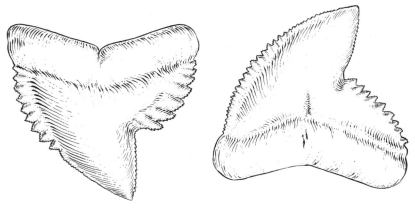

tacks in Lake Nicaragua and the Zambezi River of South Africa attest to this. In addition to its distribution, the bull shark presents a menace because of its large size (to 3 meters) and diverse food habits. Of all sharks, the bull shark is most often found to have the remains of other sharks in its stomach, along with those of sea turtles and porpoises. It normally attacks prey of human dimensions.

Most bull shark attacks on humans are in rivers and along continental coastlines of Central America, South Africa, and Queensland in Australia. It is less frequently encountered near oceanic islands. Sometimes large bull sharks are found in shallow bays, yet do not molest swimmers. One interpretation of this docility is that these are female sharks ready to give birth and are inhibited from feeding at that time. But whenever a bull shark is encountered in the water it should be treated with great respect. These are powerful, dangerous sharks.

The second category of dangerous sharks includes those that are known to attack humans, but do so relatively infrequently This list consists of the large hammerhead sharks and a number of requiem sharks such as the gray reef shark, dusky shark, lemon shark, Ganges River shark, blue shark, and spinner shark. It also includes the sand tiger, ragged tooth shark, and nurse shark.

The whaler sharks of the genus *Carcharhinus* are particularly troublesome in certain parts of the world. The dusky shark, known as the black whaler in Australia, has a bad reputation in that country. It also has attacked people in Florida. In the islands of the cental Pacific, the gray reef shark is an aggressive shark known for its defensive, territorial displays and attacks on divers and submersibles (Chapter 5). In the same region the blacktip reef shark, which grows only to 4 or 5 feet (1.2 to 1.5 meters) in length, attacks the legs of fishermen wading in shallow lagoons.

Several species of hammerheads, including the great hammerhead, smooth hammerhead, and scalloped hammerhead, should always be considered dangerous sharks. Some grow to immense size (well over 20 feet—6.5 meters—in length) and are predaceous, highly maneuverable fishes. Where they encounter swimmers, their reputations are not good.

The sand tiger and ragged tooth sharks of the genus *Odontaspis*, although responsible for few shark attacks in the Western Hemisphere, are justly feared sharks in South Africa and Australia. Blue sharks are usually found well away from beaches and coastlines, but scuba divers and others swimming in deep waters frequented by this species are sometimes harassed by them. Blue sharks often travel in groups. This means that feeding frenzies of blue sharks can easily develop—a fact that divers should respect.

Its inshore habitat in tropical and subtropical seas puts the lemon shark well within reach of swimmers and divers. Although attacks by lemons are rare, the Pacific lemon shark responds aggressively to attacks upon it. When provoked, this shark can be expected to retaliate. Another retaliatory elasmobranch is the nurse shark. Usually docile and sluggish in appearance, this species can be roused to ferocity when cornered or speared, or by pulling its tail. Its small mouth and teeth do not present a danger, but its crushing biting power does. The Ganges River shark is known to attack humans in India. Unfortunately, so little is known about the biology of this species that not much can be reported about it except to remark that, in a closely circumscribed region, it is a dangerous shark.

The final category of dangerous sharks is comprised of those for which specific data on attacks are rare, but because of their size and behavior should be treated with caution. Into this group fall the mako shark and a host of medium-sized whaler sharks such as the sandbar shark, Galapagos shark, and the oceanic whitetip shark. Most of these have oceanic distributions (sandbar shark excepted) which keep them away from centers of human activity. The scarcity of attacks attributed to them is probably related to this fact. In general, any predaceous mackerel or requiem shark species which reaches 5 feet (1.8 meters) or more in length should be treated with concern by divers and bathers.

ANTISHARK MEASURES

Shark attacks are rare events, yet they are terrifying and newsworthy, and thus have considerable economic and emotional importance. Consequently many measures have been proposed to eliminate them. The most successful have included systematic and sustained attempts to depress populations of large sharks in the regions of popular bathing beaches. This has been best accomplished in South Africa near Durban and in southeastern Australia near Sydney by programs known as "meshing." Meshing involves setting panels of gill netting at overlapping intervals offshore from and parallel to the beaches (Figure 1–5). The nets are regularly visited and maintained, sharks caught in them being killed and disposed of.

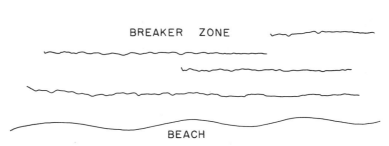

Figure 1–5. "Meshing" to protect bathing beaches from large sharks involves setting gill nets in overlapping rows outside of the breaker zone. The nets are nearly 1000 feet (305 millimeters) in length and overlap each other by about 66 feet (20 meters).

Meshing began in Durban in 1952. Twenty years later the catch of large sharks had dropped to a fifteenth of the initial catch despite nearly four times the amount of net being used. Few, if any, shark attacks have occurred at those beaches since the program began. A similar experience is reported from Australia.

Bathing beaches in some parts of the world have been protected by the permanent installation of wire and wood fencing. Although expensive, it is effective. Attempts have also been made to protect beaches by bubbling air from perforations in pipes laid on the ocean floor. Such "bubble curtains" have sometimes controlled the movements of bony fishes. Tests of this system with captive tiger sharks, however, showed it to be ineffective in altering their behavior.

Attempts to control sharks often involve chemical shark repellents, or substances or devices that ward off attacks by individual sharks. The earliest attempts to develop a repellent resulted in Shark Chaser, a combination of a presumed chemical irritant (copper acetate) and a visual mask (nigrosine dye). These components, packaged in a cake with a water-soluble wax base, were found by testing supported by the U.S. Navy in the 1940s to be effective in discouraging the approach of some species of sharks under some conditions. Accordingly, Shark Chaser was distributed as standard survival gear to U.S. military personnel and later was made available to the general public. Further testing has shown that Shark Chaser fails to repel sharks under intensive feeding conditions (feeding frenzies). The search for other chemical repellents has not been very successful. Recently, however, it was observed that sharks refuse to attack the Moses sole *(Pardachirus marmoratus)*, a small flounder native to the Red Sea. This fish secretes a material rich in a toxin, paradoxin, which is responsible for the repellent effect. Paradoxin is an unstable, expensive chemical compound. Tests show that its repellent effect is equalled or exceeded by some common industrial surfactants used as strong detergents. The surfactants are cheap and readily available. Now hope springs anew that a reliable, inexpensive chemical shark repellent can be developed to protect humans from sharks.

Aside from chemical antishark measures, a variety of electrical, sonic, and mechanical devices have been tested as defenses against shark attack. These include electrical barriers (which can be dangerous to swimmers), suits of maillike armor, broadcasts of killer whale calls, and a variety of weapons to kill or disable sharks. The weapons range from powerheads (bangsticks), which fire shotgun shells into sharks upon contact with them, to speargun-fired darts tipped with strychnine-filled syringes. Darts have been designed which inject gaseous CO_2 into the body cavity of an attacking shark, or which deploy drogue chutes. Both of these devices attempt to alter radically the swimming dynamics of a threatening shark, thereby disabling it. Most of these measures are also dangerous to the swimmer, for all of them can cause stimuli (pulsed sounds, blood, rapid movements) that can attract more sharks and trigger a feeding frenzy.

The most promising of the mechanical shark defenses is a large, dull-colored plastic bag with an inflatable collar. This device, dubbed the "shark screen," has proved to be successful in a number of field tests. The idea is for the threatened individual to deploy the bag and crawl into it. The shark screen presents a nonstimulating image to the shark and is a barrier to electrical and olfactory attractants (bleeding, etc.) emitted by the person. This may prove to be a cheap and important piece of survival gear with which to equip boats and planes.

Perhaps the best means of preventing a shark attack is to know and obey the following simple set of rules, succinctly stated by H. David Baldridge in his book *Shark Attack.*[1]

ADVICE TO BATHERS AND SWIMMERS

1. Always swim with a companion, and do not wander away from a coherent group of other bathers and thereby isolate yourself as a prime target for attack.

2. Do not swim in water known to be frequented by dangerous sharks. Leave the water if sharks have been recently sighted or thought to be in the area.

3. Although not conclusively proven, human blood is highly suspect as an attractant and excitant for sharks. Keep out of the water if possessed of open wounds or sores. Women should avoid swimming in the sea during menstrual periods.

4. It is not always convenient, but very murky or turbid water of limited underwater visibility should be avoided if possible. In any event, a particularly watchful eye should be maintained for shadows and movements in the water. If there is any doubt, get out at once.

5. Refrain from swimming far from shore where encountering a shark becomes more probable.

6. Avoid swimming alongside channels or dropoffs to deeper water which provide ready access for a shark.

7. Leave the water if fish are noticed in unusual numbers or behaving in an erratic manner.

8. Take no comfort in the sighting of porpoises, for this does not at all mean sharks are not about.

9. Avoid uneven tanning of the skin prior to bathing in the sea, for sharks apparently respond to such discontinuities of shading.

10. Use discretion in terms of putting human waste into the water.

11. Avoid swimming with an animal such as a dog or a horse, etc.

12. Take time to look around carefully before jumping or diving into the sea from a boat.

13. Particularly at low tide, take notice of a nearby offshore sandbar or reef that might have entrapped a shark.

[1] Baldridge, H.D., *Shark Attack* (Anderson, S.C.: Droke House/Hallux, Inc., 1974).

14. Avoid swimming at dusk or at night when many species of sharks are known to be searching for food.

15. It just might be a good idea to select other than extremely bright colors for swimwear.

16. Never, in any form or fashion, molest a shark no matter how small it is or how harmless it might appear.

17. Keep a wary eye out towards the open sea for anything suggestive of an approaching shark.

ADVICE TO DIVERS

1. NEVER DIVE ALONE. Not only might the very presence of your diving buddy deter the shark, but together you have a far better chance of becoming aware of a nearby shark in time to take effective countermeasures. Furthermore, if something did happen to you, at least there would be assistance close at hand.

2. Do not in any way provoke even a small shark—not by spearing, riding, hanging on to its tail, or anything else that might seem like a good idea at the time. Even a very small shark can inflict serious, possibly fatal, injury to a man.

3. Do not keep captured fish, dead or alive, about your person or tethered to you on a stringer or similar device. Remove all speared or otherwise wounded fish from the water immediately.

4. Do not spearfish in the same waters for such extended periods of time that curious sharks may be drawn to the area by either your quick movements or an accumulation of body juices from numbers of wounded fish.

5. Leave the water as soon as possible after sighting a shark of reasonable size, even if it appears to be minding its own business. Submerged divers, as opposed to surface swimmers, have a better chance of seeing a shark making investigatory passes prior to being committed to attack. Use smooth swimming strokes, making no undue commotion, in reaching the safety of a boat or the shore. To the greatest extent possible, remain submerged where chances are greater for watching the shark and countering its charge if attack occurs. Do not count on the shark either circling or passing close at hand without contact before it makes a direct run.

6. Use discretion in the choice of wetsuit colors in terms of conditions and sea life prevalent in the waters of intended operations. Do not take a chance on being mistaken for the area's natural prey of choice.

7. Carry a shark billy or plan to use the butt of a speargun for this purpose if necessary. Such devices have been shown to be very effective in holding an aggressive shark at bay until its ardor cools.

8. Take full advantage of your submerged position and limits of visibility to be aware always of nearby movements and presences. Shark attack case histories indicate that such vigilance had played a major role in lowering injuries and mortality rates among diver-victims.

9. Do not maneuver a shark into a trapped position between yourself and any obstacle such as the beach, reef, sandbar, or possibly even a boat.

10. As with swimmers, do not wander away from an established group of other divers and possibly give thereby an appearance of fair game. Avoid diving at dusk and at night.

ADVICE TO VICTIMS

1. Try to remain calm and take full advantage of weapons available to you.

2. Use any object at hand to fend off the shark while at the same time not intentionally provoking it further.

3. Keep fully in mind the limitations of such devices as power-heads, gas-guns, spearguns, etc., and do not expect them to accomplish the impossible. Such weapons, if used improperly, may serve only to further agitate the shark.

4. Use available spears and knives first to fend off the shark, and attempt to wound the fish only as a last resort. Sharks often seem to react with increased vigor to efforts at sticking it with pointed objects.

5. Discretion should be used in making aggressive movements towards a shark. One that had not yet committed itself to attack might be "turned on" by such movements if interpreted by it as a threat. On the other hand, quick movements towards a shark close at hand might produce a desirable startle response.

6. Once contact has been made or is imminent, fight the shark as best you can. Hit it with your bare hands only as a last resort. Probing the shark's eyes especially and perhaps also its gills has often turned the tide. Startle responses which at least buy valuable time have been produced occasionally by such actions as shouting underwater or blowing bubbles. Do anything that comes to mind, for the seconds or minutes of time during which the shark might withdraw as a result could be sufficient to effect your rescue.

7. Most shark attacks produce wounds that are readily survivable. Bleeding should be controlled as quickly as possible—even before the victim has been brought ashore. Because of danger of infection, treatment by a physician is indicated even where wounds are relatively minor.

Unfortunately, the question of shark attack is a subject considered far out of proportion to its magnitude. The reaction of many people to even the sighting of a distant shark borders on hysteria. Sharks of all kinds, not just the few dangerous ones, are frequently slaughtered or injured just because "they are sharks." Far more appropriate than hysteria is admiration: admiration of their grace and economy of movements, admiration of their evolutionary diversity, admiration of their physiological perfection, and admiration of an animal that is in nearly every way our superior when we enter its environment.

ADDITIONAL READING

Ames, J.A., and V. Morejohn. "Evidence of white shark, *Carcharodon carcharias*, attacks on sea otters." *California Fish and Game,* 66, no. 4 (1980), 8–22.

Baldridge, H.D. *Shark Attack.* Anderson, S.C.: Droke House/Hallux, Inc., 1974.

Brodie, P., and B. Beck. "Predation by sharks on the grey seal *(Halichoerus grypus)* in eastern Canada." *Can. J. Fish. Aquat. Sci.,* 40 (1983), 267–271.

Clark, E., and S. Chao. "A toxic secretion from the Red Sea flatfish, *Pardachirus marmoratus* (Lacepede)." *Bull. Sea. Fish Res. Sta. (Haifa),* 60 (1973), 53–56.

Coppleson, V.M. *Shark Attack.* Sydney: Angus and Robertson, 1958.

Ellis, R. *The Book of Sharks.* New York: Grosset and Dunlap, 1976.

Gilbert, P.W., ed. *Sharks and Survival.* Boston: D.C. Heath, 1963.

Gilbert, P.W. "The shark: Barbarian and benefactor." *Bioscience,* 18, no. 10 (1968), 946–950.

Gilbert, P.W., and C. Gilbert. "Sharks and shark deterrents." *Underwater Journal,* 5, no. 2 (1973), 69–79.

Gruber, S.H. "Shark repellents: Perspectives for the future." *Oceanus,* 24, no. 4 (1981), 72–76.

Martini, F.H., and K. Welch. "A report on a nonfatal shark attack in the Hawaiian Islands." *Pacific Science,* 35, no. 3 (1981), 237–240.

Miller, D.J., and R.S. Collier. "Shark attacks in California and Oregon, 1926–1979." *California Fish and Game,* 67, no. 2 (1980), 76–104.

Nelson, D.R., "The silent savages." *Oceans Magazine,* 1, no. 4 (1969), 8–22.

Randall, J.E., and G.S. Helfman. "Attacks on humans by the blacktip reef shark *(Carcharhinus melanopterus)*." *Pacific Science,* 27, no. 3 (1973), 226–238.

Seaman, W., ed. "Sharks and Man—A Perspective." Gainesville, Fla., Florida Sea Grant Program, Report Number 10 (1976).

Stimson, P.B. "Synthetic-fiber deep-sea mooring cables: Their life expectancy and susceptibility to biological attack." *Deep-Sea Research,* 12, no. 1 (1965), 1–8.

Zahuranec, B.J., ed. "Shark repellents from the sea," AAAS Selected Symposium Series 83, Boulder, Col.: Westview, 1983.

2

Sharks— The Positives

For animals that are symbols of things sinister and which inspire almost universal fear and distrust, elasmobranchs have a surprising amount of value and number of uses. Products produced from sharks, skates, and rays run from human and animal food to leather, curios, biomedical products, and educational uses (Figure 2–1). The list grows longer every year.

The harvest that provides these products is not without its consequences on natural populations of sharks and rays, and the history of such ventures has been one of boom and bust. Elasmobranchs have low reproductive capacity, and it has proved easy to reduce significantly the stocks of sharks targeted for exploitation.

ELASMOBRANCHS AS FOOD

The single greatest use of sharks has been for their meat. The flesh of elasmobranchs is not oily (most fats and oils are stored in the liver), so it is easy to salt or dry—a major consideration in tropical climates where perishability is a factor. In the United States the public has been reluctant to accept shark meat as food, although today it is beginning to be found more frequently on restaurant menus and in fish markets.

World shark fisheries landed about 400,000 metric tons of elasmobranchs annually through the middle part of the 1970s. Total landings have risen since because of increased exploitation of elasmobranchs in the Indo-Pacific. Much of this meat is dried, salted, or minced and prepared in a variety of dishes favored in Oriental cuisine.

The mackerel sharks are probably the most flavorful, with the flesh of makos, thresher sharks, white sharks, and porbeagles comparing favorably with that of swordfish. The salmon shark of the northern Pacific is particularly delectable. Its meat is salmon red, just like that of its favorite food. Other sharks and rays esteemed for

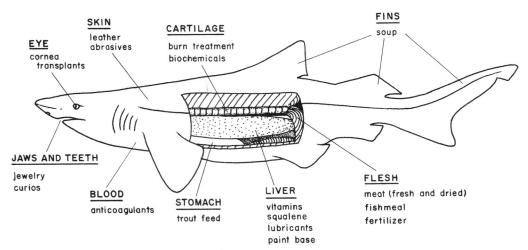

EYE
cornea
transplants

SKIN
leather
abrasives

CARTILAGE
burn treatment
biochemicals

FINS
soup

JAWS AND TEETH
jewelry
curios

BLOOD
anticoagulants

STOMACH
trout feed

LIVER
vitamins
squalene
lubricants
paint base

FLESH
meat (fresh and dried)
fishmeal
fertilizer

Figure 2–1. The usable shark. Some of the products available from sharks.

their flesh include the spiny dogfish, which is marketed as "flake" in England and is much sought after by Norwegian fishermen. Sixgill sharks, sawfish, blue sharks, school sharks, and other requiem sharks have been or are now utilized as human food. The edibility of the dasyatid rays is not well known, although the thick pectoral fin musculature of these animals is exceedingly delicious. The larger species of electric rays also make a tasty dish, particularly in a fish chowder or stew. So delicious are the pectoral fins of skates that they historically have been utilized as a substitute for scallop meat.

Despite its good taste, people are reluctant to try eating shark meat. In the early part of this century, I.A. Field, who studied elasmobranchs at the Marine Biological Laboratory at Woods Hole, Massachusetts, promoted the culinary qualities of smooth dogfish. He had these sharks cooked in the laboratory commissary and served to the staff under a disguised name. Encouraged by the success of this venture, Field sent smooth dogfish to northern New England resort hotels, where the guests enjoyed their meals—until they found they had been eating shark! Later attempts by the U.S. Fish & Wildlife Service to market spiny dogfish in the United States under the label "grayfish" met with about the same result.

One cause for the lack of enthusiasm about eating elasmobranchs is due to uncertainty about how it should be prepared. In particular are concerns about the removal of urea from the meat be-

28

fore cooking. This is not a problem if the shark is properly eviscerated, butchered, and refrigerated shortly after catching. Prolonged soaking of the meat in cold, salted water is not necessary unless the shark was not bled or cleaned promptly after being caught. One cooks elasmobranch steaks or fillets just like any other fish, and a delicious, nourishing meal results.

Consumer studies supported by the Texas A & M University Sea Grant College Program surveyed acceptance of and prejudices about eating shark meat. Three species of shark—Atlantic sharpnose, bonnethead, and blacktip—were sampled along with a favored teleost, redfish (channel bass). Tasters did not know what kind of fish they were eating. Sharpnose shark was rated with the redfish, and only slightly ahead of the bonnethead and blacktip shark. Meat from larger sharks was preferred over that from smaller sharks of the same species; unsoaked meat was preferred over that soaked in fresh water for one hour.

Elasmobranchs can be cooked just like teleosts. Some representative recipes follow:

Shark Teriyaki[1]

2 pounds fresh shark fillets, cut in one-inch chunks
1 can (16 ounces) pineapple chunks
½ cup soy sauce
¼ cup sherry (optional)
2 tablespoons brown sugar
1 teaspoon ground ginger
1 teaspoon dry mustard
1 clove garlic, crushed
1 green pepper, cut in one-inch squares
Cherry tomatoes, mushrooms, onions (optional)
Bamboo or metal skewers

Drain pineapple chunks reserving ¼ cup of juice. Make marinade by combining pineapple juice, soy sauce, sherry, brown sugar, ginger, mustard and garlic. Pour marinade over fish chunks. Cover and refrigerate fish for at least one hour. Drain fish and reserve marinade. Thread fish chunks, pineapple chunks and green pepper squares alternately on skewers. Include cherry tomatoes, fresh mushrooms and onion wedges, if desired. Cook over hot coals or under broiler about four inches from heat for five minutes. Baste with marinade. Turn and

[1] Recipe courtesy of Texas A&M University Sea Grant College Program.

cook for five minutes more or until fish flakes easily when tested with a fork. Serve as a main dish on a bed of rice or alone as an hors d'oeuvre. Makes six entree servings or 18 to 20 hor d'oeuvres.

Barbecued Shark Steaks[2]

2 pounds shark or other fish steaks, fresh or frozen
¼ cup choped onion
2 tablespoons chopped green pepper
1 clove garlic, finely chopped
2 tablespoons oil or melted fat
1 can (8 ounces) tomato sauce
2 tablespoons lemon juice
1 tablespoon Worcestershire sauce
1 tablespoon sugar
2 teaspoons salt
¼ teaspoon pepper

Thaw frozen steaks. For sauce, cook onion, green pepper, and garlic in oil or fat until tender. Add remaining six ingredients and simmer for 5 minutes, stirring occasionally. Cool.

Cut steaks into serving-size portions and place them in a single layer in a shallow baking dish. Pour sauce over fish and let stand for 30 minutes, turning fish once.

Remove fish, reserving sauce for basting. Place fish in well-greased, hinged wire grills. Cook about 4 inches from moderately hot coals for 8 minutes. Baste with sauce. Turn and cook for 7 to 10 minutes longer, or until fish flakes easily when tested with a fork. Serves six.

Oven-Fried Shark or Skate[2]

2 pounds shark fillets or skate wings
½ cup milk
1½ tablespoons salt
1 cup fine bread crumbs
⅓ cup cooking oil or melted fat

Wipe fillets or chunks of skate wings with a damp cloth and dry thoroughly. Add salt to milk; stir until dissolved. Dip each

[2] Recipe courtesy of the California Sea Grant Advisory Program, and the University of California Cooperative Extension, Division of Agricultural Sciences.

fillet first in milk, then in bread crumbs, and place on a greased shallow baking pan. Top each piece of fish with oil or melted fat, and bake in a preheated oven at 375°F for 25 minutes.

Grilled Oriental Shark Steaks[2]

2 pounds shark or other fish steaks, fresh or frozen
¼ cup orange juice
¼ cup soy sauce
2 tablespoons catsup
2 tablespoons oil or melted fat
2 tablespoons chopped parsley
1 tablespoon lemon juice
1 clove garlic, finely chopped
½ teaspoon oregano
½ teaspoon pepper

Thaw frozen steaks. Cut into serving-size portions and place in a single layer in a shallow baking dish. Combine remaining ingredients, pour over fish, and let stand for 30 minutes, turning fish once.

Remove fish, reserving sauce for basting. Place fish in well-greased, hinged wire grills. Cook about 4 inches from moderately hot coals for 8 minutes. Baste with sauce. Turn and cook 7 to 10 minutes longer, or until fish flakes easily when tested with a fork. Serves six.

Skate Kabobs[2]

2 pounds skate wings or other fish fillets, fresh or frozen
⅓ cup french dressing
3 large, firm tomatoes
1 can (1 pound) whole potatoes, drained
1½ teaspoons salt
Dash pepper
⅓ cup oil or melted fat

Thaw frozen wings or fillets. Skin wings, if necessary, and cut into strips approximately 1 inch wide by 4 inches long. Place fish in a shallow baking dish. Pour dressing over fish and let stand for 30 minutes.

Wash tomatoes. Remove stem ends, and cut into sixths.

[2] Recipe courtesy of the California Sea Grant Advisory Program, and the University of California Cooperative Extension, Division of Agricultural Sciences.

Remove fish, reserving dressing for basting. Roll fish strips and place on skewers alternately with tomatoes and potatoes until skewers are filled. Place kabobs in well-greased, hinged wire grills.

Add salt, pepper, and remaining dressing to oil or fat, and mix thoroughly; baste kabobs. Cook about 4 inches from moderately hot coals for 4 to 6 minutes, basting with the sauce. Turn and cook for 4 to 6 minutes longer, or until fish flakes easily when tested with a fork. Serves six.

Oriental cuisine is famous for its shark fin soup. What is eaten here is not the shark meat, but a product extracted and prepared from the cartilaginous supports (ceratotrichia) of the fins. After drying, the skin and meat are removed from the fins. The ceratotrichial rays are pressed into disks or cubes which, when simmered in stock, produce the slightly glutinous, many-flavored soup so famous in the East. The dried fins of virtually any shark command a respectable price from Oriental importers, although those from the nurse shark are unacceptable.

Methods of preparing shark meat for eating reach their pinnacle of complexity in an Icelandic delicacy, *hàkall* (also written *hàkarl*). This is prepared from the flesh of the Greenland shark, which is rumored to be poisonous if prepared conventionally. The carcass of a butchered shark is buried in a pit dug in the shore above the high-tide mark. Because this process results in bacterial modification of the flesh, certain pits, harboring proven cultures of bacteria, are favored over others. After several months of ripening in the cold pit, the shark is exhumed and its flesh cut up into large chunks. These are then hung in the open air of a barn—preferably one that recently housed sheep. After six months or so of curing, the flesh develops a tough rind. It is then eaten in the following manner: *Hàkall* is sliced into thin slivers and eaten without further preparation, but is washed down with copious amounts of aquavit, Iceland's national drink. Some people report that eating *hàkall* is much like eating smelling salts, so rich in ammonia is the shark. They conclude that eating *hàkall* is just an excuse to drink aquavit!

On occasion other parts of elasmobranchs are consumed. The brains, dried and ground to a fine powder, have been alleged to have aphrodisiac (and emetic) qualities. The liver of some species is supposedly rich and succulent when fried or roasted. But the real value of shark liver in modern times has been its oil and vitamin content.

SHARK LIVER OIL

Many species of sharks have livers that exceed one third of the entire weight of the fish. The fats and oils stored there add considerable buoyancy to the shark (Chapter 7). This oil is valuable as a lubricant and as a base for paints. In addition, it often has considerable vitamin A dissolved in it. When supplies of cod liver oil from northern Europe were disrupted by World War II, shark liver oil became an important source of vitamin A. Until about 1950, when commercially synthesized vitamin A became available, several fisheries for sharks existed principally to obtain vitamin A. One of these fisheries was off the coast of Florida. This was a mixed-species fishery, preying on a number of large galeoid sharks. Another fishery developed around the soupfin shark off California, and later included the northern Pacific spiny dogfish. A third shark fishery arose at this time in Australia; it depended mainly on the Australian school shark. These fisheries and others, such as the northeast Atlantic spiny dogfish fishery and the protective meshing fishery off South Africa, all share a similar history of the difficulty of managing a sustained, profitable fishery for elasmobranchs.

COMMERCIAL EXPLOITATON OF SHARKS

As you will see in Chapter 8, reproduction in elasmobranchs is different from that of most of the commercially important teleost fishes. Most grow slowly, lead long lives, and give birth to few young at a time. Teleosts such as cod can produce millions of eggs per female. When environmental conditions enhance the survival of these eggs, the young fish are "recruited" into the commercial stock en masse and can reconstitute a badly exploited population in short order. Although there is evidence that overfished populations of sharks may produce more pups per litter than do dense populations (density-dependent reproduction), the recruitment reservoir for elasmobranchs populations simply is not large. Intensively fished sharks are inevitably eliminated as a commercial resource.

As an example, the California-based soupfin shark fishery can be examined. The soupfin shark is medium-sized, with females reaching a little more than 6 feet in length (2 meters) and about 100 pounds (45 kilograms) in weight. Males are smaller. Females bear 35 embryos per litter, with a gestation period of about one year. Small fishes (sardines, anchovies, midshipmen, rockfish, mackerel) and squid are the principal items in their diet. Growth is slow. Prior to 1937 just under 600,000 pounds of soupfins were landed annually in California, primarily for their fins and fresh meat. In 1937 a market developed for the liver oil of this shark, which was found to contain exceptionally rich quantities of vitamin A. The fishery increased explosively.

In the first years of the expanded fishery the sharks were captured by set lines from about 600 vessels. The value of the catch rose from an initial price of $40 to $60 per ton in the round, to a high of $2,000 per ton in 1941. After that year the livers were removed by the fishermen and brought prices as high as $13 per pound. The six-pound liver of a male soupfin (males have the highest quality livers) was thus worth as much as $78 during the early 1940s.

Shark landings in California leaped to a peak of 9,228,187 pounds in 1939, just two years after the fishery expanded and was converting to sunken gill nets. From this peak, the catch plunged to about 5 million pounds in 1941, and by 1944 had fallen back to the preboom level of 600,000 pounds per year. The catch per unit effort during this period fell from as many as 60 sharks per 20-hour set of a 1,000 fathom gill net in 1939, to a low of about 1 shark per set by 1944. The population had, for all practical purposes, been eliminated. Fortunately for the soupfin shark, the industrial synthesis of vitamin A became a reality by 1950, and the fishing pressure eased as prices fell. Thirty years later, however, this formerly abundant shark had still not regained its former numbers.

This catastrophic effect on a shark population by overfishing is not an isolated one. Similar effects have been felt by populations of spiny dogfish in the northeastern Atlantic and by several populations of basking sharks as well as by carcharhinids in Florida and South Africa. Occasionally shark populations have been managed. One example is that of the Australian school shark, a close relative of the soupfin and one which has a similar life history. The school shark was commercially sought for its tasty flesh in the 1920s in Victoria, Australia. By the late 1940s the stocks had declined to the point that a minimum size limit of 91 centimeters (36 inches) was established. Even with the size limit in place, the fishery continued to decline until the 1960s, when catches rose once again.

In the early 1970s it was discovered that unacceptably high levels of mercury existed in the flesh of the larger school sharks. Concentrations of mercury are not unusual in shark muscle, even from species occupying oceanic regions that remain unpolluted. This is probably due to the long lifetime and slow growth of most elasmobranch species. They have more time to accumulate mercury from the dilute background levels. As a result of this discovery, a maximum size limit of 104 centimeters (41 inches) was placed on the school shark fishery in 1972. This meant that legally landed sharks could only fall in the narrow band between 91 and 104 centimeters. School sharks in this size range are immature. Under these restrictions, the catch fell once again.

School sharks reach a maximum age of at least 40 years. They mature in about 10 years. Females produce fewer than 30 pups per litter, after a gestation period of between 10 and 16 months.

The strict size limit imposed in 1972 had such an adverse effect on the Victoria fishery that it was relaxed in 1976 so that fish between 91 and 112 centimeters could be landed legally. Recent studies of the school shark stocks suggest that a sustained-yield fishery about double the present landings could be tolerated, but uncertainties exist about the biology of the species (gestation period, natural mortality, etc.) that make this recommendation equivocal.

Because of the low fecundity of elasmobranchs, fisheries would benefit from protection of the females and greater exploitation of the males. Because many species segregate by sexes, this option often exists. Conflicting interests, however, can conspire to make this management concept unworkable. A case in point is the North Atlantic spiny dogfish fishery conducted off the coasts of Norway and Scotland. From 1909 to 1931 the northeast Atlantic landings of spiny dogfish were always less than 2,850 tons per year. As the fish became more marketable, the landings rose by 1937 to 12,300 tons per year, with Norwegian longline fishermen contributing about 9,000 tons of the total. After a hiatus during World War II, this fishery expanded to a peak of 41,802 tons in 1963. It has declined ever since despite a steady increase in effort.

The Norwegian segment of the fishery is concentrated on large, mature female dogfish, which are found over rocky bottoms fishable by set and baited longlines. The Scottish segment depends upon smaller males and immature females, which are caught by trawling over smooth bottoms. All of the fish are dressed and shipped to the fish-and-chips market in London and southeast England. Unfortunately for the spiny dogfish, the larger and more meaty female carcasses are the most desirable, so the Norwegian fishery, concentrated on the mature females, is stimulated. In lieu of complex international fisheries agreements, the only saving act for the shark was a reevaluation of the Norwegian krone, which made the Norwegian imports more expensive and had the effect of stimulating the Scottish fishery for the male sharks. The decline of the entire fishery continues, however, and has resulted in recommendations for size and catch limits. Only time will tell if such measures can put this fishery on a sustained-yield basis.

In 1970 a new fishery developed for the unique population of largetooth sawfish that inhabits Lake Nicaragua in Central America. This fishery was primarily for the meat, which was marketed locally as well as exported to countries as far away as the United States. In 1971 the combined production of meat and fins from both bull sharks and sawfish (but mainly the latter) was 178,300 pounds (81,045 kilograms). The catch exceeded 700,000 pounds (318,182 kilograms) in 1974 and 1976, but dropped to slightly more than 100,000 pounds (45,454 kilograms) by 1980, when the catch per unit effort was but a small fraction of that of the peak years.

In 1981 a two-year moratorium on this fishery was enacted by the Nicaraguan government after it became apparent that sawfish had practically been exterminated from the lake. Because the lake population is thought to receive little recruitment through the Río San Juan system from the Caribbean Sea, and because sawfish do not grow rapidly (sexual maturation at 9 to 10 years, life span of 25 to 30 years), much time will be required for this population to recover, if indeed it can.

The experience of these boom-and-bust fisheries for elasmobranchs argues that better life history and population dynamics information are needed by fishery managers before elasmobranch populations are devastated by overfishing. We need to know the real extent of these resources. To this purpose, the National Marine Fisheries Service of the National Oceanic and Atmospheric Administration has for many years supported a shark-tagging program, which is centered in the southern New England and middle Atlantic region of the east coast of the United States. Basic life history information is gradually being accumulated on such species as blue, mako, sandbar, dusky, hammerheads, and white sharks.

Meanwhile, the U.S. commercial landings of elasmobranchs continue to rise. In 1979, 10.2 metric tons of sharks were caught in the United States. Surveys indicate that exploitable shark populations exist off California, in the Gulf of Mexico, and the Atlantic east coast. Estimates of the value of a single shark weighing 125 pounds (56.8 kilograms), sold for fresh meat, fishmeal, liver oil, leather, fins, and curios, range from $75 to $100. With this kind of incentive it is no wonder that more intensive exploitation of elasmobranchs looms in the future.

SHARK LEATHER

Shark fisheries supply more than just oil and meat. A third sought-after product is leather. Sharkskin can be tanned and produces a superior product. The thick dermis contains tannable collagenous fibers that are long and complexly intermeshed when compared to those of the hides of mammals. After tanning, shark leathers commonly exceed 150 percent of the tensile strength of cowhide and pigskin, and outwear them by at least 100 percent.

Sharks larger than about 5 feet (1.5 meters) are preferred for leather. Those animals having mating scars (carried by the females of many species, including sand tiger sharks and blue sharks) are rejected because holes develop in the hide during the tanning process. After the skin is removed and partially fleshed, it is preserved by salting and is then shipped to the manufacturer (Figure 2–2).

At the tannery, the dermal denticles are removed by prolonged soaking in a series of lime solutions. The skins are "bated" with proteolytic enzymes to hydrolyze the dermal fibers and swell the skin. After bating, the skins are tanned by a vegetable tanning process. They are then lubricated with oils, dyed, shaved, ironed, and dried.

The primary use of sharkskin leather is for tough footwear (toe scuffs on children's shoes and work boots used in harsh environments). One disadvantage to its use in shoes is that it is so dense that moisture does not breathe through it easily. Shark leather is also commonly used in the manufacture of leather accessories such as wallets and belts.

In centuries past, particularly exquisite shark-leather-crafted items were produced in Europe and Japan. The eighteenth-century Galluchats of France, in particular, were known for their shark-leather products (book bindings, instrument cases, etc.), which featured leather with the dermal denticles intact. The denticles were ground and polished to achieve striking effects in the finished products. The art of making "galuchat" has been all but lost today, and those antique items containing it are often not recognized for what they are.

Shark leather with the denticles in place was once used on the

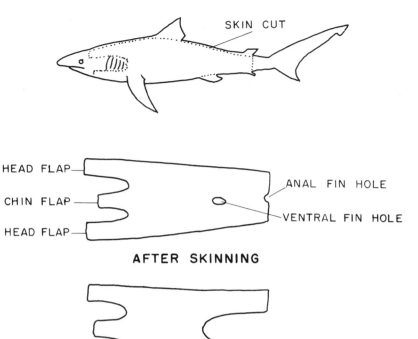

SKIN CUT

HEAD FLAP

CHIN FLAP

HEAD FLAP

ANAL FIN HOLE

VENTRAL FIN HOLE

AFTER SKINNING

FINAL FORM

Figure 2–2. The manner of skinning a shark for the production of leather. (Diagram courtesy of the Ocean Leather Corp., 42 Garden Street, Newark, New Jersey.)

hilts of swords in Japan to provide slip-proof grips. Today small quantities of this form of the leather are produced as *borosso*—an exceptionally fine and beautiful leather product. Shark leather with dermal denticles is also used as a curiosity to make pickpocket-proof wallets which, because of the denticle alignment, are difficult to remove from one's pocket.

Dried sharkskin, known as *shagreen*, was used in olden days by European cabinetmakers to sand and polish wood. With superior modern sandpapers this use has all but disappeared, although Italian stoneworkers are said to use sharkskin for polishing marble.

Sharkskin, because of its exceptional toughness and resistance to wear, has also been utilized for a number of special uses. Fish-

38

ermen wrap it around oars to reduce the wear on the oars and tholes. Eskimos cut strips of skin from Greenland sharks to make lines and ropes.

SHARK CURIOS

A long list of curios is obtained from other parts of sharks. These feature the teeth and jaws of large sharks, which, after cleaning and drying, make interesting—if dangerous to dust—conversation pieces. The teeth can be easily removed from a shark jaw after boiling it in water with detergent or caustic soda for a few minutes or until the teeth loosen. Where large sharks are abundant, the teeth are sometimes mounted in gold or silver settings and worn as jewelry items. Shark jaws can be easily removed from the carcass. To dry them, they must first be scraped clean of all flesh and fatty tissue, and then soaked in seawater to remove all blood. The cleaned and soaked jaws then are tied in an open position to a frame of crossed sticks and are dried in open shade for several days. The best jaws for drying are those from large sharks with heavily calcified jaws such as tiger sharks, bull sharks, makos, and white sharks. The jaws of smaller sharks, or those with little calcification, like blue sharks, frequently warp badly as they dry.

Before metal was introduced by foreign traders into Polynesia, Pacific inslanders used the large serrated teeth of tiger sharks and whaler sharks to make knives and weapons. Whaling museums in the United States are repositories of many beautiful and ingenious implements fashioned from these teeth (Figure 2–3). Other curios

Figure 2–3. These swords, studded with the teeth of whaler sharks, were fashioned in the South Pacific (probably the Gilbert Islands) in the nineteenth century. (Photo courtesy of the Whaling Museum, New Bedford, Massachusetts.)

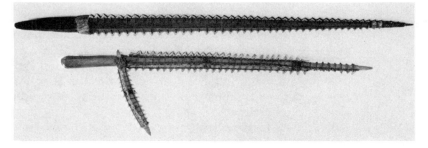

obtained from sharks include canes made from dried vertebral columns and earrings fashioned from the scleras of the eyeballs! But more interesting and useful shark products exist, especially a host of biomedical uses and products.

SHARKS IN MEDICINE, EDUCATION, AND BIORESEARCH

For years the anatomical education of would-be physicians has begun with the study of comparative vertebrate anatomy. A standard dissection specimen in such courses is the spiny dogfish, which is preserved in formaldehyde and prepared by injecting its vascular system with colored latex to demonstrate arteries and veins. Tens of thousands of these sharks are used every year in the United States for this purpose, along with lesser numbers of smooth dogfish, sevengill sharks, and several species of skates. Other elasmobranchs are sought for experimentation by physiologists. The California electric ray is now in great demand by researchers, who have found that the neural junctions with the electroplaques are excellent preparations to use in the study of the synaptic transmission of nerve impulses. The shovelnose guitarfish is another California species that is shipped long distances to provide physiologists with a preparation useful for studying the equilibrium functions of the inner ear.

Other scientists have directed attention to elasmobranchs as sources of biochemicals which might have antitumor or antibacterial activity. Although it is frequently mentioned that malignant tumors are unknown in elasmobranchs, such is not the case. Tumors have been described from a number of species, and antitumor agents have not been found. One chemical often mentioned in this regard is squalene, which is concentrated in the liver oil of sharks. While the biochemical efficacy of squalene remains a question, its presence in shark liver oil allowed unscrupulous oil mongers at one time in the past to dilute olive oil (which also contains squalene) with shark liver oil.

Worthwhile medical uses of elasmobranchs include the use of shark corneas as successful substitutes for human corneas (Chapter 5). Some sharks, such as the spiny dogfish, are rich sources of heparinlike anticoagulants. The development and exploitation of this resource lies fallow. Most recently it has been learned that cartilage derived from elasmobranchs can be of extraordinary use to human burn victims.

In a new process developed at the Massachusetts Institute of

Technology and the Massachusetts General Hospital, a synthetic skin is constructed and placed over charred areas of skin on severely burned patients. The immediate goal is to prevent infection and fluid loss from the burned area. A secondary goal is to provide a template for new dermal cells to invade and begin to divide and grow. The artificial skin is composed of collagen (a fibrous protein) obtained from cowhide, and chondroiten-6-sulfate chemically bonded to the collagen. The chondroiten is extracted from the cartilage of sharks. This temporary "skin" is applied to a thin sheet of silicon rubber, which provides a moisture barrier. After the synthetic skin is grafted into place, the chondroiten-collagen complex biodegrades while new dermal cells are infiltrating it. After about 20 days the silicon backing is removed and epidermis is grafted onto the new dermis. The resultant new skin has a good blood and nerve supply—it is hot, cold, and pain sensitive—but it lacks sweat glands and hair follicles.

The importance of this use of elasmobranch cartilage is that every year in the United States alone there are 130,000 burn victims who require hospital teatment—and each year about 10,000 of them die. With the development of this artificial skin, many if not most of these lives can be saved—and with much less disfigurement than produced by older treatments. This use of sharks may thus save many more human lives than the few these predators manage to take.

In view of the various interactions we have with sharks—some negative, and many positive—it makes sense to explore the natural history of these animals in some detail. An understanding of the current knowledge of the origins, evolution, anatomy, behavior, and physiology of sharks can influence our future interactions with them, with an accent on the positive. But, more important, this understanding can help us better appreciate sharks as animals uniquely adapted to fulfill certain roles in their ecological setting. The following chapters are dedicated to this purpose.

ADDITIONAL READING

Branstetter, S. "Shark fishery potential for the northern Gulf of Mexico." *Dauphin Island Sea Lab Technical Report*, no. 81-001 (1981), 1–21.

Casey, J., H. Pratt, and C. Stillwell. "The Shark Tagger. Newsletter of the Cooperative Shark Tagging Program." *National Marine*

Fisheries Service. Northeast Fisheries Center, Narragansett, Rhode Island. Annual.

Grant, C.J., R.L. Sandland, and A.M. Olsen. "Estimation of growth, mortality and yield per recruit of the Australian school shark, *Galeorhinus australis* (Macleay) from tag recoveries." *Aust. J. Mar. Freshwater Res.* 30 (1979), 625–637.

Holden, M.J. "Elasmobranchs." In *Fish Population Dynamics,* ed. J.A. Gulland, London and New York: John Wiley & Sons, 1977, 187–215.

McCormick, H.W., T. Allen, and W.E. Young. *Shadows in the Sea.* New York: Weathervane Books, 1963.

Olsen. A.M. "The biology, migration and growth rate of the school shark, *Galeorhinus australis* (Macleay) (Carcharhinidae) in south-eastern Australian waters." *Aust. J. Mar. Freshwater Res.,* 5 (1954), 353–410.

Olsen, A.M. "The status of the school shark fishery in south-eastern Australian waters." *Aust. J. Mar. Freshwater Res.,* 10 (1959), 150–176.

Ripley, W.E. "The soupfin shark and the fishery." *California Division Fish and Game Fish Bull.,* 64 (1946), 7–37.

Ronsivalli, L.J. "Sharks and their utilization." *Mar. Fish. Rev.,* (MFR Pap. 1281), 40, no. 2 (1978), 1–13.

Seaman, W., ed. "Sharks and Man: A Perspective." Gainesville, Fla., Florida Sea Grant Program, Report no. 10.

Thorson, T.B. "The impact of commercial exploitation on sawfish and shark populations in Lake Nicaragua." *Fisheries,* 7, no. 2 (1982), 2–10.

3

Shark Diversity and Evolution

Sharks are usually pictured as large, streamlined fish with malevolent eyes, undershot jaws equipped with sharp teeth, and a tendency to unpredictable, sometimes menacing behavior. Dispassionate weighing of the evidence, however, does not always confirm this image of the shark. True, some sharks are large; some present ferocious appearances; and a few are unparalleled predators that can attack human swimmers. But the great majority of sharks do not fit this stereotype.

Sharks are classified in the vertebrate class Chondrichthyes (cartilaginous fishes), characterized by the conspicuous presence of cartilage as the main structural material of their skeletons. Within the Chondrichthyes are two subclasses known as the Holocephali (fused skull) and Elasmobranchii (plate gills). The holocephalans—also known as chimaeras, or rattails—are bizarre fishes seldom encountered by most people. They have peculiar rabbitlike mouths, large heads, and slender, tapering tails. Each gill chamber is covered by a single gill flap or operculum. The upper jaw is fused immovably to the braincase—hence the name Holocephali. There exist only about 35 species of chimaeras. Occasionally they may be found in comparatively shallow coastal water—one species, *Hydrolagus collei*, inhabits Washington's Puget Sound—but most are caught in deep oceanic water on the edges of the continental slopes.

The more speciose and more interesting chondrichthyans are the Elasmobranchii—known popularly as sharks, skates, and rays. Elasmobranchs have gills that are closely attached to a supporting septum (Figure 3–1), and gill chambers that open separately to the outside through from five to seven gill slits. The upper jaw is often separate from the rest of the skull. Indeed, this jaw is only loosely connected to the braincase in most sharks—a condition that is an important feature of shark feeding. These fishes also have unique toothlike denticles, known as placoid scales, found on the outer surface of the body as well as on the buccal and pharyngeal linings of the mouth and gill cavities. These scales are modified as teeth on the biting surfaces of the jaws—teeth that are unique because they are

45

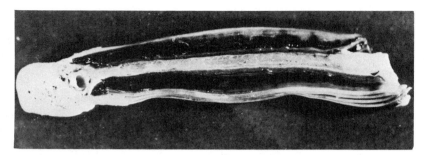

Figure 3-1. Segment of a gill arch from a shortfin mako shark. The gill filaments are supported along most of their length by a plate of connective tissue characteristic of all elasmobranchs. The inner or medial side of the gill is to the left.

Figure 3-2. Sharks characteristically replace their teeth in an unending series from the inner sides of the jaws. Here, replacement teeth from the upper jaw of a silky shark can be seen awaiting their turn to become functional.

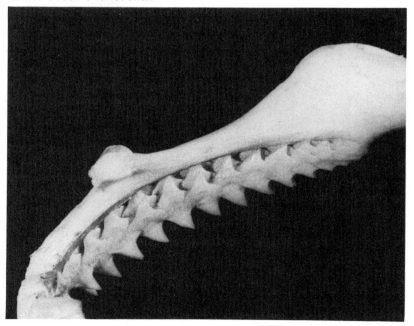

only loosely anchored in skin and are replaced continuously throughout the life of the fish (Figure 3–2). Other prominent external characteristics shared by most elasmobranchs include a caudal fin in which the vertebral column extends through the upper (epichordal) lobe, giving rise to the familiar "sharklike" (heterocercal) tail; and modifications of the inner edges of the male pelvic fins to form claspers, which are the inseminating structures used in reproduction.

Although many people distinguish between sharks on one hand and skates and rays on the other, the scientific reasons for doing so are not overwhelmingly compelling. Most skates and rays are flattened as an adaptation for benthic life—but so are many sharks. Some sharks are as distantly related to each other as they are to the skates and rays. All elasmobranchs could thus be considered "sharks." Because of the deeply rooted popular image of sharks, however, this simplification might be confusing. It is better, perhaps, to speak of "sharks and their allies" when referring to elasmobranchs. In this context, sharks and their allies are classified into the following four superorders:

1. Squalomorphii. Six- and sevengilled sharks, frill sharks, saw sharks, and dogfish sharks.
2. Squatinomorphii. Angel sharks.
3. Batoidea. Skates, rays, and guitarfish.
4. Galeomorphii. Hornsharks, carpet sharks, mackerel sharks, requiem sharks, and hammerheads.

SQUALOMORPHII

The Squalomorphii contain some of our most familiar and also some of our rarest sharks. This is a diverse group, including the familiar spiny dogfish (which, as mentioned in Chapter 2, is often used as a dissection specimen in comparative anatomy laboratories) as well as some large sharks like the sleeper or Greenland sharks of high latitudes. Of the 80 species found here, 70 of them belong to one suborder, the Squaloidei or dogfishes. The dogfish sharks are characterized by the absence of an anal fin and the presence of short, transverse jaws in which the teeth are often arranged in sawlike bands (Figure 3–3). Many species have a spine (with an associated venom gland) in front of each of the two dorsal fins. Some squaloids—Greenland sharks, for example—grow to 20 or more feet (7

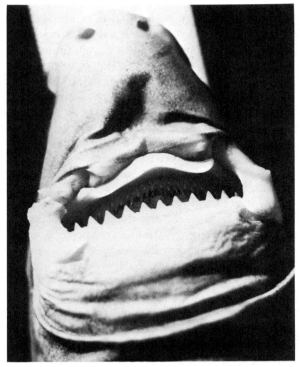

Figure 3–3. In many sharks the teeth are arranged in sawlike bands passing from side to side, as in the lower jaw of the cookie-cutter shark.

meters) in length. Another squaloid, *Squaliolus laticaudus*, matures at only 6 inches (15 centimeters) and is thus the smallest species of shark. Like *Squaliolus*, many squaloid sharks are confined to the deeper pelagic and benthic realms of the ocean, where some species have evolved bioluminescent organs.

Included in the Squalomorphii are three families of sharks that have six or more gill slits: the Chlamydoselachidae, Hexanchidae, and Pristiophoridae. Most of the sharks in these families live in deep oceanic water on the continental shelves and slopes, and present a mix of unusual, and in some respects primitive, features. The fabulous frill shark, *Chlamydoselachus anguineus*, is a rarely caught shark that grows up to 6 or 7 feet (2 meters) in length. Its operculi are extended into pleated folds or frills (Figure 3–4). This deep-sea shark has features reminiscent of fossil paleozoic sharks, including a terminal mouth with long jaws and an array of multicusped teeth. Little is known of its biology, but because of the frill shark's apparent antiquity it is placed at the beginning of nearly all systems of shark classification.

The six- and sevengilled sharks (family Hexanchidae), like frill sharks, have a single dorsal fin and an upper jaw less movable than that of other groups of sharks. The sixgill shark, *Hexanchus*, is another shark of the continental shelf and slopes. Some grow to large size (in excess of 15 feet—almost 5 meters) and, because they are esteemed for food, have been the object of intensive fisheries. The sevengill shark, *Notorhynchus*, is found close inshore and has been recorded as the most abundant shark in San Francisco Bay.

The Squalomorphii include the curious sawsharks of the family Pristiophoridae. These small (3 feet; 1 meter) sharks have their snouts extended into swordlike blades edged with toothlike denticles, and thus superficially resemble their larger cousins, the sawfish (which are rays). There are only five species of sawsharks. They have long barbels in front of their mouths and, like the dogfishes, lack anal fins. Most live in continental shelf and slope areas in the Southern Hemisphere, where they are especially numerous off Australia and South Africa. The members of one genus, *Pliotrema*, have six gill slits.

As a rule, squalomorph sharks are viviparous, giving birth to live young which have been nourished by nutrients included in the yolky eggs from which they hatched *in utero* (Figure 3–5). These sharks also have a generalized pattern of brain structure which until recently was considered the norm for elasmobranch fishes. Indeed, the reliance on spiny dogfish for studies on shark morphology and physiology tended to bias our understanding of sharks. Although the Squalomorphii show remarkable diversity of form throughout the 80-odd species that comprise them, they represent only one radia-

Figure 3–4. The head of the seemingly primitive frill shark. Captured only rarely in deep oceanic water, the frill shark has a terminal mouth, multicusped teeth, six gill slits that are continuous from one side to the other, and a long, eellike body.

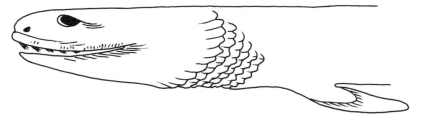

Figure 3–5. An embryonic spiny dogfish. This fetus, about half term, has hatched from its egg case and will be born when it has absorbed all the yolk from its pendant yolk sac. Pads of tissue cover the fin spines. These protect the mother during gestation and birth.

tion of the Elasmobranchii. It can be argued that their abundance in the colder latitudes and less favorable ocean depths is due to their failure to compete successfully with other, and perhaps more recent, radiations of sharks that now occupy the more shallow, warmer, and more species-rich regions of the oceans. The oceanic distribution of squalomorph sharks parallels the distribution of unspecialized teleost fishes such as the herrings and salmoniforms, the majority of which have found refuge in the deep sea—a habitat not yet fully exploited by the more recently evolved bony fishes.

SQUATINOMORPHII

Anyone seeing an angel shark *(Squatina)* for the first time could easily mistake it for a skate or a ray. This small group of about a dozen species is flattened for a life spent on the ocean floor. The pectoral fins are expanded, although not to the extent of pushing the gill slits completely to the ventral surface of the animal, as in the Batoidea. Like the squalomorph sharks to which they seem most closely related, angel sharks lack anal fins and are viviparous. They have some peculiar features, however, that justify their special position in a sep-

50

arate superorder. Angel sharks have nearly terminal mouths with highly protrusile upper jaws. They also have unique tails among elasmobranchs in that the lower lobe of the caudal fin is actually larger than the upper lobe. Angel sharks behave like angler fish, for they partially bury themselves in the sand or mud of the bottom and ambush the small fishes that make up their diet. Most angel sharks grow to lengths of from 3 to 6 feet (1 to 2 meters). They also are found in deeper continental shelf regions, although some species are taken well inshore in shallow water.

BATOIDEA

The sharks that we know familiarly as skates and rays comprise the most speciose group of elasmobranchs. There are roughly 435 species of batoids that share the following easily observed characteristics: reduced or absent anal fin; flattened, depressed body with greatly expanded pectoral fins; five external gill slits on the ventral surface of the body; and a single pair of enlarged spiracles (hyoidean gill slits) on the dorsal surface of the body. The mouth is usually small and on the ventrum, except in the devil rays (mantas), where it is large and terminal. The pelvic fins are widely separated from the vent. In addition to these external characteristics, batoids show a number of internal ones involving details of jaw suspension, skull structure, and the fusion of the pectoral fin skeleton to the skull and vertebral column.

The batoids are divided into four orders: Rajiformes (skates and guitarfishes), Torpediniformes (electric rays), Pristiformes (sawfish), and Myliobatiformes (stingrays, eagle rays, devil rays, cownosed rays). They have been most successful in the warmer, shallow regions of the oceans where they are conspicuous and frequently caught by fishermen. The vast majority of batoids are decidedly benthic in habit; they eat a variety of invertebrates, although many also include fish in the diet. A few rays have adopted an actively swimming, pelagic existence. The devil rays in particular are noted for their large size, filter feeding, and planktonic diet.

Familiar to fishermen of inshore, sandy-bottom waters around the world are the skates of the order Rajiformes, suborder Rajoidei. They are extremely flattened, and most of them have enlarged placoid scales irregularly scattered over the dorsal surface, giving them a spiny appearance (Figure 3–6). There are nearly 200 living species of skates, making them the single most successful group of elasmo-

Figure 3–6. An example of a skate—the little skate.
As a group of elasmobranchs, the skates contain
more species than any other.

branchs. Skates (the genus *Raja* is typical) have long, slender tails
with the dorsal fin reduced or sometimes absent. The anal fin is small
if present. The nostrils are connected to the mouth by prominent
oronasal grooves. The skates are all oviparous, laying horny-shelled,
four-corner eggs familiar to beachcombers as "mermaid's purses."
Although most skates are small, measuring a foot or two (0.5 meter)
across the pectoral disc, a few species, such as the barndoor skate
(Raja laevis), grow to 5 feet or more in diameter. This last species,
which is found on both sides of the North Atlantic, is captured in the
ground fishery for cod, haddock, and halibut. Because the barndoor
skate grows and reproduces slowly, its numbers have declined in recent years as fishing has intensified. There is concern that it may become endangered.

The fifty species of guitarfishes (rhinobatoids) have thickened
52 postanal bodies with two dorsal fins, "sharklike" heterocercal tails,

reduced pectoral fins, and no oronasal grooves. Guitarfishes are viviparous, bearing live young. Indeed, they look like descendents of a skate that decided to become a shark (although in truth, the evolutionary history is the other way around).

The shovelnose guitarfish *(Rhinobatos productus)* found off central and southern California is fairly typical of the group. This fish prefers shallow coastal water, where it feeds principally on crabs and clams. The shovelnose guitarfish grows to about 4 feet (1.3 meters) in length. It is often caught by sport and commercial fishermen and is considered a nuisance by them. Other guitarfishes are known to reach lengths of 10 feet (3 meters) and weights of about 500 pounds (227 kilograms).

The electric rays of the order Torpediniformes have distinctive electrogenic organs formed of modified branchial (gill) muscle tissue. The forty species of them have short and stout postanal tails with one or (usually) two dorsal fins and superficially symmetrical caudal fins. The eyes are reduced, and so are the placoid scales, giving these rays a smooth, spineless appearance (Figure 3–7). The lethargic electric rays rest cryptically on the bottom of shallow coastal waters, awaiting their prey. Small fish are conspicuous in the diet, lending credence to the idea that the rays use their electric organs offensively. Large members of the genus *Torpedo* reach lengths in excess of 3 feet (1 meter) and weigh 50 to 60 pounds (22 to 27 kilograms). Large specimens are respected by commercial fishermen for

Figure 3–7. A lesser electric ray, taken from the Gulf of Mexico.

their ability to deliver electric shocks when handled. In recent years electric rays have been sought by cellular biologists and neurobiologists. Preparations from their electric organs are revealing much information about the details of synaptic transmission of nerve impulses.

The spectacular sawfishes of the order Pristiformes are represented by fewer than ten species found in tropical and subtropical shallow seas as well as in the freshwater rivers draining into them (Chapter 9). They are easily identified by their "saws"—long rostral expansions of the skull, tipped on the lateral edges by expanded placoid scales or "teeth." In addition to the obvious saws, these rays are distinctive for their sharklike appearance, with modest pectoral fins and stout, only slightly flattened bodies. Sawfishes make side-to-side swipes with their saws when feeding, striking at small fish with them. Sawfish also stir up the bottom with their saws and eat the invertebrates thus dislodged. The lateral mobility of the head is reflected in unusually large occipital condyles where the rear of the skull articulates with the vertebral column. Sawfishes grow to large sizes and have been reported to reach 20 feet (6 meters) in length. Those 10 to 15 feet (3 to 4.5 meters) in length are common. These rays often penetrate into fresh water in tropical areas and frequently occur in such places as Lake Nicaragua and the Amazon, Zambezi, Ganges, and Mekong rivers. Here they are susceptible to intense fishing pressure, and their populations have consequently declined dangerously in some areas.

The remaining group of batoids (Myliobatiformes) are the elasmobranchs popularly known as rays. There are nearly 150 species of these fishes divided among the stingrays, butterfly rays, eagle rays, cownosed rays, and devil rays. All but a few of these are characterized by the presence of a serrated spine (often associated with a venom gland) on the whiplike tail (Figure 3–8). The rays also have a curious arrangement of the nostrils. The inner edge of each nostril is expanded into a flap that is fused medially with the nasal flap from the other side. The effect is to create a nasal curtain that reaches back to the mouth. The rays are viviparous, giving birth to live young.

The rays most familiar to bathers and fishermen are the stingrays (stingarees) of the families Dasyatidae and Urolophidae. These fish inhabit shallow waters of coastal embayments, where they are frequently captured by fishermen and are occasionally stepped on by bathers. The tail spine can inflict an exceedingly painful and dangerous wound and is wisely feared by people frequenting waters where these fish abound. Multiple spines are not unusual in sting-

Figure 3–8. The "business" end of a tail spine from a large southern stingray. With their recurved barbs and capacity for venom injection, these spines give stingrays a formidable defensive armament.

rays and represent stages in the replacement of spines. The round stingrays of the genus *Urolophus* are small—usually less than 1 foot (0.3 meter) across the disk—and have well-developed caudal fins. The larger and more speciose genus *Dasyatis* contains some members that grow to large size. For example, a specimen of the southern stingray captured at Bimini, in the Bahamas, was 5 feet (1.9 meters) in disk diameter and weighed 300 pounds (136 kilograms). A ray this size may have a stinging spine six inches (13 centimeters) long. The stingrays have low, molarlike teeth and normally eat invertebrates such as mollusks and crustaceans, although fish are also sometimes eaten. Stingrays often penetrate into brackish and even fresh waters. Indeed, there is a family of rays, the Potamotrygonidae, which are exclusively freshwater and inhabit rivers draining into the Caribbean and Atlantic from South America (Chapter 9). At least one species of stingray, the pelagic stingray, has gone the other way and lives in the open seas of the tropical and subtropical Atlantic and Pacific oceans.

The butterfly rays of the family Gymnuridae are represented by fewer than ten species and are closely related to the stingrays. They have short tails and pectoral fins that are much expanded laterally, giving them a "butterfly" appearance. Some of these rays are vividly marked with purple and green coloration. Several species lack the tail spine typical of stingrays. *Gymnura altavela*, from West Africa, reaches 13 feet (4 meters) across the pectoral fins.

The remaining rays—cownosed, eagle, and devil—are all pelagic in existence. They swim by graceful flapping motions of their pectoral fins and have thus forsaken the benthic life of their batoid relatives.

The eagle rays of the family Myliobatidae are moderate-sized rays with a peculiar head set apart from the pectoral fins. The eyes and spiracles are on the sides of the head, and forward rostral expansions give some of these rays a curious ducklike appearance. The pectoral "wings" are long and pointed. The tail is also long and

55

whiplike. Some of the fewer than 20 species have venomous spines at the bases of the tails, while others lack them. The teeth of these rays are shaped like flat pavement stones designed to crush the bivalve mollusks that they root out of the bottom. Several species grow to 7 or 8 feet (1.5 to 1.8 meters) across the pectoral fins and have been estimated to weigh over 400 pounds (181 kilograms). Like all of the Myliobatiformes, they are viviparous.

The cownosed rays, family Rhinopteridae, are a group of perhaps 10 species that are similar to eagle rays. The principal difference between the two families is that the cownosed rays have a divided rostral expansion of the head, giving them a curious cleft-head appearance. These medium-sized rays, which average about 4 feet (1.3 meters) in width, are found in warm coastal waters—sometimes right in the surf—and crush clams and oysters with their flat, pavement teeth. Cownosed rays can be abundant in areas such as the Chesapeake Bay, and large schools of them wreak havoc with commercially important shellfish beds.

The final and most spectacular of the batoids are the devil rays of the family Mobulidae. These often large rays have terminal *(Manta)* or subterminal *(Mobula)* mouths flanked by curious cephalic fins (Figure 3–9). The teeth are reduced or absent, and the gill rakers are expanded to produce a filtering apparatus by which plankton and small fishes are strained from the water as the rays swim forward. The five species of this family range in size from the lesser devil ray, which matures at 4 feet (1.2 meters) in diameter, to the fabulous At-

Figure 3–9. The head of a devil ray, showing the curious cephalic appendages that flank the mouth.

lantic and Pacific mantas, which grow to widths greater than 22 feet (6.7 meters) and weights of 3000 pounds (1370 kilograms). They thus rank among the largest of fishes.

GALEOIDEA

The galeoid sharks are the fishes most people think of when the word *shark* is mentioned. Although there is much diversity in this group, many of these animals are conspicuous for their size and predatory habits. There are about 250 species known in this large group, which is divided into four orders: Heterodontiformes (horn-sharks), Orectolobiformes (carpet sharks), Lamniformes (mackerel sharks), and Carcharhiniformes (requiem and hammerhead sharks).

The hornsharks are a curious group of about eight species of small, odd-looking animals. These sharks have two dorsal fins with spines (but have anal fins, separating them from the squaloids). They also have crests above the eyes and a peculiar dentition with large molars at the back of the jaws and sharp biting teeth in the front. This feature gives them the name heterodont, which means "different teeth." The living species are confined to the Indo-Pacific region, where they inhabit inshore rocky or reef areas and eat hard-shelled invertebrates and some fish. They are oviparous, laying distinctive eggs which possess prominent spiral flanges on the horny egg cases.

The Orectolobiformes include the nurse and carpet sharks. These broadly flattened, bottom-loving animals are found in shallow tropical seas and are distinguished by small eyes and mouths, two large dorsal fins set well back on the body, nostrils connected to the mouth by oronasal grooves, and a pair of short preoral barbels (Figure 3–10). The powerful jaws are equipped with small, sharp teeth to grasp invertebrates, which are sucked into the mouth by rapid expansion of the large pharyngeal cavity. Some of the carpet sharks grow to substantial size. The nurse shark of the tropical western Atlantic reaches lengths of 12 feet (4 meters) and may weigh several hundred pounds. Even though it is a docile, indolent shark, the nurse shark puts up a powerful and tenacious struggle when hooked. Many sharks in this order, particularly the wobbegongs of the family Orectolobidae, are brightly colored in variegated patterns, belying the notion that sharks are uniformly drab animals.

The incredible whale shark, *Rhiniodon typus*, is also a member of the Orectolobiformes. This enormous animal is reported to reach lengths of 60 feet (18 meters) and weights in excess of 15 tons. Like

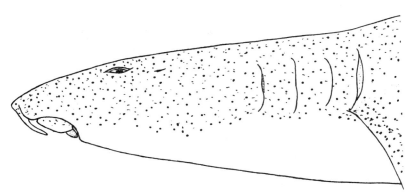

Figure 3–10. A drawing of the head of a nurse shark, demonstrating the preoral barbels typical of many orectolobiform sharks. Notice also the small eye, spiracle, and heavy labial cartilages around the small mouth.

the large mobulid rays, it has forsaken a benthic existence for the life of a pelagic plankton feeder. *Rhiniodon* is the largest living fish in the world.

Altogether there are fewer than 30 species of carpet sharks worldwide. They present a mix of reproductive modes. Some, like the whale shark, are oviparous, while others (including the nurse shark) are viviparous and give birth to live young.

The mackerel sharks (order Lamniformes) form a small group (14 species) of spectacular elasmobranchs. Most are wide-ranging, fast-swimming predators of the open oceans of the world. They are typical sharks in appearance, with conical, pointed snouts and lateral keels ahead of the often nearly symmetrical caudal fins. The mouth is large with sharp, sometimes widely spaced teeth (Figure 3–11). The deep-sea goblin shark *(Mitsukurina)* is atypical, being a sluggish, inactive shark. This order includes the mako sharks *(Isurus)* of sport-fishing fame, the great white or man-eater shark *(Carcharodon),* the long-tailed thresher sharks *(Alopias),* the sand tiger sharks *(Odontaspis),* and at least two large planktivorous forms—the basking shark *(Cetorhinus)* and the newly discovered and described megamouth *(Megachasma pelagios).*

The remaining group of sharks is the large and successful order Carcharhiniformes. This assemblage of about 200 species shares a body plan similar to the mackerel sharks (Figure 3–12). Many also have nictitating membranes (eyelids) which can move to cover and protect the eyeball (Figure 3–13). Carcharhiniform sharks are found in all tropical and temperate oceans. Some, particularly the catsharks

Figure 3–11. A recently captured shortfin mako showing the sharp snout, large gill slits, sleek shape, and large, widely spaced teeth typical of many lamniform sharks.

(Scyliorhinidae), are found in deep oceanic waters on the continental slopes (Figure 3–14). Others, such as the smoothhounds (Triakidae) are common in estuaries and embayments (Figure 3–15). Nearly 25 percent of carcharhiniform sharks belong to the family of requiem sharks, the Carcharhinidae. These predaceous sharks are the ones most often encountered by bathers and divers. Some, such as the bull shark, penetrate into fresh water in tropical regions. Others, like the tiger shark, grow to impressive size and can menace swimmers.

Rounding out the Carcharhiniformes are the hammerhead sharks of the family Sphyrnidae. These fishes have skulls laterally expanded into the remarkable "hammers" that serve to separate the eyes and nostrils widely, and additionally act as bow planes to increase maneuverability (Figure 3–16). Some species grow to lengths of 20 feet (6 meters), and at that size are feared predators.

Figure 3-12. An adult lemon shark—typical of the requiem shark family—swims in the clear waters of the Bahamas.

Figure 3-13. A lemon shark striking at a bait at the surface. Its nictitating membrane occludes and protects the eye at the instant of the bite.

60

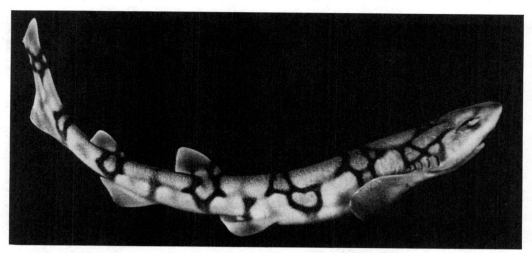

Figure 3–14. An example of the catshark family, the chain dogfish. This handsomely marked species is caught in the deeper parts of the Atlantic continental shelf of North America.

Figure 3–15. Smooth dogfish are often caught by fishermen along the Atlantic coast of North America. They are members of the family Triakidae, closely allied to the requiem sharks. Other familiar triakids include the gray smoothhound and leopard shark of California waters.

Figure 3–16. A catch of scalloped hammerheads taken from the Gulf Stream off the coast of North Carolina in late February. The "hammers" serve to widely separate the eyes and nostrils, and provide abundant planing surfaces for swimming control.

EVOLUTIONARY HISTORY

Sharks are nearly universally thought of as archaic, primitive creatures that have survived hundreds of millions of years without change. Paleontology, however, simply does not support this interpretation of shark evolution (or lack of it). The fossil record is spotty and scanty—especially so for animals like sharks, which have few hard parts to fossilize. Teeth, fin spines, and placoid scales make up most of the fossil remains of sharks. Occasionally a fortuitous imprint of skull, jaws, fins, or axial skeleton has been found to help flesh out our understanding of earlier elasmobranchs. Some of the recent finds have been rich indeed.

Most of the available evidence points to an origin of the class Chondrichthyes about 400 million years ago. The Chondrichthyes are not ancestral to the bony fishes, but arose from a common ancestor to that group. By the late Devonian (360 million years ago), a number of elasmobranch genera—already distinct from the holocephalans—were present. They included *Xenacanthus* and *Cladoselache* (Figure 3–17). These earliest recognizable sharks had terminal

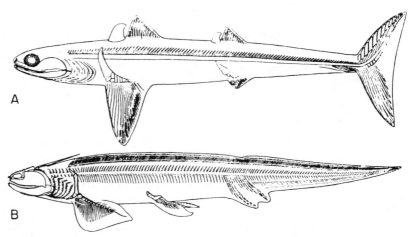

Figure 3–17. Examples of Cladodont-level elasmobranchs,
Cladoselache (A) and *Xenocanthus* (B). Note the long, terminal jaws
and poorly formed vertebrae. (From Schaeffer, 1967)

mouths with long upper jaws that were firmly attached to the skull.
Each tooth had several pronglike cusps which projected from the
flattened base. The fins were supported by an axial series of cartilages much different from those of modern elasmobranchs.

These Devonian sharks were denizens of the warm shallow
seas that covered much of what is now North America. Some of
them—*Cladoselache*, for example—grew to substantial size: greater
than 6 feet (2 meters) in length. Both *Deanea* and *Cladoselache* were
streamlined fish with well-developed, symmetrical caudal fins. They
appear to have been fast-swimming, predaceous fish. These sharks
existed at a time of momentous evolutionary events, for the rhipi-
distian bony fishes were then giving rise to the earliest amphibians,
which soon after produced the first reptiles. Thus, these earliest
sharks have a history not much longer than amphibians.

In the Carboniferous, approximately 310 million years ago, a
rich and diverse chondrichthyan fauna developed. Recent finds in
central Montana's Bear Gulch limestone formation, for example, include an assemblage of no fewer than 35 species of chondrichthyans
(20 of them elasmobranchs), which apparently lived contempora-
neously. These paleozoic sharks show a level of organization substantially different from modern elasmobranchs.

Late in the Paleozoic and during the Mesozoic many sharks
achieved new levels of organization. Some of the principal adaptations included a pectoral fin skeleton supported at its base by three
stout cartilages, the development of an anal fin, and the addition of

63

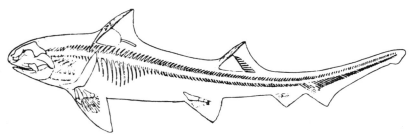

Figure 3–18. A Hybodont-level elasmobranch, *Hybodus*.
(From Schaeffer, 1967)

new ventral elements to the vertebral column. Much experimentation occurred in the skull and jaw structure, but the jaws were basically still elongate and reached to the front of the snout. This hybodont level of organization, as opposed to the earlier cladodont level, is seen in such fossil genera as *Ctenacanthus* from the Mississippian, *Lissodus* (early Triassic to late Cretaceous), and *Hybodus* (early Triassic to late Cretaceous) (Figure 3–18). Thus, during the Mesozoic (between 225 and 65 million years ago), while the dinosaurs and other ruling reptiles had their fling and while both birds and mammals were first appearing, the Elasmobranchii were undergoing a lot of experimenting. They were evolving the mix of adaptations necessary to survive in an increasingly complex world.

In the lower Jurassic of the Mesozoic (about 170 million years ago), coincident with the first birds in the fossil record, a shark of distinctly modern appearance made its entry into geologic history. *Paleospinax* had a modern hyostylic jaw suspension, a shortened upper jaw, and well-developed vertebrae (Figure 3–19). The protrusile upper jaws were equipped with sharp, single-cusped teeth.

A significant radiation of modern-level elasmobranchs continued through the Jurassic, so that by late in this period separate radiations assignable to squaloids and galeoids occurred—although

Figure 3–19. *Paleospinax*, one of the earliest fossils to show the shortened jaws, inferior mouth, and well-formed vertebrae typical of modern sharks. (From Schaeffer, 1967)

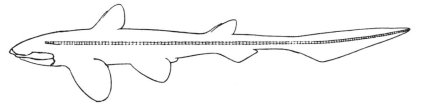

the truly recent forms were not yet in evidence. The upper Jurassic also saw the earliest, primitive batoids, represented by *Spathobatis* and *Belemnobatis*. At about the same time, fossils ancestral to the modern angel sharks also appeared.

The achievement of the modern level of elasmobranch organization in the Jurassic set the stage for a radiation of sharks that continued until recent times. The number of recognized elasmobranch genera in the fossil record increased through the Jurassic and Cretaceous, with many modern genera appearing in the Tertiary and Quaternary periods of geologic history—that is, during the last 25 million years. The appearance of sharks in a truly modern form is thus a more recent phenomenon than generally seems to be recognized. In fact, their ultimate radiation coincided with that of both birds and mammals.

Just as surviving older levels of organization are found in most living groups—grebes among the birds, and monotremes among the mammals, for instance—so exist living sharks which harken back to some of their earlier ancestors. *Chlamydoselachus* and the hexanchid sharks have some uniquely modern characteristics, yet they also retain some cladodont-level characters, particularly in details of tooth structure and jaw suspension. Many biologists also believe the heterodont dentition and jaw structure of hornsharks to be reminiscent of the hybodont level of organization. In the main, however, modern elasmobranchs are not "primitive" animals that represent some bygone day etched into an immutable form. Rather, they are products of several adaptive radiations, the most recent of which was coincident with the mammalian radiation that ultimately produced ourselves.

The adapatations that make sharks such successful and interesting animals involve a number of anatomical and physiological systems. These include sensory and nervous systems; locomotor, reproductive, and excretory systems; and systems pertaining to the ingestion of food. The feeding apparatus is especially interesting, both because of its importance to a predatory mode of life and because its evolutionary history has been partially preserved in the fossil record.

ADDITIONAL READING

Bigelow, H.B., and W.C. Schroeder. "Sharks," Fishes of the western North Atlantic. *Memoirs of the Sears Foundation for Marine Research*, 1, no. 1 (1948), 56–576.

Bigelow, H.B., and W.C. Schroeder. "Sawfishes, guitarfishes, skates and rays," Fishes of the western North Atlantic. *Memoirs of the Sears Foundation for Marine Research,* 1, no. 2 (1953), 1–514.

Castro. J.L. *The Sharks of North American Waters.* College Station, Tex.: Texas A & M University Press, 1983.

Campagno, L.J.V. "Interrelationships of living elasmobranchs." In *Interrelationships of Fishes, Zool. J. Linn. Soc.,* ed. P.H. Greenwood, R.S. Miles, and C. Patterson. 55, supp. no. 1 (1973), 15–61.

Compagno, L.J.V. "Phyletic relationships of living sharks and rays." *American Zoologist* 17 (1977), 303–322.

Compagno, L.J.V. "Legend versus reality: The jaws image and shark diversity." *Oceanus* 24, no. 4 (1981), 5–16.

Moy-Thomas, J.A., and R.S. Miles. *Palaeozoic Fishes,* 2nd ed. Philadelphia: W. B. Saunders Co., 1971.

Schaeffer, B. "Comments on elasmobranch evolution." In *Sharks, Skates and Rays,* ed. P.W. Gilbert, R.F. Mathewson, and D.P. Rall, 3–35. Baltimore: Johns Hopkins Press, 1967. (Figures 3-1, 3-18, and 3-19 are from this work.)

Schaeffer B., and M. Williams. "Relationships of fossil and living elasmobranchs." *American Zoologist,* 17 (1977), 293–302.

4

How Sharks Eat

If the nearly 800 living species of elasmobranchs are compared, two features of their feeding mechanisms are striking. First, all sharks with teeth (the planktivorous *Manta* has none) have them arranged in series of replacement rows in the jaws. As early as 1846, Sir Richard Owen, a prominent English anatomist, vividly described the elasmobranch successional series of teeth as a "phalanx . . . ever marching slowly forward in rotatory progress over the alveolar border of the jaw." The second characteristic, shown by all but a few species, is the location of the mouth, which seems to be tucked out of the way on the ventral surface of the shark's head. Another biologist, William Beebe, called attention to this feature when he colorfully—but not accurately—labeled sharks "chinless cowards."

The first of these characteristics—an unending replacement series of teeth—has been a chondrichthyan hallmark since the origin of the group 400 million years ago. The basic mechanism for replacing teeth seems not to have changed during the entire evolutionary history of sharks, although tooth form and structure have. More dramatic changes occurred in the location of the mouth—changes that help us understand the adaptations that make sharks successful predators.

JAWS

The ancient elasmobranchs of the Paleozoic, like *Cladoselache* (Figure 3–17), had mouths that opened at the tips of the snouts (terminal mouth). The jaws were formed of the palatoquadrate (upper) and Meckel's (lower) cartilages (Figure 4–1), which seem to be derived from an anterior gill arch in the ancestral jawless fish. These jaws were long, with the upper ones supported by tight connections with the cartilaginous braincase lying inside and above them. The second gill arch in the series, the hyoid arch, helped to brace the jaws from behind. The remaining gill arches supported gills and did not assist

69

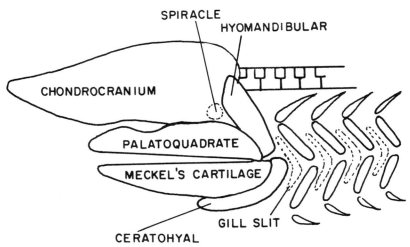

Figure 4–1. The skeletal elements of a shark skull. The *chondrocranium* houses the brain. The jaws consist of the *palatoquadrate* cartilages (upper jaw) and *Meckel's* cartilages (lower jaw). These are supported from behind by the *hyomandibular* and *ceratohyal* cartilages. The jaws and hyoid elements represent modified gill arches. Between them is often found a hyoidean gill slit or *spiracle.*

in the suspension of the jaw apparatus. This form of jaw support, in which the upper jaw is anchored by ligamentous connections—not outright fusion—to the braincase, is known as an amphistylic suspension, and is a characteristic of cladodont- and hybodont-level sharks. It did not allow much independent movement of the upper jaw. In the early chimaeras, fusion of the upper jaw to the braincase occurred, producing the so-called holostylic or autostylic jaw suspension. Mammals, including humans, have autostylic suspensions.

Living sharks that retain upper jaw suspensions capable of limited movement include the frill shark, *Chlamydoselachus*, the six- and sevengilled sharks of the family Hexanchidae, and the hornsharks (Heterodontidae). The frill shark is interesting because in addition to its primitive jaw suspension it has a terminal mouth with multicusped cladodontlike teeth (Figure 4–2). In these respects *Chlamydoselachus* resembles reconstructions of paleozoic, cladodont sharks.

Predators with long jaws, terminal mouths, and grasping, pronged teeth can be limited to feeding on prey they can consume at a single bite. The feeding strategies of bony fish so equipped (like the pikes, pickerels, basses, barracudas, etc.) are to open the large mouth and rush at the intended prey, literally surrounding it with

70

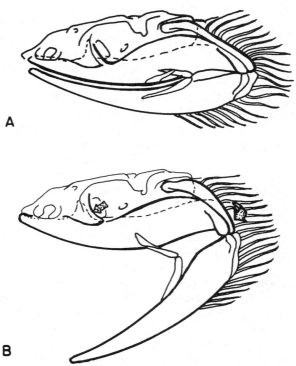

A

B

Figure 4–2. Jaw suspension of the frill shark. The long, terminal jaws of this shark are buttressed by hyomandibulae that swing outward when the mouth is opened. There is little forward movement of the upper jaw, which is tightly braced against the braincase. (From Maisey, 1980. Courtesy of The American Museum of Natural History.)

the mouth. Because the jaws are long and closed by a muscle—the adductor mandibulae—located near the hinge, little power is generated at the front of the jaw. The mechanical advantages do not favor cutting large prey into smaller chunks. Similar limitations in prey selection may occur in the frill shark and in those paleozoic sharks that had long jaws and grasping teeth.

The fossil record chronicles a series of changes in the early shark feeding mechanism. First, in the hybodont radiation, the jaws shortened and the teeth were modified both for crushing and cutting. The mouth appears to have remained terminal. The shortened jaws would have made possible a more powerful bite. Modern teleost an-

71

alogs are predaceous forms such as bluefish and piranhas that are able to chop up prey with short powerful jaws equipped with blade-like triangular teeth. The hybodont feeding mechanism opened up new food resources that fueled this radiation of sharks. The more powerful jaws, for instance, allowed hybodonts to crush hard-shelled invertebrates such as crustaceans and mollusks. This change in diet is reflected by the dentition of these animals, which often featured flattened grinding and crushing sorts of teeth.

The most important change in the evolution of the elasmo-branch feeding apparatus occurred in the Mesozoic, when the upper jaw was loosened from its connections with the cranium. The jaws became more firmly buttressed by the hyoid arch, and the forward ligamentous connections became less restrictive. The upper element of the hyoid arch, the hyomandibula, served to brace the back part of the upper jaw against the chondrocranium, producing the modern hyostylic form of jaw suspension shared by most living elasmo-branchs (Figure 4–3).

Additional shortening of the jaws also occurred, making the bite more powerful. The spatial requirements of having the hyo-mandibula brace the short jaws resulted in the move of the mouth back from the tip of the snout to the underside of the head—to the "inferior" position in which the mouth is now found in all but a few elasmobranchs.

The inferior mouth is seen in the fossil record in *Paleospinax* from the Jurassic (Figure 3–19). This shark was a streamlined, hy-drodynamically efficient fish, indicating that the location of the mouth may not (as some suggest) have been a primary adaptation to

Figure 4–3. The jaw suspension of a requiem shark. The upper jaw (pq) is only loosely attached to the braincase (stippled) by ligaments from the orbital process (obp). (From Moss, 1972a)

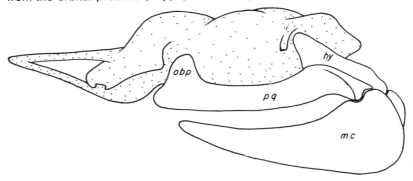

benthic feeding. In fast-swimming, pelagic sharks such as *Paleospinax* and modern carcharhiniforms and lamniforms, hydrodynamic considerations dictate the maintenance of an extended, flattened or conical snout to give additional "lift" when swimming (Chapter 7). The ventral mouth must have made bottom feeding easier, for its appearance was soon followed by the batoid radiation that featured benthic feeders like the living stingrays and skates.

The importance of short but powerful jaws, loosely suspended from the chondrocranium and buttressed against it by the hyomandibulae, can be illustrated by considering in detail the feeding mechanism of modern carcharhiniform sharks. In these sharks the upper jaw is slung from the chondrocranium by a pair of ligaments (ethmopalatine ligaments) that pass from the underside of the skull to a prominent knob (orbital process) on the anterior third of each upper jaw. The posterior end of the jaw projects well behind the skull and, where it articulates with the lower jaw, it is loosely attached to the end of the long hyomandibular cartilage. This latter element arches forward inside the upper jaw to brace against the side of the back part of the chondrocranium. In its resting, nonbiting position, the upper jaw lies on a level with, or slightly below, the chondrocranium. In this position the ethmopalatine ligaments are slack and do not physically restrain the upper jaw.

Several muscles serve this skeletal system. The most important is the quadratomandibularis muscle mass, which runs between the upper and lower jaws just in front of their articulation. This group of muscles produces the main biting force. Also important to the feeding mechanism are additional muscles. The preorbitalis muscle group runs back from the chondrocranium, where it arises in front of the eye, to insert on the back of the jaw complex. When it contracts, it pulls the jaw apparatus forward. The levator hyoideus and levator palatoquadratii arise from attachments high on the chondrocranium, above the eye, and run back to insert on the hyomandibula and palatoquadrate. When contracted, the levator hyoideus pulls on the hyomandibula, causing its farther end to swing out and forward, more firmly bracing the jaws. The levator palatoquadratii pulls the jaw complex forward and rotates the upper jaw down and out, protruding it (Figure 4–4).

The overall effect of the actions of these muscles is astonishing. When they contract, the jaw complex, composed of a number of cartilages loosely connected to each other, is stiffened and buttressed into a rigid entity. The upper jaws are pulled and pushed forward with the preorbitalis and levator hyoideus muscles acting in concert.

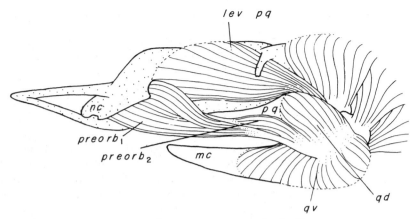

Figure 4–4. Jaw musculature of a requiem shark. The *quadratomandibularis* muscle mass (qv and qd) are the principal jaw-closing muscles. The *preorbitalis* muscles (preorb₁ and preorb₂) and the *levator palatoquadratii* (lev pq) help pull the jaw complex forward, protruding the upper jaw. (From Moss, 1972a)

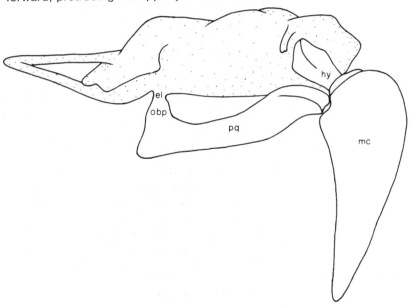

Figure 4–5. When requiem sharks (or other modern-level elasmobranchs) bite, the jaws and the hyomandibulae are pulled forward and rotated, protruding the upper jaws to the limit allowed by the ethmopalatine ligaments (el). This feature of the shark feeding apparatus allows a deep bite so that chunks can be gouged from large prey. (From Moss, 1972a)

74

The upper jaw rides forward and down in a groove in the front of the chondrocranium ahead of it. The result is that the upper jaw is protruded and protracted from the mouth to the limit allowed by the ethmopalatine ligaments (Figure 4–5).

The effectiveness of this feeding mechanism can be appreciated by watching what happens when a shark attacks its prey. A large shark such as a lemon or tiger shark can circle and examine its prey for some time before attacking. During this examination it may bump or nudge the prey with its snout or pectoral fins. The final attack is made swiftly, with the shark taking on a stiffened, jerky, and curious "hunchback" appearance. During this ultimate rush the mouth may be rapidly opened and closed. When the shark reaches its victim the trailing edges of the large pectoral fins are depressed, braking the forward speed and lifting the head and forepart of the body. The mouth is further exposed by muscles in the nape region, which lift the head and snout. The teeth of the depressed lower jaw first encounter the prey; a purchase is gained with these teeth. In many carcharhiniform sharks the teeth of the lower jaw are often spikelike holding teeth, whereas the upper jaw teeth are broader, blade-shaped cutting teeth.

With the prey securely impaled on the lower jaw teeth, the upper jaw protracts and its teeth begin a sawing action powered by violent side-to-side swings of the shark's head and forebody. As the sharp upper-jaw teeth carve through the prey's flesh, the upper jaw continues its protraction, entering the kerf made by its teeth (Figure 4–6). Using both jaws actively, the shark is able to gouge a chunk out of what otherwise might be an unassailably large animal.

The mobility of the upper jaws of the most modern elasmobranchs can also function in a different manner when they feed on the benthos. Sharks can pick up prey from the bottom with more precision using a protrusile upper jaw. Rather than indiscriminately scooping up material from the bottom with the lower jaw, a shark with a mobile upper jaw can pick up items, almost fingerlike, with its jaws. This mode of feeding is particularly important to the skates and rays, where the upper jaw has lost its ligamental connections to the skull, allowing even greater jaw protrusion.

The significance of the appearance of the modern hyostylic jaw suspension in Mesozoic elasmobranchs is considerable. It signaled the evolution of a feeding mechanism that opened a great range of feeding possibilities—from precise feeding on small and tough benthic organisms to eating chunks of large prey that could be gouged due to the power of the shorter jaws and the new mobility of the

Figure 4–6. A tiger shark biting a bait at the surface. The upper jaw is maximally protruded. (From Moss, 1972a)

upper jaw. This fundamental change in the mechanical system of feeding heralded a radiation of elasmobranchs—often referred to as neoselachians—that occurred in the most recent third of their evolutionary history.

TEETH

The other noteworthy feeding adaptation of elasmobranchs involves the mode by which their teeth are periodically replaced. The serial replacement of teeth in sharks is of great antiquity, for it is found in the earliest Paleozoic sharks. The continual replacement of teeth is, in part, made possible by the fact that the teeth are not set in sockets, nor are they cemented to the underlying skeletal elements of the jaws. Cartilage, even the heavily calcified cartilage found in the jaws of some of the larger sharks, makes a poor base in which to anchor teeth. Shark teeth are consequently bedded in a collagenous membrane—the tooth bed—which is stretched over the jaw cartilage (Figure 4–7).

76   Elasmobranch teeth (and placoid scales) are similar in con-

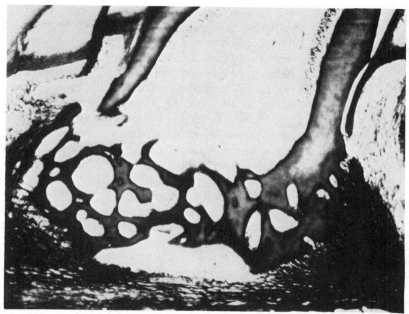

Figure 4–7. Microscopic view of the base of a lemon shark tooth held in position by the collagenous fibers of the tooth bed. The bottom of the tooth is eroding, preparatory to its loss and subsequent replacement.

struction to the teeth of other vertebrates. Each contains a central pulp cavity supplied by blood vessels and nerves. The pulp cavity is surrounded by a core of dentin secreted by cells known as odontoblasts. The dentin is expanded at the base of each tooth where it is anchored in the tooth bed. The exposed crown of the tooth is covered with clear enamel secreted by epithelial cells that surround the tooth during its development.

The variation of form found in the teeth of living elasmobranchs is immense. What these teeth have in common, however, is that they are replaced by having them ride up on the inner side of the jaw, where they rotate into position as they reach its crest.

The developmental sequence of a tooth begins deep in a groove that runs around the inside of each jaw cartilage. There tooth buds form in their respective replacement series. Cells called odontoblasts in the tooth buds begin secreting the dentin of the bases and cores of the teeth. Meanwhile, the embryonic tooth moves ahead, to be replaced by the formation of yet another tooth bud behind it (Figure

4–8). As each tooth moves forward, more dentin is deposited and the epithelial cells surrounding the tooth (ameloblasts) begin secreting the enamel that will cover the cusp of the tooth. Eventually the tooth will erupt from the tooth groove and emerge through the soft tissue lining the mouth, to fold into place as a functional tooth. At this time resorption of the base of the tooth begins. Eventually the tooth will fall or be knocked out during feeding.

In sharks such as many squaloids, the teeth of adjacent replacement series are overlapped and imbricated in such a fashion that an entire functional row of teeth may be lost at once. For instance, in the cookie-cutter shark it is not unusual to find an entire set of this shark's lower teeth (Figure 3–3) in its own stomach, apparently swallowed as the teeth fell out while eating.

The exact mechanism by which the teeth move is not understood by students of shark biology. One notion is that the growth and expansion of cells packed between the developing teeth tend to push them apart. According to this hypothesis, this force, because it is confined within the tooth groove, results in net movement of the teeth up and out of the tooth groove. The teeth must move through the stationary tooth bed by means of continual rearrangement of the anchoring collagenous connections to their bases. This hypothesis does not explain how the teeth continue to move after they have erupted from the tooth groove.

A second mechanism by which teeth could move involves motion of the tooth bed itself. The bed could be pulled up over the jaw by resorptive forces occurring on the outer (labial) surface of the jaw, where the scars of departed teeth can be seen to merge with one another. Whatever the exact mechanism of tooth movement, it is clear that the teeth move—and at surprising rates in some elasmobranchs.

Directly measured rates of tooth replacement in several species of requiem sharks demonstrate that in the first year of life these sharks renew each functional tooth every eight to fifteen days. These rates of tooth replacement undoubtedly slow down as body growth rates decline with sexual maturity. Even so, sharks must produce many thousands of teeth in a lifetime. It is little wonder that shark teeth are so abundant in the fossil record!

Tooth replacement rates have not been measured in rays having large, flat pavement teeth. The rates of replacement of these teeth, especially in mature animals, are probably quite slow.

A good set of teeth is especially important to a predator like a shark. Because of the poor skeletal support and fragility of shark teeth (broken teeth are commonly observed—Figure 4–9), the evolu-

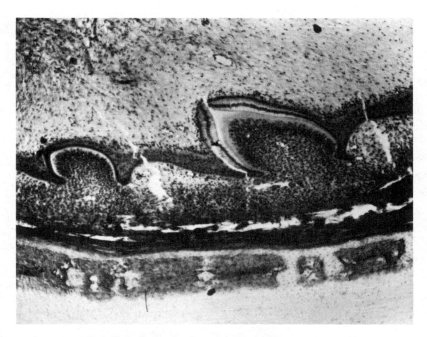

Figure 4–8. Tooth buds in the lower jaw of a lemon shark. The younger bud on the left has just formed. The older bud on the right precedes it in development by eight or ten days.

tionary success of elasmobranchs must be explained, in part, by their rapid tooth replacement.

Despite the common mode of tooth replacement and jaw suspensions shared by most sharks, they are not the indiscriminate feeders that many people believe them to be. True, the general features of the feeding mechanism allow most sharks to be opportunistic feeders when necessity requires. But secondary specializations—such as details of tooth structure, jaw shape and strength, dental pattern, muscle arrangement and behavioral patterns—produce sharks that are often real dietary specialists. Each species has a battery of specializations that fine tunes it for a distinctive predatory role. Some of this fine tuning can be seen in the details of tooth structure, for example.

So distinctive are the teeth of sharks that they form an important taxonomic character by which a species may be described and identified. In most cases sharks can be positively identified from a single tooth or even a fragment thereof. In certain species (particularly some skates, stingrays, and catsharks) the teeth of males and females are so different that sex may be identified from a single tooth as well.

Myliobatid rays, like the cownosed rays, are completely specialized in their flat pavement teeth for a diet of bivalve mollusks. Other noteworthy dietary specialists include shortfin mako sharks, which preferentially eat bluefish, and smooth dogfish, which specialize in eating crabs and lobsters. Hammerhead sharks prefer stingrays as food (Figure 4–10), while the bonnethead shark is a shrimp-eating specialist. The great white shark is adapted for feeding on marine mammals such as seals, sea otters, and whales. Tiger sharks, with their massive, heavily calcified jaws and strong, deeply serrated teeth, are known to include sea turtles in their diets, although this species also has gained a reputation for scavenging offal and carrion. The bull shark is another opportunistic feeder. It will eat a number of large items, including rays, other sharks, garbage, and sea turtles.

Figure 4–9. The lower jaw of a smooth dogfish, showing the low-cusped, crushing dentition of this species. Damaged teeth can be seen, indicating the importance of rapid tooth replacement. (From Moss, 1972b)

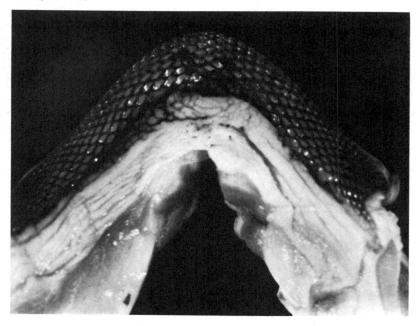

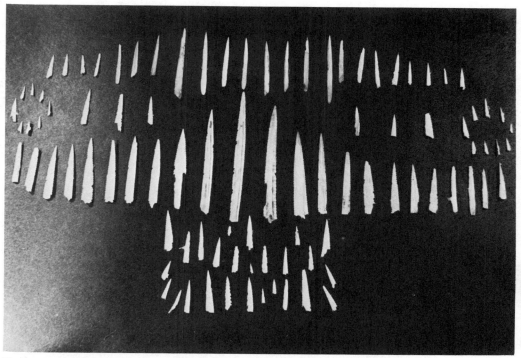

Figure 4–10. Stingray spines recovered from the head and jaws of a single smooth hammerhead.

FEEDING BEHAVIOR

Many elasmobranchs specialize to the degree that 75 percent of their diets may be made up of a single type of food. Perhaps the most restricted diets are found in those sharks that have evolved specializations for plankton feeding. These animals, which include the mobulid rays, the whale shark, the basking shark, and the newly discovered megamouth, have independently derived adaptations, including: (a) an extremely large mouth and its return to a terminal or near-terminal position (Figure 4–11); (b) the reduction of the size and importance of the teeth; and (c) the elaboration of the gill rakers on the inner faces of the gill bars into filters that are used to strain plankton and small fishes from the water (Figure 4–12).

81

Figure 4–11. The enormous mouth of the basking shark allows it to strain plankton from great quantities of water.

The feeding behavior of these planktivorous sharks seems simple. They open their large mouths and swim slowly forward until the gill rakers are clogged with food. This is swallowed and the process repeated. The stomach contents of basking sharks feeding on concentrations of copepods in the North Atlantic look like gallons upon gallons of orange juice because of the quantities of these tiny crustaceans in the diet. But basking sharks are also enormously selective in what they swallow, suggesting that the filter feeding mode may not be as simple as it looks. An interesting variation of filter feeding has been observed in whale sharks. Where dense patches of plankton exist near the surface, these great sharks may hang, tail downward, in the water column and drive straight up through the mass of food. The momentum developed carries their heads well out of water before they sink back down for another pass through the plankton. Tunas, feeding on the same masses of plankton, have been seen to leap inadvertently into the open mouths of the sharks. They

82

must have added bulk to the whale sharks' diets! The stomach contents of whale sharks are less homogeneous than those of basking sharks, indicating that they may not be as selective in their feeding habits and mechanisms.

Other behavioral modifications during feeding can further enhance the adaptability of the basic shark feeding mechanism. Blue sharks are known to adopt several strategies for feeding on small schooling organisms such as anchovies and squids off the coast of southern California. These sharks have the typical carcharhiniform gouging feeding mechanism and, in fact, are known for their attacks on captured whales. They most often feed, however, on small (5 to 25 centimeter) prey. They can approach a school of squid rapidly and directly, swimming through it with mouths wide open—in effect, filter feeding. At other times they slowly and sinuously swim through a school, capturing squid or anchovies in the corners of their mouths with lateral swings of their heads. Yet another strategy

Figure 4–12. The closely spaced, long gill rakers of basking sharks make effective plankton filters.

occurs when these sharks feed on stationary surface schools concentrated under a light at night. Blue sharks then hang below the school, tail down, and repeatedly rise up through it, capturing as many as thirty small squid before sinking below the school once again.

Even closely related species of elasmobranchs can have distinctive differences in their dietary habits. For example, two species of skates, the little skate and the winter skate, coexist over much of their ranges off the east coast of North America. Winter skates grow to more than twice the adult size of little skates, but the immature sizes are difficult to distinguish from one another. Yet when the diets of individuals of these two species, taken from the same habitat, are analyzed, important differences are found. Little skates eat more crabs, fewer fishes, and fewer polychaete worms than do winter skates. When the habits of the prey are compared, it turns out that winter skates feed more often on animals that burrow in the sandy bottoms (infauna), while little skates eat prey that sit on or above the substrate (epifauna). The largest winter skates eat a number of fish, but even these are often sand lance (*Ammodytes*), which also burrow in sandy bottoms.

The popular literature on the feeding habits of sharks is full of stories of unusual items being recovered from the stomachs of sharks—including tin cans, lumps of coal, and even a suit of armor! Although sharks occasionally swallow inappropriate items, this does not happen very often. Of the many hundreds of shark stomachs I have examined, the only unusual item found was the remains of a paper cup taken from a spiny dogfish. It is possible that the electric fields created by metal objects in seawater may make them attractive to sharks, which rely on their sensitive electrosensory apparatus for feeding (Chapter 5), so that stories of license plates, cans, and so on in shark stomachs are probably not fabrications or exaggerations.

The mechanical strength of the jaws of a large shark is impressive. The combination of short jaws and bulky muscles produces biting forces capable of shearing through firm flesh and bone. Free-swimming tiger, lemon, and dusky sharks, 7 to 10 feet (2 to 3 meters) long, produced biting forces measured during experiments to be as high as 132 pounds (60 kilograms) per tooth. Considering the area of the tooth in contact with the measuring device, this translates to forces of 3 metric tons per square centimeter (21 tons per square inch). It is little wonder that chips of shattered shark teeth are commonly found embedded in the remains of their prey!

DIGESTION

Once food has been taken into the mouth, a shark swallows it after a minimum of manipulation. Bottom-feeding sharks and those that crush mollusks are adept at separating sand and bits of shell from the edible portion of their intake. Infaunal-feeding skates, for example, almost never have sand in their stomachs. The rejected inedible material is expelled from the gill slits.

When the food is swallowed it passes to a large stomach, where the digestive process begins. Here gastric juices consisting of peptidases and hydrochloric acid begin the chemical breakdown of the food. Although numerous reports exist of objects residing undigested for days or even weeks in the stomachs of sharks, the dissolution of prey usually is rapid. Small fishes eaten by blue sharks, for example, are reduced to a few vertebrae and eye lenses within 24 hours. On the other hand, some sharks may not have to eat very frequently. Based on the estimated metabolism of a white shark, determined from telemetry of its movements and body temperature changes (Chapter 10), and the energy content of a known meal, it was estimated that white sharks may need to eat but once in one or two months! Indeed, this shark showed no signs of feeding for a period of three days following its monitored meal, even though opportunities for it to eat existed. Captive sharks may stop feeding for weeks or months—usually after a significant shift in temperature. The more usual observation, however, is that most sharks seem to eat regularly at one- or two-day intervals, and that an average meal consists of about 3 to 5 percent of the body weight.

Not much is known about the digestive physiology of elasmobranchs. The gastric juices of autopsied sharks are potent, however. If stomach contents are handled without gloves, biologists and fishermen do not experience immediate discomfort, but the cornified epidermis of their hands will peel away several days later.

Sharks hooked during fishing operations not infrequently evert portions of their stomachs from their mouths. This has given rise to the claim that unfettered sharks may do the same to rid their stomachs of indigestible or unwanted material such as parasites. If sharks can evert their stomachs, it must occur only infrequently for a number of reasons. First, the mechanism for stomach eversion can only be through violent contractions of the body musculature that

85

squeeze the viscera to the point of expelling the stomach. Such contractions must be desperate measures that likely occur only during
capture. Secondly, the everted stomachs could be impaled on the
teeth and might suffer dangerous lacerations. Finally, the eversions
raise havoc with the normal blood supply to the stomach (indeed, to
the entire digestive tract). The rupture of visceral blood vessels could
have severe consequences.

The dissolved and partially digested food is ultimately passed
through the narrow fundal region of the stomach to the pylorus,
where it goes through a sphincter valve to enter the intestine. The
upper portion of the intestine receives the bile duct from the liver
and pancreatic ducts from the pancreas. The secretions entering here
further aid and complete the digestive process. The material leaving
this short portion of the intestine (which is comparable to the duode-
num of mammals) then enters an absorptive segment of the intestine
known as the spiral valve, which is found in chondrichthyans and a
few generalized bony fishes.

The spiral valve (Figure 4–13) is variously arranged in different
elasmobranchs, but its basic pattern is that of a spiral staircase,
auger, or helical ramp enclosed within an outer cylinder. The products of digestion are moved along this ramp and are exposed to a
great deal of intestinal surface area as they go, facilitating their absorption into the blood. The result is that abundant surface area can
be provided for absorption in what is, by comparison to other verte-

Figure 4–13. The spiral valve of a sand tiger shark. This species has
a tightly wound spiral valve. Several tapeworms can be seen in the
valve.

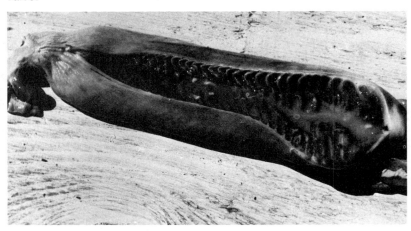

brates, a short, compact intestine. Abdominal space given over to intestinal volume in other vertebrates can be used by sharks for the large stomach, liver, and, in the case of females, uteri with developing young.

The form of the spiral valve varies from that having a tight twist to the alimentary channel, with many revolutions per unit of length, to valves that are arranged as a scroll of paper with long, broad revolutions. Examples of these extremes are found in the basking shark, which has a tightly coiled intestine, and the blue shark, which has the scroll type. A range of intermediate forms exists. There is little correlation among food preferences, systematic relationships, and the exact morphology of the spiral valve. Sharks with a scroll type of spiral valve have been observed to evert the intestine through the cloaca, for reasons that can only be guessed at.

At the hind end of the intestinal tract the spiral valve opens into the cloaca—a common chamber into which empty the genital and urinary ducts as well as the intestine. Near its termination at the cloaca, the intestine receives secretions from a gland unique to cartilaginous fishes. This structure, known as the digitiform or rectal gland, projects anteriorly from the dorsal surface of the intestine. It excretes a viscous solution rich in salts into the intestine, to be eliminated with the feces. Its role is that of a special salt-secreting gland (Chapter 9).

DIVERSITY OF FEEDING MECHANISM

If the food-handling capabilities of elasmobranchs are impressive, the diversity of their feeding mechanisms is even more so. As noted before, the modern or neoselachian feeding mechanism was defined during the Mesozoic era by the appearance of a jaw suspension featuring short jaws, an inferior mouth, and a movable, protrusile upper jaw. During the Mesozoic and later, in the Cenozoic, this basic feeding mechanism was modified in a number of ways along the separate lines of the modern elasmobranch radiation (Figure 4–14).

In the batoids, for example, the mouth became very small and was armed with many small, sharp teeth. The small mouth, combined with an expandable pharyngeal cavity, produced a mechanism capable of sucking small benthic organisms into the mouth and then grasping them with the prickly dentition. The loss of the anterior (ethmopalatine) connection between the upper jaw and braincase allowed the upper jaw to aid in directing the suction currents.

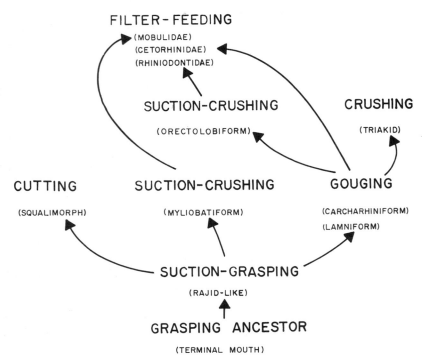

Figure 4–14. The diversity of elasmobranch feeding mechanisms. (From Moss, 1977)

The addition of broader, stronger molariform teeth and heavier jaws in the myliobatiform rays allowed this suction-grasping apparatus to be transformed into one that can be called a suction-crushing mechanism—one capable of dealing with hard-shelled mollusks and crustaceans.

In a few groups of batoids, further adaptations allowed the utilization of more diverse food resources. These include the evolution of a toothed rostral expansion in the sawfishes and electrogenic organs in the torpediniform rays. While both adaptations have a defensive character, they also allow these rays to immobilize fish, which can then be sucked into their small mouths. The ultimate feeding adaptation in the batoids, of course, is that of the plankton-feeding mobulid rays.

Another kind of feeding mechanism was developed early in the squalomorph radiation. Many of these sharks have short jaws positioned transversely across the body axis. These jaws are supported by short, heavy hyomandibular cartilages and long orbital processes from the upper jaw. These ride against the braincase in the orbits, behind the eyes. The teeth in squalids are often low, sharp, and tightly overlapped to form a continuous knife edge that runs from one side of the mouth to the other. This "cutting" feeding apparatus is admirably suited for attacking prey too large to be swallowed whole and slicing it up into bite-size pieces. Spiny dogfish eat herring and squid in just this manner.

The gouging apparatus of the carcharhiniform sharks is another basic feeding mechanism. With their relatively large jaws and bladelike upper-jaw teeth (Figure 4–15), these animals can gouge chunks out of much larger prey. Modifications on this theme are seen in a number of carcharhiniform and lamniform sharks. The Triakidae, a family of carcharhiniform sharks known as smoothhounds, have forsaken a sharp-toothed dentition for raylike molars (Figure 4–9). These animals have a crushing feeding apparatus designed to deal with their preferred food—crabs, lobsters, and other crustaceans. The Orectolobiformes, including the nurse and carpet sharks, have developed a feeding mechanism that in some ways is similar to that of the skates and stingrays. With a small, almost tubular mouth, small-cusped grasping teeth and a huge, expandable pharyngeal cavity, these sluggish sharks are adept at sucking benthic invertebrates into their mouths.

A few groups of sharks depend on structures outside of the

Figure 4–15. Upper-jaw teeth of a blue shark. The scimitar-shaped, serrated teeth are effective cutting tools, but are fragile, breaking often.

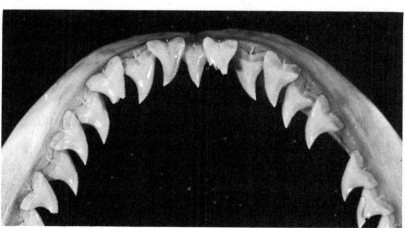

Figure 4–16. The long upper lobe of the bigeye thresher's tail is used to stun the small fish and squid on which it feeds.

mouth to assist in catching prey. The sawsharks and sawfishes feature rostral expansions tipped with teeth for this purpose. Another example is found in the thresher sharks, which have greatly elongated epichordal lobes of the caudal fins (Figure 4–16). Based on the observation that these sharks are often foul-hooked by the tail on longline fishing gear, it is thought that they use the long tails to stun or kill the small fishes on which they prey.

The history of the radiation of the modern elasmobranch feeding mechanism is thus a complex one. It involved a substantial array of distinct adaptations in a small group of vertebrates. At the same time, it provides a number of examples of parallel and convergent evolutionary pathways.

The success of an elasmobranch's feeding apparatus, however, is not just a function of the animal's ability to attack and swallow food. First, it must perceive the presence of the prey. To that purpose, sharks have a battery of senses which becomes more impressive as our understanding of them grows. The next chapter will deal with those senses.

ADDITIONAL READING

Alexander, R.McN. *The Chordates.* 2nd ed. New York: Cambridge University Press, 1981. (Figure 4–1 is modified from this work.)

Gilbert, P.W. "The behavior of sharks." *Scientific American,* 207, no. 1 (1962), 60–68.

Maisey, J.G. "An evaluation of jaw suspension in sharks." *American Museum Novitates*, 2706 (1980), 1–17.

McEachran, J.D., D.F. Boesch, and J.A. Musick. "Food division within two sympatric species-pairs of skates (Pisces: Rajidae)." *Marine Biology*, 35 (1976), 301–317.

Moss, S.A. "Tooth replacement in the lemon shark, *Negaprion brevirostris.*" In *Sharks, Skates and Rays*, ed. P.W. Gilbert, R.F. Mathewson, and D.P. Rall, 319–329. Baltimore: The Johns Hopkins Press, 1967.

Moss, S.A. "The feeding mechanism of sharks of the family Carcharhinidae." *Journal of Zoology* (London), 167 (1972), 423–436.

Moss, S.A. "Tooth replacement and body growth rates in the smooth dogfish, *Mustelus canis* (Mitchill)." *Copeia*, 1972(4) (1972), 808–811. (Figure 4–9 is from this work.)

Moss, S.A. "Feeding mechanisms in sharks." *Amer. Zool.*, 17 (1977), 355–364.

Moss, S.A. "Shark feeding mechanisms." *Oceanus*, 24, no. 4 (1981), 23–29. (Figure 4–14 is from this work.)

Springer, S. "Dynamics of the feeding mechanism of large galeoid sharks." *Amer. Zool.*, 1 (1961), 183–185.

Stillwell, C.E., and N.E. Kohler. "Food, feeding habits, and estimates of daily ration of the shortfin mako *(Isurus oxyrinchus)* in the northwest Atlantic." *Canadian J. Fish. Aquatic Sci.*, 39, no. 3 (1982), 407–414.

Strasburg, D.W. "The diet and dentition of *Isistius brasiliensis*, with remarks on tooth replacement in other sharks." *Copeia* (1963), 33–40.

Tricas, T.C. "Relationships of the blue shark, *Prionace glauca*, and its prey species near Santa Catalina Island, California." *Fishery Bulletin*, 77, no. 1 (1979), 175–182.

Tricas, T.C. "Feeding ethology of the white shark, *Carcharodon carcharias.*" *Bulletin of the Southern California Academy of Sciences* (1984), In Press.

5

Shark Sense

Sharks are often considered by scientists and the public alike to be "living noses"—that is, animals whose behavior is dominated by their sense of smell (olfaction). Early experiments conducted on captive smooth dogfish in the first decades of this century showed that these fish find food with difficulty when their sense of smell is impaired.

Today evidence is rapidly accumulating that shows sharks do not live by smell alone. Instead we are learning that they have a battery of senses perhaps unparalleled by any other vertebrate. Facts about the visual system, chemoreception, hearing, and the ability to perceive minute electrical and magnetic fields now cause us to revise our analysis of how a shark may sense its environment. This chapter will explore sensory perception in elasmobranchs and emphasize the new understanding and appreciation we have for this subject.

VISUAL SYSTEM

The orthodox view of shark vision was that it didn't matter too much. Elasmobranchs were known to have a typically vertebrate eye—one with a rigid eyeball or sclera protecting a pigmented choroid membrane which, in turn, supports the light-sensitive retina. The anterior, or outer, side of the eye has a nearly transparent cornea that directs and refracts light through the anterior chamber of the eye past the iris and through the lens, which helps to focus the image on the retina (Figure 5-1). Sharks were thought to have a retina that included only one type of photoreceptive unit—the rod cell. Vertebrate rod cells, while sensitive to small absolute amounts of light, absorb light from a broad frequency spectrum and are not suited for chromatic or color vision. Sharks, therefore, were not expected to distinguish colors.

About the only thing for which shark eyes were noteworthy, in the older view of things, was their mechanism of accommodation. Accommodation is the ability to change the focal length of the eye,

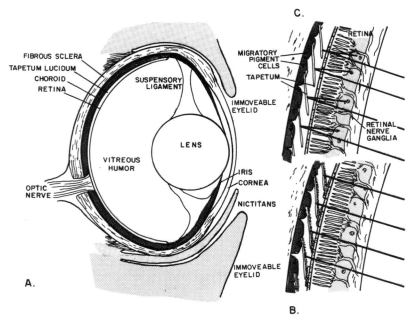

Figure 5-1. (A) General structure of an elasmobranch eye. (B) In the dark-adapted eye, light that passes through the retina is reflected back through it by mirrors in the tapetum lucidum. (C) In bright light, pigmented cell processes cover the mirrors. (From Gilbert, 1962. Copyright © 1962 by Scientific American, Inc. All rights reserved.)

allowing it to focus the image of near or far objects on the retina. This is effected in our eyes by altering the shape of our highly refractive lenses. Sharks were thought to have a lens with a fixed spherical shape that accommodated by moving back and forth due to intrinsic muscular contractions.

Modern analysis shows that much of this earlier view of elasmobranch vision is wrong. To discuss the current findings, let us enter the eye of a typical shark as if we were a ray of light, pausing to consider structures as we encounter them.

Shark eyes come in a variety of sizes and shapes. Benthic, lethargic forms like the skates, stingrays, hornsharks, and carpet sharks have small eyes, the diameters of which are usually less than 1 percent of the body length. In the flattened skates and stingrays the eyes periscopically project above the dorsal outline of the fish, allowing vision even while the animal is partially buried in sand or mud (Figure 5-2).

96   More active sharks, cylindrical in shape, have larger eyes located on the sides of the head, in front of and well above the mouth. The bigeye thresher shark has an eye diameter fully 10 percent of its body length. The eyes in this shark are directed upward, perhaps allowing a better view of its prey as it attacks them with the epichordal lobe of its tail.

Most elasmobranchs have eyes rimmed with immovable lids. Some, such as the smoothhounds of the family Triakidae, have distinct subocular folds of skin that are slightly movable. The development of this subocular fold reaches its zenith in the highly movable nictitating membrane, which can completely cover the eye in carcharhinid sharks (Figure 3–13).

As in other vertebrates, the cornea of the shark is a transparent, avascular structure that plays an important role in refracting light so that it may be focused on the retina. In the cytological details of its structure the elasmobranch cornea is similar to that of mammals. Almost uniquely, the shark cornea does not swell when placed in distilled water. This mechanical stability in the face of osmotic stress has made the shark cornea a candidate for corneal heterografts. Several successful shark-to-human corneal transplants have already been performed!

The iris is found in the anterior chamber of the eye, behind the cornea and ahead of the lens. This structure is markedly occlusible in most elasmobranchs, in contrast to the iris of bony fishes, which

Figure 5–2. The eyes of many benthic elasmobranchs, such as this clearnose skate, project above the body so that the animal can see while lying partially buried in the bottom sediments.

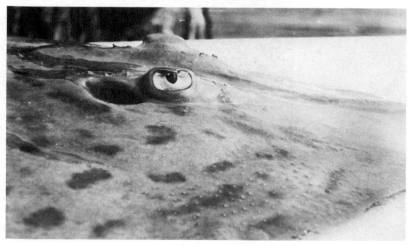

does not dilate or contract. The expansion of the iris narrows the pupillary aperture and reduces the amount of light that enters the posterior chamber of the eye and ultimately impinges on the retina. The iris thus helps adjust the eye to dim light (scotopic vision) and bright light (photopic vision) conditions. Iridial movements are rapid—95 percent complete in five minutes in many species—and result from the direct stimulation of light on the eye. An eye dissected from a shark will remain capable of iridial movements.

The shape of the pupil varies greatly among elasmobranchs. A circular pupil is found in sharks like the Atlantic sharpnose shark, although most sharks have slitlike pupils oriented horizontally (hammerheads) or vertically (whaler sharks). Many batoids have curious dorsal appendages, the operculum pupillare, in front of the cornea. These structures expand during light adaptation to occlude the pupil like a deeply scalloped shade. The effect may be to cast a series of shadows across the retina (stenopaic apertures) that provide great depth of field and may cause the retina to become more responsive to movement of an image (Figure 5–3). A similar effect is

Figure 5–3. This light-adapted eye of a little skate demonstrates the operculum pupillare, which permits vision through narrow slits (stenopaic apertures).

created in the eyes of birds, particularly hawks, by the intraocular pecten, which may be partly responsible for the great visual sensitivity to movement shown by these animals. The operculum pupillare is found in many elasmobranchs that spend most of their time resting motionless on the bottom.

The lenses of most sharks appear not to be spherical as stated in the older literature. Careful measurements show them to be 8 to 10 percent thinner than they are wide. Moreover, there is doubt that the lens moves to cause accommodation in many sharks. There is controversy here, with some workers reporting lens movement and others not. Most measurements of the eyes of sharks show them to be hyperopic (farsighted) and incapable of accommodation.

When sharks are held in captivity, it is striking that normally pelagic sharks (dusky sharks, blue sharks, etc.) are difficult to maintain because they persist in abrading their snouts and pectoral fins against the walls of the tanks or pens in which they are confined. Sharks more littoral in habitat (lemon sharks, nurse sharks, sandbar sharks) and which encounter more structure in their natural environments are adept at avoiding fin and snout abrasions. Perhaps the latter group of sharks is either myopic or is capable of accommodation—and hence can see the near, confining walls—while those from the pelagic realm are permanently hyperopic and unable to focus on near objects.

In batoids like the skates and stingrays, the eyeball is oblong rather than round. This has the effect of molding the retina so that all parts of it are not equidistant from the lens. The "ramp retina" that results makes possible visual accommodation without lens participation. By looking at an object from slightly different angles (by movement of the eye), a skate can project the image onto different parts of the retina, altering the focal length of the eye and thus accommodating.

The shark retina is a structure that, in its complexity, rivals that of mammals. The innermost layers of the retina, through which light passes almost unimpeded, consist first of axons converging to form the optic nerve that projects to the brain and then of alternating layers of nerve cell bodies and regions of synaptic connections. These inner layers of the retina support a substantial integrative function that reflects its developmental origin—an outgrowth of the embryonic brain. The outermost retinal layer consists mainly of the photoreceptive cells.

The older view—that sharks have retinas populated purely by rod cells—is refuted by cytological and physiological investigations in a number of elasmobranch species (rajid skates, which have all rod retinas, are exceptions). Most elasmobranchs have duplex retinas, with both rods and photoreceptive cones. The rod-to-cone ratio among these animals ranges from four to one in the white shark to one hundred to one in the smooth dogfish. These ratios represent small numbers of cones by human or teleost fish standards, and it remains to be learned what is the function of elasmobranch cones. Cone cells are traditionally considered to represent the anatomical basis for color vision, but they also are connected to the brain more independently than rods, allowing greater visual acuity under bright-light conditions.

Experimental conditioning of some sharks shows them capable of distinguishing between sets of shapes, but the threshold of visual acuity has not been convincingly demonstrated. What behavioral and physiological experimentation does reveal, however, is that most sharks see well under dim-light conditions. Light levels experienced underwater during moonlight are sufficient for shark vision. The ability to adapt from photopic to scotopic vision must, therefore, be substantial, and proves to involve more than just iris movements.

The pigmented choroid membrane, which lies just outside of the retina, is important in the processes of dark and light adaptation by sharks. This tissue contains a layer, the tapetum lucidum, that is equipped with crystalline reflecting plates of guanine. Under dim-light conditions, light that passes unabsorbed through the retina is reflected from the guanine mirrors back through the retina a second time. The opportunity to strike a photoreceptor is thus doubled. Moreover, the mirrors are angled in such a way that light reflecting from them will traverse nearly the same path out through the retina as it took coming in (Figure 5–1B). Visual acuity is thus preserved.

Many animals, particularly nocturnally active ones, have reflecting tapetums (the eye-shine of domestic cats is a familiar example). What makes many sharks unique, however, is that their tapetal mirrors can be covered by pigment granules dispersing in the cytoplasmic processes of cells facing the mirrors. Some sharks, especially those found in brightly lit surface waters, are capable of drawing a light-absorbing curtain across the tapetal mirrors during the process of light adaptation (Figure 5–1C). This process is reversed during the conversion to scotopic vision when light levels fall.

Not all sharks have occlusible tapetums. Deep-sea squalomorphs, which live in constant darkness, have permanently reflecting tapetums and preserve their eye-shine when captured. Other benthic sharks, like the catsharks, have choroids that are permanently pigmented in some areas and reflecting in others. These sharks may dark- or light-adapt by focusing images on the appropriate part of the retina.

Vision plays a more important role in the lives of sharks than earlier scientists realized. These animals have eyes that are well suited to seeing in dim light, and many have unique mechanisms for converting to photopic vision as well. Much is yet to be learned about this system, and the role vision plays in the lives of sharks will be determined only through additional behavioral observation and experimentation.

CHEMORECEPTION

Chemoreception, the ability to sense chemicals in the environment, involves at least three separate sensory systems in most aquatic vertebrates. These include the senses of smell (olfaction), taste (gustation), and general chemical sense. Sharks include a fourth chemoreceptive sense mediated through so-called pit organs, which are distributed over their bodies. Of these four chemical senses, gustation and olfaction are the best studied and of primary importance to elasmobranchs.

Gustation is carried out through taste buds located in the mouth and pharynx of sharks. The chemoreceptive cells are associated with sensory neurons that collect and pass to the brain through the facial (VII), glossopharyngeal (IX), and vagus (X) cranial nerves. The sense of taste has not been studied extensively in sharks, although the distributions of taste buds have been reported for a few species.

The cells responsible for taste are mounted on small papillae scattered over the mucosal lining of the mouth and pharynx. Their greatest density occurs on the soft tissue just inside the teeth. External taste buds, like those known from bony fishes (catfish, eels, etc.), have not been described in elasmobranchs. If such external taste buds exist, a good place for them would be on the oral barbels of sawsharks, carpet sharks, and some of the catsharks. Taste allows the shark to make a final discrimination about the palatability of prey before it is swallowed. Cases of sharks rejecting food conceivably result from its taste.

Sharks are famous for their feats of olfactory discrimination and are often referred to as "living noses." Actually, many of the experiments and observations that provided this view are confounded by our newer understanding about the visual, auditory, and electroreceptive capabilities of these animals.

Modern behavioral and physiological experiments confirm that sharks do have acute senses of smell and are able to detect slight concentrations of chemicals important to them. The olfactory apparatus of elasmobranchs consists of paired nasal sacs found on the ventral surface of the head in front of the mouth. The single opening of each sac is guarded by a flap of skin that effectively divides it into an incurrent (outer) side and an excurrent (inner) side (Figure 5–4). As the shark swims forward, water is forced into the nasal sac and perfuses the olfactory organ that lies therein. In sedentary sharks, including most batoids, an oronasal groove connects the nasal sac with the mouth. As these sharks rest motionless on the bottom, the

Figure 5–4. The nostrils of elasmobranchs are divided externally by a skin flap, as in this sand tiger shark. Water flows into the olfactory organ through the lateral part of the opening and out through the medial side.

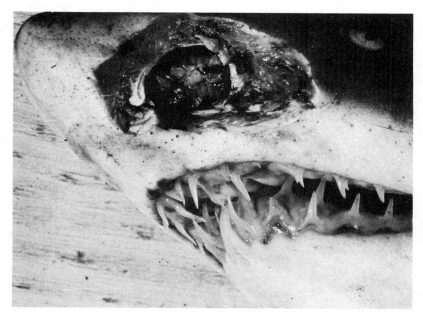

Figure 5–5. The nasal capsule of a sand tiger shark is opened to show the large, much-folded olfactory organ within.

olfactory organ can be irrigated by ventilation currents generated in the mouth and pharynx.

The olfactory organ consists of a series of thin, platelike folds or lamellae that provide abundant surface area for the intimate contact of water with the numerous olfactory receptor cells contained in it (Figure 5–5). Although the olfactory organs of elasmobranchs differ considerably in their relative sizes, and probably in importance, even the smallest of them is large when compared with the olfactory organs of most bony fish.

The sensory nerves that supply the olfactory sensory cells together form the olfactory nerve (cranial nerve I). These project a short distance to the olfactory bulb, which is the most anterior part of the brain and the first site of olfactory integration. The olfactory bulbs connect to the olfactory lobes of the forebrain by long olfactory tracts (Chapter 6). The size of the forebrain of the shark used to be taken as a measure of the importance of olfaction. Today, however, we know that more goes on in this region of the brain than the mere integration of olfactory information (Chapter 6).

103

A great deal is now known about the capabilities of the shark sense of smell. Not unexpectedly, sharks are most sensitive to chemicals produced by the sorts of prey they usually eat. Amino acids, amines, and small fatty acids are more stimulating than are simple sugars or other carbohydrates. Lemon sharks and nurse sharks are most responsive behaviorally and neurophysiologically to extracts of "oily" fishes such as tunas and jacks. Of the pure chemicals tested, there are positive responses to concentrations as low as one part per billion of amino acids such as glycine and glutamic acid, as well as to amines like betaine, trimethylamine, and trimethylamine oxide. Responses to polyhydric alcohols, large fatty acids and oils, and carbohydrates are either nonexistent or ambiguous.

Tests on sharks held captive in large pens confirm that these animals negotiate olfactory corridors to locate the sources of attractive odors. A naive view of the mechanism by which any shark is able to locate a prey by olfaction alone has the shark comparing the intensity of odor between its two nostrils and turning toward the side of the "stronger" odor until the prey is reached. This probably does not happen because odor trails are extremely dilute from all but very near prey. The nostrils of most sharks (hammerheads excluded) are set close together, and the small concentration differences between them are not easily detectable. Experiments on several species of sharks reveal that when a shark encounters the odor of a potential prey it turns into the current. The olfactory stimulus releases a positive rheotaxis (movement into the current flow). By repeated turns (upcurrent whenever the scent is perceived), the shark is able to arrive at or near the prey in short order (Figure 5–6).

A lot of research on shark olfaction has been directed toward finding chemical compounds that sharks avoid, and which therefore may have repellent activity (Chapter 1). Such compounds appear to be rare. Indeed, if olfactory repellent substances exist, practical considerations (general toxicity, difficult delivery, etc.) would make a workable chemical repellent unlikely.

Sharks, like most vertebrates, respond to irritating chemicals (such as acids) when these are placed on the general surface of the skin. This general chemical sense may be mediated by bare nerve endings in the skin. In addition to such unspecialized receptors, sharks have unique sensory organs known as sensory crypts or pit organs, which are distributed in particular patterns (usually over the head and back) in each species. A sensory crypt consists of a slight depression in the skin which is guarded by a pair of enlarged placoid scales. At the bottom of each crypt is a small cluster of sensory cells

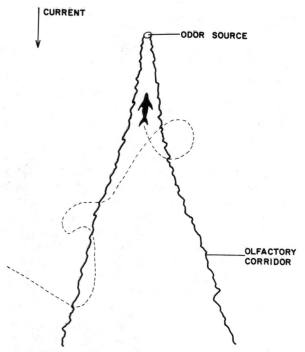

CURRENT

ODOR SOURCE

OLFACTORY CORRIDOR

Figure 5-6. Sharks locate an odor source by turning into the current whenever they encounter an olfactory stimulus.

that resemble both taste buds and receptors of the lateral line system. The precise function of these sensory crypts has not been determined. Their resemblance to taste buds argues for a chemoreceptive function. Their distribution over the dorsal body surface, however, does not favor this interpretation.

MECHANICAL SENSE

Sharks are abundantly endowed with batteries of receptors that are responsive to mechanical forms of energy such as touch, vibration, water currents, sound, and hydrostatic pressure. Most of these senses are studied from the perspective of shark feeding, but mechanical senses are also important in swimming, reproductive behavior, and perhaps social behavior.

105 When deciding whether or not to attack a prey, a shark may nudge or bump it with its snout or a pectoral fin. The shark could be getting useful information about the resilience or other mechanical properties of the prey. It also might learn something about the ability of the prey to defend itself. Bumps against human swimmers are sometimes reported as shark attacks. Indeed, the consequences of being hit by several hundred pounds of speeding shark can be severe. The rough, scale-studded skin can cause significant abrasions and gashes. These attacks are really the final investigatory phases of feeding behavior.

No specialized mechanoreceptors in the snout and fins of sharks have been described that are related to this behavior. Naked nerve endings in the skin or other receptors such as pit organs and lateral line neuromasts can provide the sensory information necessary for the shark or judge the palatability of prey so bumped.

The main mechanoreceptors of elasmobranchs, like other fishes, are the neuromast cells of the acoustico-lateralis system (lateral line system). These sensory cells are sunken into the skin and communicate with each other and the watery environment through a series of tubes that comprise the head and lateral line canals (Figure 5–7). Movement of water created by turbulence, currents, and vibration displaces the water in these canals through pores that communicate with the outside. The water displacement stimulates neuromast cells to initiate nerve impulses, which are conveyed to the brain via the lateral line nerves.

Neuromast hair cells have an anatomy that makes them responsive to slight water displacements. Projecting from the free end of the cell into the cavity of the lateral line canal are a patch of hair-like processes called cilia. These consist of many shorter stereocilia and usually one longer klinocilium. The stereocilia are often graded

Figure 5–7. The lateral line systems of sharks include neuromast-containing canals that ramify over their heads. (From Gilbert, 1962. Copyright © 1962 by Scientific American, Inc. All rights reserved.)

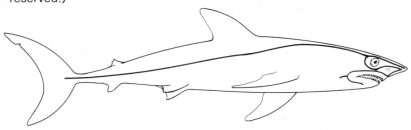

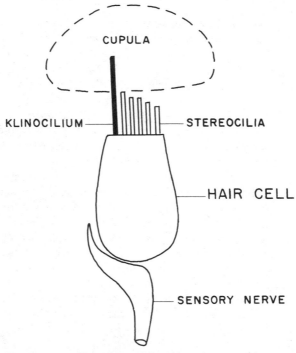

Figure 5–8. The hair cell is the major sensory cell of the neuromast organs found in lateral lines, the labyrinth of the inner ear, and in pit organs or sensory crypts. Displacement of the gelatinous cupula strains the klinocilium embedded within it and causes an electrical change in the hair cell. This information is passed to a sensory nerve and travels to the central nervous system.

in length, the shortest ones on one side of the patch, the longest on the other (Figure 5–8). The klinocilium is found behind the longest stereocilia, which buttress it and allow it to bend only in the direction away from the stereocilia. The klinocilia from closely adjacent hair cells are embedded in a single gelatinous mass, known as the cupula, which projects into the canal. Water movement in the canal displaces the cupula, which then stretches or shears those klinocilia embedded in it. It is this mechanical force that causes the neuromast cells to initiate nerve impulses.

The sensitivity of this system depends upon the number of neuromast cells, the orientation of their stereocilia, and the connections between the nerve cells they serve. Experiments on captive sharks show that the lateral line and head canal system is sensitive indeed. The rheotactic (current-seeking) behavior of sharks can be good, allowing them to distinguish water current differences of about 1 centimeter per second or less. Blinded sharks held in large tanks are able to discern the walls of these tanks without touching them—probably by sensing reflections of water waves of their own making. Sharks are also sensitive to vibrations in water, particularly of the sort set up by injured or otherwise distressed fish. Vibrations in the "near field"—that is, close enough to displace water particles—could be sensed by lateral line detectors.

It has been suggested that the swimming motions of sharks cause displacement of water in the enclosed canals of the lateral line. If neuromasts respond to these self-induced displacements, they could provide information to the shark about its own postural changes. This kind of position sense (proprioception) is important to muscular coordination. Tetrapods like mammals and birds have sophisticated proprioceptors of types undescribed for fishes, including sharks. The lateral line neuromasts could be useful in allowing motor coordination in these superbly coordinated elasmobranchs.

The inner ear or labyrinthine system of elasmobranchs is developmentally and anatomically related to the lateral line system. The basic sensory cell of the labyrinth is the hair cell. In all vertebrates but the lampreys and hagfishes (cyclostomes), the labyrinth consists of three semicircular canals connected at their bases to a system of chambers, which in fish consists of a central sacculus, an anterior utriculus, and a posterior lagena. Within this system are patches of hair cells with their klinocilia embedded in cupulae or, in the sacculus, utriculus and lagena, in concentrations of calcareous material known as otoliths (Figure 5–9).

The cupulae of the semicircular canals are found in expansions of the canals near their bases known as ampullae. As the head of the shark turns or rolls, fluid (endolymph) in the canals lags in its movement due to its inertia. The relative displacement between the cupulae and the neuromasts provides information about the angular velocities and directions of head turning. We have a similar system and appreciate its normal function best when it malfunctions, producing sensations of dizziness or vertigo.

The otic capsule (the part of the skull containing the labyrinth) is accessible in most sharks because it is embedded in soft, uncalcified cartilage. A block of cartilage containing the inner ear can be cut from the chondrocranium, further dissected, and then placed on a special turntable. Electrodes record the nerve impulses generated as

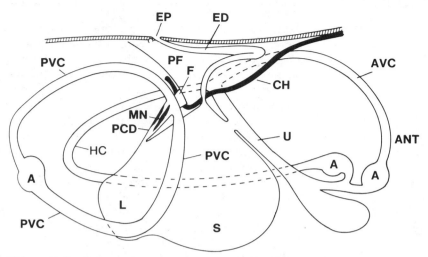

Figure 5–9. Schematic diagram of the left inner ear of a gray reef shark. The endolymphatic duct (ED) tortuously passes from its pore (EP) in the skin through the parietal fossa (PF) to enter the sacculus (S) beneath the chondrocranium (CH). The lagena (L) and posterior vertical canal (PVC) communicate to a fenestra (F) in the parietal fossa through the posterior communicating duct (PCD). The posterior communicating duct houses the macula neglecta (MN), a suspected sound-sensitive receptor. A = ampulla; U = utriculus; AVC = anterior vertical canal; HC = horizontal canal; ANT = anterior. (From Tester, *et al.*, 1972)

the labyrinth is rotated in different planes. Because of this accessibility, more is known of the neurophysiology of the elasmobranch semicircular canals than those of any other group of animals. For fortuitous reasons, most of the experiments on this system have used guitarfishes of the genus *Rhinobatos.* This otherwise unpopular elasmobranch is coveted by researchers who seek to better understand our own sense of balance and equilibrium.

The central chambers of the inner ear are dominated in elasmobranchs by the sacculus. This is filled in most sharks by packed spherules of calcium carbonate embedded in a matrix of mucopolysaccharides. Unlike the dense, bonelike saccular otolith of teleost fishes, the shark otolith has the consistency of thick cream. It rests on a large collection of neuromasts at the bottom of the sacculus. The klinocilia of these neuromasts are embedded in the otolith.

The inner ear of elasmobranchs is unique among that of vertebrates because the fluid within the labyrinth communicates with the outside environment through a pair of ducts—the endolymphatic ducts. These run from the top of the sacculus on each side through the top of the braincase and, after a tortuous but short course, emerge through the skin of the head to the outside. The endolymphatic pores are found on either side of the midline in the otic region of any shark's head. The exact function of the endolymphatic ducts is still not known.

The region of the braincase through which the endolymphatic ducts pass is depressed into a parabolic recess known as the parietal fossa (Figure 5–9). There is a hole (fenestra ovalis) through the cartilage on the ventrolateral wall on each side of this fossa. The fenestra ovalae are covered by tightly stretched membranes, producing a double-paned window effect. The fenestra ovalis lies just behind the top of the sacculus near a short duct, the posterior communicating duct, which runs from the posterior wall of the sacculus to the posterior vertical semicircular canal. Within the short posterior communicating duct are one or two maculae (depending upon the species) with a gelatinous cupula that fills the duct. This *macula neglecta* was unappreciated by shark biologists for many years. Now it is recognized as having an important hearing function in some sharks (Figure 5–9).

The inner ear of most land vertebrates as well as many teleosts is modified to receive sound in addition to its basic accelerometer and gravity detection functions. The reception of sound is a particular problem because of its physical nature. Sound can be thought of as having two properties—waves of net particle displacement (vibration) and waves of particle displacement in all directions (pressure). The energy in sound quickly dissipates as it propagates from its source, so that the vibration property is soon lost. What remains is "far-field" sound, which, to be sensed, must be converted back into vibrations. This is done in most vertebrates by some sort of transducer that works by passing sound through two phases (solid–gas or gas–liquid) that transmit pressure waves at unequal velocities. The resulting displacement reestablishes vibrations that excite the neuromasts of the inner ear. This is done in our ears by eardrums and middle ear ossicles. In bony fishes the inflated swim bladder that is often directly connected to the labyrinth does the same. Sharks have no swim bladders, however, nor other phase interfaces to interact with far-field sound. They should, in theory, be transparent to sound and deaf to all but near-field sound with its vibration component. Yet experiments show that not only can sharks hear, but that they are remarkably responsive to certain frequencies, particularly those less than about 375 Hertz.

Field experiments demonstrate that some sharks are attracted to sound sources from distances as great as 250 meters. The most attractive frequencies are those in the range of 25 to 100 Hertz. The responses of sharks to these frequencies can be enhanced if they are emitted as bursts or pulses of sound rather than continuous tones. Sharks are thus attracted to sounds of the sort produced by fish in distress (either struggling or rapidly accelerating). Sound reception is used in the location of food by sharks and may be as important as olfaction in the distant perception of prey.

The observation that sharks can hear prompted a closer look at the inner ears of these animals to determine the mechanism of this sense. Two potential sound receptors have been discovered. The first of these, the macula neglecta, has highly orientated neuromasts that could respond to sound waves focused on it by the parietal fossa—fenestra ovalis system. Indeed, sharks that prey on fish have larger and better organized macula neglecti than benthic, invertebrate-feeding sharks. In theory, the macula neglecta sound receptor is most responsive to sounds originating above the shark and would be unable to distinguish the true direction of the source (180-degree error). Neurophysiological experiments disclose, however, that the large inertial mass of the saccular otolith allows the saccular macula also to be a sound receptor. The presence of two distinct sound receptors could allow the shark to determine with precision the direction of the source of sound energy.

ELECTRORECEPTION

If any elasmobranch is closely examined, one of its pervasive features is a system of pores in the skin, particularly richly distributed around the head and mouth (Figure 5–10). In fresh specimens these pores exude a jellylike substance when the nearby skin is pressed. These pores are the surface openings for long, jelly-filled tubes that connect to a few congregations of ampullary organs located in the heads of all elasmobranchs. These organs are composed of the "ampullae of Lorenzini"—curious sensory receptors that receive information conveyed by the ampullary canals. Each ampulla consists of a cluster of several saclike alveoli, continuous with the jelly-filled canal (Figure 5–11). In the walls of the alveoli are the sensory cells themselves. Each ampulla produces about five sensory nerves that pass to the brain.

Not many years ago the ampullary system was thought to be

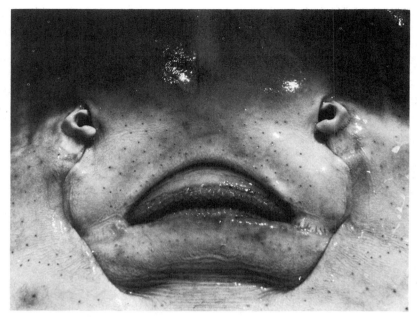

Figure 5–10. The external pores of the ampullary system can be seen around the mouth of this clearnose skate.

responsible for either temperature sense or hydrostatic pressure sense. Today we know that this is an electroreceptive system that is sensitive to small electric fields, responding to voltage gradients of less than 0.01 microvolt per centimeter.

The significance of this sensitive electrosensory system is apparent when it becomes known that fishes and invertebrates normally produce electric fields around them which, for a distance of about 25 centimeters, greatly exceed the sensory limits of the ampullary system. Indeed, elasmobranchs such as smooth dogfish, spotted dogfish, swell sharks, blue sharks, and certain skates can locate food based on its electrical characteristics alone. Smooth dogfish, for example, when given a choice of biting the source of an olfactory attractant or electrodes emitting an appropriate electric field, will nearly always bite the electrodes (Figure 5–12).

The results of a growing number of experiments with more species of sharks demonstrate that the electroreceptive powers of sharks are important to them in the final stages of prey capture. Because the pattern of pore openings on the underside of batoids are

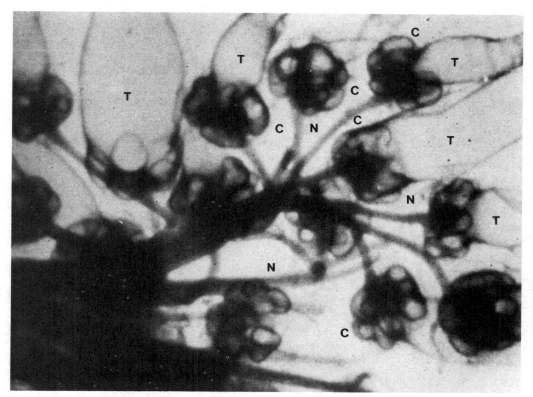

Figure 5–11. Each ampullary tube (T) ends at a cluster of ampullary cells (C) deep in the heads of elasmobranchs. Sensory nerves (N) carry information to the brain about weak electric fields sensed by the ampullary cells.

usually symmetrical around the mouth, it is likely that these animals are able to bite prey with precision using just electrical information (Figure 5–13).

Some species of elasmobranchs, including the spiny dogfish and many species of skates, are notoriously difficult to feed in captivity. It is likely that the large electrical fields present in confined situations and associated with metal aquarium fixtures, pumps, and filters, effectively jam the captive sharks' electroreceptive systems, rendering it difficult or impossible for them to recognize food.

Biologically generated electrical fields are not the only ones found in the oceans. The earth's magnetic field, and saltwater currents moving through this field, create voltage potentials large

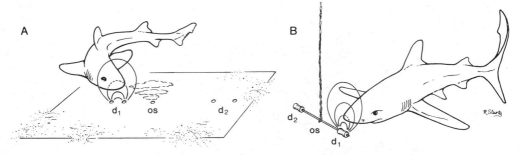

Figure 5–12. Both smooth dogfish (A) and blue sharks (B) will attack electrodes (d_1), passing a current of only 8 microamps in preference to a nearby odor source (os) or control electrodes (d_2). (From Kalmign, 1982. Copyright 1982 by the American Association for the Advancement of Science.)

enough to be sensed by elasmobranchs. Round stingrays can be conditioned to distinguish compass direction based solely on their orientation to magnetic fields. The electrosensory system of sharks may thus allow them to orientate and navigate in an otherwise featureless ocean using just electromagnetic cues.

In terms of breadth as well as sensitivity, the sensory world of elasmobranchs is a rich one indeed. Endowed with good eyesight; excellent senses of olfaction, hearing, and mechanoreception; and an extraordinary electrical sense, sharks are acutely tuned to their environments. More than any other group of fishes, they display a broad spectrum of sensory excellence. Sensory information provides the raw material for behavior. The conversion of sensory experience to behavior requires the interposition of a decision maker—the central nervous system. So, in the next chapter, we'll look at the brain of sharks and its output—behavior.

Figure 5–13. The ventral ampullary pores of the little skate (left) and winter skate (right) are geometrically symmetrical around the mouths of these fish. (From Raschi, 1978)

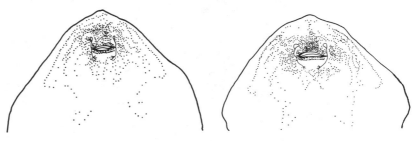

ADDITIONAL READING

Cohen, J.L. "Vision in sharks." *Oceanus*, 24, no. 4 (1981), 17–22.

Hodgson, E.S., and R.F. Mathewson, eds. *Sensory Biology of Sharks, Skates, and Rays.* Arlington, VA, Office of Naval Research, Department of the Navy (1978).

Kalmijn, A.J. "Electric and Magnetic Field Detection in Elasmobranch Fishes." *Science,* 218 (1982), 916–918. (Figure 5–12 is from this work. Copyright 1982 by the American Association for the Advancement of Science.)

Myrberg, A.A., S.J. Ha, S. Walewski, and J.C. Banbury. "Effectiveness of acoustic signals in attracting epipelagic sharks to an underwater sound source." *Bulletin of Marine Science*, 22, no. 4 (1972), 926–949.

Raschi, W. "Notes on the gross morphology of the ampullary system in two similar species of skates, *Raja erinacea* and *R. ocellata.*" *Copeia*, 1978, no. 1, (1978), 48–53. (Figure 5–13 is from this work.)

Tester, A.L., J.I. Kendall, and W.B. Milisen. "Morphology of the ear of the shark genus *Carcharhinus,* with particular reference to the macula neglecta." *Pacific Science*, 26, no. 3 (1972), 264–274. (Figure 5–9 is modified from this work.)

Tricas, T.C. "Bioelectric-mediated predation by swell sharks, *Cephaloscyllium ventriosum.*" *Copeia*, 1982, no. 4 (1982), 948–952.

6

Shark Brains and Behavior

The receptor systems discussed in Chapter 5 provide the raw material for decisions made by the elasmobranch central nervous system (brain plus spinal cord). The sensory input flows through spinal and cranial nerves directly to the CNS. Nerve pathways direct and redirect this information through the brain in circuits about which we have only the most cursory information. At different levels sensory input is matched and compared with that of various receptor systems, and this information is correlated with the stored traces of experiences past. This continuous integration can be modified by the hormonal environment of the brain as well as by the responses of sensory receptors. What emerges after finite periods of time are decisions—neural commands to specific muscles to contract or to relax—and chemical commands to glands and physiologically responsive tissues. We see the results of these decisions as behavior—what the shark does. Our desire to know with some certainty what a shark *will* do—and *when* it will do it—can be best satisfied by learning as much as we can about the structure and functions of the shark brain.

Most of the traditional thinking about the brains and behavior of sharks can be summed up in two words—primitive and unpredictable. There is scarcely a textbook in comparative neurology that does not start with the brain of the shark as the example of a "primitive" vertebrate brain. Most general references on sharks label their behavior as "unpredictable," and infer that "unpredictability" is a necessary consequence of "primitiveness." This is a result of shoddy logic and ignorance of shark anatomy. Sharks, it turns out, are more competent intellectually than is generally recognized.

THE ELASMOBRANCH BRAIN

In the study of shark brains, that of the spiny dogfish is a good place to start. It is not compact—most of the parts are easy to see—and it has few of the special distinctions that mark the brains of so many

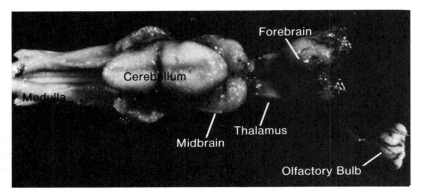

Figure 6–1. The brain of a squalomorph shark, the spiny dogfish.

other elasmobranchs (Figure 6–1). The rearmost portion of the brain, the hindbrain or medulla oblongata, merges imperceptibly with the spinal cord where the latter emerges from the chondrocranium. The medulla receives the fifth through the tenth cranial nerves. In sharks the eighth (auditory) and tenth (vagus) nerves bring sensory input from the acoustico-lateralis system, while the fifth and seventh nerves contribute neural information gleaned from the ampullary system of electroreceptors in the shark's head.

Ahead of and above the medulla is a discrete lobe, the cerebellum. In spiny dogfish the cerebellum is undistinguished, it being an oblong, smooth-walled projection. In many sharks, however, the cerebellum is enlarged and foliated. It has classically been regarded as a site of muscular coordination, and animals with large, complex cerebella are good runners, swimmers, or fliers, and are capable of precisely coordinated movements. On either side of the dogfish's cerebellum is an earlike appendage, the auricle of the cerebellum, which receives input from the lateral line nerves. Injury to either of the auricles impairs the swimming performance of a shark.

Ahead of the cerebellum is the mesencephalon or midbrain. In most sharks the roof of the midbrain (tectum) is formed by a pair of prominent swellings, the optic lobes, which appear to integrate visual information.

The diencephalon, part of the forebrain, lies in front of the mesencephalon. In it are found the thalamus, the epithalamus, and the hypothalamus. It also contains a cavity, the third ventricle, which is filled with cerebrospinal fluid and is continuous with the fourth ventricle of the medulla through a narrow tube, the cerebral aque-

120

duct, which passes through the midbrain. The epithalamus is interesting because in some elasmobranchs one of its dorsal projections, the epiphysis, reaches up and forward to terminate in a structure that has cells resembling the rods of the retina, and which has been discovered to be light sensitive. Oceanic sharks such as the blue shark have exceptionally thin and clear "windows" in the roofs of the skull directly over the epiphysis. Information about length of day or sun position gathered by the epiphysis could provide navigational aids useful to these wide-ranging, migrating sharks.

The hypothalamus on the underside of the diencephalon is marked by the entrance of the optic nerves (second cranial nerves) which send pathways to the thalamus. The hypothalamus also supports the pituitary (hypophysis), the master endocrine gland of the elasmobranch. Much of the activity of the hypothalamus relates to both hormonal and neural control of the pituitary, but electric stimulation of this region of the brain can produce biting movements, indicating that important elements of feeding behavior also are controlled here.

The anterior part of the forebrain (telencephalon) consists of a pair of cerebral hemispheres, each of which produces an olfactory tract terminating in an olfactory bulb at the base of the nasal capsule. Short olfactory nerves (first cranial nerves) bring sensory information from the olfactory organs to the olfactory bulbs.

Each cerebral hemisphere contains a cavity (lateral ventricle) continuous with the third ventricle of the diencephalon. In skates (*Raja*) and advanced batoids, the enlarged cerebral hemispheres have reduced lateral ventricles. The function of the ventricular system of the vertebrate brain has long perplexed biologists. Evidence now indicates that the cerebrospinal fluid that circulates through the ventricles carries hormones that help coordinate brain activity. In several parts of the elasmobranch brain (the midbrain, for example) there exist groups of cells that may secrete hormones into the ventricular system.

The olfactory bulbs in most vertebrates are connected to the front of the cerebral hemispheres by the olfactory tracts. Sharks uniquely have the olfactory tracts coming into the sides of the cerebral hemispheres. The meaning of this peculiarity is not known. What is clear, however, is that the roles of the cerebral hemispheres in sharks (and other fishes) have been misunderstood by most biologists. They are traditionally considered to be centers of olfactory integration. This view holds that the relative size of the cerebrum in sharks is an indication of the importance of the sense of smell to these animals. Indeed, most textbooks label the cerebral hemispheres as the "olfactory lobes."

New techniques in the microscopic examination of shark forebrains, along with behavioral experiments, demonstrate that as little as 10 percent of the cerebral hemispheres integrate olfactory information. Exactly what the remaining part does is conjectural. We know, however, that the cerebrum in teleost fishes also is not completely given over to olfaction. In these fishes an intact forebrain is necessary for learning and memory, just as the forebrain is used for these "higher" functions in birds and mammals. In many sharks the cerebral hemispheres are large, prominent structures. Perhaps this marks them not so much as "living noses," but as perceptive animals capable of sophisticated integration and information retention.

The spiny dogfish brain described here is like those found in several other groups of sharks. The angel sharks, six- and sevengill sharks, and the frill shark share a similar brain anatomy. Because these sharks resulted from the earliest radiation of modern sharks, this brain pattern may represent a general level of elasmobranch neural organization. Other elasmobranchs have strikingly different central nervous systems, both in terms of gross morphology and the cellular details of their brains. For example, several groups of sharks evolved a convoluted, foliate cerebellum that superficially bears little resemblance to that of squaliforms. The cerebella of the mackerel sharks, requiem sharks, and myliobatiform rays are highly convo-

Figure 6–2. The brain of an advanced galeomorph, the sandbar shark. Note the complex cerebellum and large cerebrum.

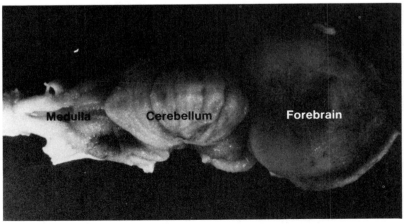

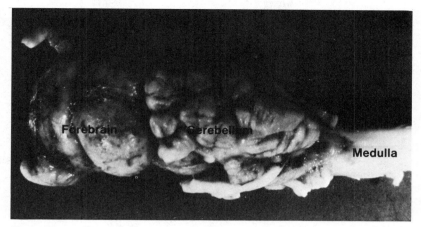

Figure 6–3. The brain of the roughtailed stingray has a large, complex cerebellum and a large, subdivided cerebrum.

luted, subdivided, and twisted to the point that they are decidedly asymmetric (Figure 6–2). The cerebral hemispheres also vary in their sizes and appearances. Again, the requiem sharks (including hammerheads) and myliobatiform rays have the largest forebrains (Figure 6–3). The kinds of differences found among shark brains are indicated by the relative weights of brain segments for several species in Figure 6–4.

BRAIN SIZE

When the microscopic structure of the brains of batoids and galeomorph sharks are compared with those of squalomorphs, a picture of enhanced complexity emerges. Cellular groups (nuclei) within the brain are more discrete and better organized in batoids and galeomorphs. Another measure that can be made of brains is the ratio of the weight of an animal's brain to the weight of its body. Comparative brain-body weight ratios are available now for a variety of sharks. Some sharks have small brains relative to their body weight. These include basking sharks, angel sharks, thornback guitarfish, electric rays, spiny dogfish, and clearnose skates. Sharks with the largest brain weight-body weight ratios include the stingrays (*Dasyatis, Potamotrygon*), the dusky shark, and scalloped hammerheads. The range of values is impressive. Batoids have both large (stingrays) and small brains (skates, electric rays). Squalomorph and squatino-

123

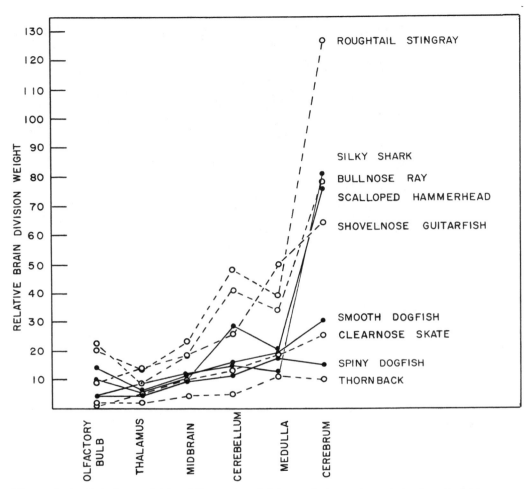

Figure 6-4. Relative weights of the major divisions of elasmobranch brains. Batoids are indicated with dashed lines and open circles, squalomorph and galeomorph sharks with solid lines and closed circles. (Data from Northcutt, 1978.)

morph sharks have small brains, although crucial data from large squalomorphs such as the Greenland and sleeper sharks *(Somniosus)* are missing. Some galeomorph sharks have relatively small brains (basking shark, nurse shark, horn shark), while many (whaler sharks, hammerheads) have large ones.

One correlation with brain size is the activity of these fishes. The swifter pelagic sharks have larger brains than more indolent,

124

bottom-oriented ones. Although the large-brained stingrays can be lethargic, some are migratory and others show complex behavior. All are capable of active defense. Many myliobatiforms have taken up the actively swimming pelagic existence.

To be active requires an enhanced sensory picture of the environment that is being explored and a greater degree of muscular coordination to move effectively within that environment. More sensory input with heightened decision-making obligations demand a more complex and larger brain. Such appears to be the case among elasmobranchs.

When the brain weight-body weight relationships of sharks are compared with those of other vertebrates, an interesting picture emerges. Comparative studies on vertebrates other than sharks indicate that homeothermic vertebrates (mainly birds and mammals) have distinctly larger brains than poikilotherms (bony fishes, reptiles, and amphibians). The traditional view of sharks predicts that their brain-body weight ratios should be comparable to those of bony fish, if not smaller. This is not the case. While small-brained sharks overlap the brain-body weight ratios of poikilotherms, many elasmobranchs prove to have brains fully as large or larger than many birds and some mammals of equivalent body weight (Figure 6–5). While the fact that sharks can have large brains relative to other vertebrates may surprise some people, it does not impress those who have had a chance to study carefully the behavior of these fishes. In view of the superb senses of elasmobranchs and their active roles in the environment, their large brains make sense.

ELASMOBRANCH BEHAVIOR

The complexity of the brain can be estimated by the behavioral repertoire of an animal. Those with limited behavior (due perhaps to limited neural substrate) respond to particular situations in characteristic and predictable ways. These animals are said to be stereotyped in their behavior. Most bony fishes present examples of stereotyped behavior and, because of this, have been frequent subjects of behavioral studies. Sharks, on the other hand, are legendary for their "unpredictability," both in the natural environment and in captivity. Their stereotypical behavior is not prominent. Curiously, this richness of response (including decisions not to do what is expected of them) is often taken as evidence of their "primitiveness."

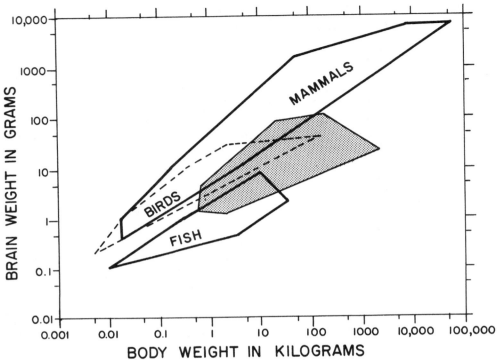

Figure 6–5. The brain- and body-weight relationships of four groups of vertebrates. Those for elasmobranchs fall within the stippled area, overlapping some birds and mammals. (Modified from Northcutt, 1977)

Swimming. Perhaps the most generalized of all shark behavior is locomotion. The mechanism of the basic swimming movement has been analyzed in detail for a few sharks, particularly in the spiny dogfish (a squalomorph) and the smooth dogfish (a galeomorph). These studies reveal a high degree of stereotypy in the fundamental locomotor pattern. This pattern consists of waves of contraction and relaxation that pass along alternate sides of the body, causing the sinusoidal body movements that will be analyzed in more detail in the next chapter. The immediate neural control of these movements occurs in the spinal cord itself, rather than in the brain. This is shown by experiments in which the spinal cord is severed just behind the skull. Such "spinal" sharks maintain normal rhythmic swimming movements. Of course the brain is necessary for changes in the rate or amplitude of these waves of muscle contraction. Similar experiments, in which the nerves from the lateral line are severed, result in no appreciable changes in the locomotor rhythms, indicating that the proposed proprioceptive function of the lateral line is not necessary for normal swimming movements.

These experiments tell us that the brains of sharks are not burdened with making repetitive, routine decisions that can be made at lower integrative levels. The brain is freed of an onerous chore and can devote itself to making more novel decisions. At the same time the brain retains its control of locomotion in ways analogous to the control our brains have over our own heart rates.

Activity Rhythms. Another behavior common to most elasmobranchs involves rhythms of activity. Studies of feeding, direct observations of their activities in captivity and the natural environment, and radiotelemetric recording of the movements of tagged sharks all suggest that most sharks undergo daily activity rhythms, with greatest activity during twilight and dark hours. Laboratory studies of two benthic species, the swell shark and hornshark, show that under constant dark or constant light these circadian periods of activity disappear—that is, the responses are to changes of light levels in the environment.

For sharks that eat benthic invertebrates, the dark hours are when the crustaceans they savor are accessible. For sharks that feed on actively swimming bony fish, darkness may give a predatory advantage. Studies of vision in bony fish show that during the hours of dawn and dusk there are times when these fishes are in transition between light and dark adaptation. It is then that fish act as if they cannot see well, and are especially susceptible to predation. Elasmobranch eyes, which dark- and light-adapt by different mechanisms (Chapter 5), can be competent when those of bony fishes are not. The crepuscular (dawn and dusk) and nocturnal activity patterns of elasmobranchs are thus adaptive. The epiphysis or pineal organ, with its photosensitive cells and hormonal response to light, is probably the source of the overall control of activity rhythms. Even though most sharks show daily patterns of activity, they can be active at any time. Sharks will take a baited hook day or night, although the best catches are made at night.

Feeding Frenzy. In Chapter 4 the feeding mechanisms and details of feeding behavior of sharks showed that the feeding patterns of large pelagic sharks involve a variable amount of circling while the prey is examined visually, olfactorally, acoustically, and electrically. A tentative pass followed by a bump or nudge provides mechanical information. The ultimate charge at the victim is swift and is made in a stiff, almost jerky, fashion with a "hunchback" appearance and rapid gaping of the jaws. When the prey is seized most sharks swing their heads from side to side in a manner characteristic for each species in order to cut off chunks from prey too large to swallow whole.

One frequently mentioned aspect of shark feeding behavior is the "feeding frenzy." In a true feeding frenzy a group of sharks appear to throw all caution to the winds and indiscriminately attack any moving or bleeding object—even each other. The violence and ferocity of a group of large sharks engaged in such a slaughter is an impressive sight to see—so impressive, in fact, that a feeding frenzy is often considered to be a special behavior, one that could only be carried out by "senseless, primitive" brutes like sharks! The feeding frenzy, however, is only one example (albeit a spectacular one) of a general phenomenon in animal behavior known as social facilitation. For instance, a group of aquarium-held goldfish, when fed, will be provoked into "senseless" behavior—to the point of attacking the gravel on the bottom of the tank. A flock of crows or bluejays will mob an owl or hawk in another display of behavior in which inhibitions and shyness appear to be lost. We ourselves, in crowds, can behave in ways that as individuals we would never condone. All of these are examples of social facilitation.

When a number of sharks feed together, the array of sensory experiences, spanning olfaction, vision, vibration, and electrosense, build to a crescendo as the feeding experience proceeds. The magnitude of sensory input appears to overwhelm the brain until inhibitions are lost, with a feeding frenzy the result. Observers comment that the sharks lose all sense of pain, rendering them insensible to their own sometimes catastrophic wounds. Usually these observations are made in a manner meant to enforce the notion that sharks are insensible, "low" forms of life.

One of the hallmarks of our normal behavior is inhibition—the reluctance to engage in behavior that might be immediately rewarding (gluttony, avarice, sex) but which also could be construed as antisocial. The shark too appears to be normally a creature under a good deal of inhibitory control, not so much because of social awareness, we can suppose, but for reasons having to do with survival. The changes that occur when the inhibitions are overcome may not be so much a signpost of the shark's primitiveness as of its sophistication.

As for pain—what is it, anyway? A precise neurological understanding of pain is still wanting for our own species, let alone careful analysis in elasmobranchs. At present it seems that humans have different and variable pain thresholds relating to the activity of neural pathways in the brain that produce analgesic compounds identical with the narcotic opiates. To suggest that sharks (like humans) can become insensible to otherwise "painful" stimuli is to acknowledge that the fundamental physiological plan of the shark brain is not all that different from our own! The feeding frenzy is not something basically different in sharks. Rather it is typical of behaviors shared by most, if not all, social vertebrates. In it are demonstrated neurological attributes found in even the most complex of these animals.

Reproductive Behavior. One of the fundamental features of elasmobranch biology is the fact that all sharks conceive by implanting the sperm of the male into the body of the female, where fertilization then takes place. Mating requires muscular coordination and cooperation between the two sharks. Other vertebrates that have internal fertilization also show elaborate courtship behavior to ensure both the partnership necessary for mating and the simultaneous ripening of eggs and sperm. Although studies of elasmobranch courting behavior are few in number and anecdotal in nature, the evidence favors complex courtship.

Courtship appears to start with the selection of a female by one (or sometimes two) males. The pair then swim in a coordinated fashion, with the male alongside or slightly behind the female. In some sharks the male appears attracted to the vent of the female, suggesting that she produces olfactory attractants to which the male responds. The males of most sharks and rays then often nip the females' pectoral fins or backs with their teeth. In the larger sharks these "nips" can cause obvious wounds on the fins and flanks of the females (Figure 6–6). Not surprisingly, both sexes of many sharks and rays have special adaptations for this behavior. In some sharks and many batoids, the teeth of the males are longer, more slender, and sharper than those of females (Figure 6–7). Careful studies of prey selection by skates *(Raja)* that have this dental dimorphism have found no differences in food preferences by males and females. The longer teeth of the males are adaptations for courtship and mating. In some sharks, such as the blue shark, the females are ensheathed with skin on the back and flanks that is more than twice as thick as that of the male. This is an adaptation in the female to withstand the courting attacks of the male.

The biting, nudging, and other body contact that occurs be-

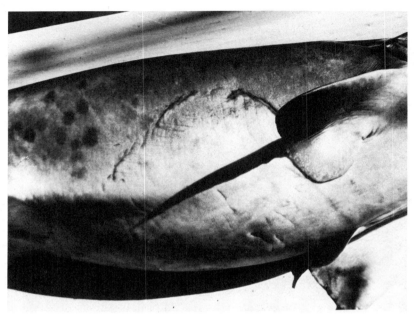

Figure 6-6. Courtship wounds on the side of a female
sand tiger shark.

tween courting pairs have been considered by biologists to constitute
"releasers," which in turn allow copulation to occur. The insertion
by the male of a clasper into the cloaca of the female (Chapter 8) is
accomplished in different positions in different elasmobranchs.
These include ventrum to ventrum (many rays and some sharks),
male above the female (some stingrays, skates), male wrapped
around the female (some small sharks), and male and female side by
side (some large sharks). In many cases the male grasps the pectoral
fin of the female with his mouth during copulation. In skates the
male has enlarged scales known as alar spines on the pectoral fins.
These are used to anchor the male to the female while clasper insertion occurs.

Often one or both of the copulating sharks or rays will be upside down while intromission occurs. Sharks, like other vertebrates,
can go into a state of tonic immobility when held upside down. Mating elasmobranchs remain quiescent while *in copula* for periods as
long as an hour or more, perhaps because of the state of tonic immobility induced by upside-down mating positions.

There is not much information available on the sensory sys-

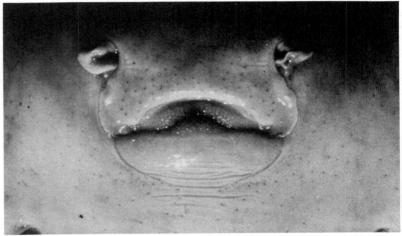

Figure 6–7. Teeth of male little skates (above) are sharper than those of females (below).

tems important to sexual recognition and courtship behavior in elasmobranchs. Sound production is unknown in sharks, and obvious sexual dimorphism or dichromatism is rare, although in the nurse shark the male is darker than the female during courtship. This seems to rule out hearing and vision as major senses associated with courtship. Some myliobatid ray males are known to display in front of females, so vision may be an important sense for some courting elasmobranchs. The degree of body contact during courtship indi-

131

cates that mechanoreception is important, and the orientation of males to the female vents demonstrates that olfactory cues are also important.

One sense that deserves closer consideration in mating is electroreception. Courting elasmobranchs approach each other closely enough to be in range of their electrosensory capabilities. At least one group of elasmobranchs, the rajid skates, are known to have electric organs in their tails. The function of these organs has not been discovered (see Chapter 9). Perhaps they are used in courtship.

Social Behavior. Having mated, sharks, skates, and rays resume what appear to be asocial lives. The males often occupy different ranges from the females, giving rise to pronounced segregation of the sexes. The utility of this behavior is that it isolates the pregnant females from males and the immatures. Females can give birth to young that are not likely to be preyed upon by older members of their kind. The pre- and postpartum females appear inhibited from eating anything at this time.

This sexual segregation suggests to some observers that the social organization and social behavior of sharks is of a low order. Actually, there are indications that at times, some elasmobranchs demonstrate surprising degrees of social behavior. Certain sharks and rays are ordinarily encountered in distributions that range from simple aggregations to discrete, well-organized schools. For example, groups of spiny dogfish and school sharks *(Galeorhinus australis)* exist as sexually segregated aggregations. The pelagic cownosed rays form visually oriented schools, as do scalloped hammerheads.

Large groups of elasmobranchs are infrequently encountered under conditions that suggest interaction. A good example of this was described for scalloped hammerheads in the Gulf of California. Here, true schools of up to 100 of these magnificent sharks gather regularly near submerged seamounts. During the daytime when they can be seen, they swim in a coordinated fashion, close together, and do not appear to be feeding. Radio telemetry of tagged sharks suggests that they disperse at night, probably to feed. While swimming in these schools, individual sharks display and seem to communicate visually. The displays include swiming on the side, head shaking, and rapid "corkscrewing" swimming motions. All have the effect of flashing the white underbellies of the sharks. These flashes can be seen for long distances underwater. Other behaviors include jaw gaping and ramming the backs of other sharks.

The function of these schools and the meaning of the behaviors going on in them are not immediately clear. Perhaps the daytime schools represent groups of waiting, resting sharks holding position for individual nocturnal forays to nearby food resources. Because the ramming behavior is directed almost totally at females, at least this behavior may have a courtship function—although small, immature females are also rammed.

Other sharks known to gather in groups include hornsharks, many species of requiem sharks (Carcharhinidae), basking skarks, and whale sharks. Although we know little about these groupings, the observations on scalloped hammerheads and gray reef sharks suggest that elasmobranchs may be more socially sophisticated than has been thought.

Among the most common kinds of behavior observed in highly social animals like birds, mammals, and bony fish are defense of territory and social interactions that result in dominance hierarchies (pecking orders). Careful study is demonstrating that these signposts of sociality exist among elasmobranchs too. Bonnethead sharks (a small hammerhead) are known to develop dominance hierarchies in efficient and subtle ways, using rare bumps and "hunch" displays. The hierarchies are size-dependent (larger sharks dominate smaller ones) and are established with a minimum of aggressive interactions.

Territorial defense has been observed several times in the gray reef shark, a common requiem shark throughout the tropical Indo-Pacific. The gray reef shark is frequently observed in groups—it is one of the most social of sharks. These sharks will often greet scuba divers and underwater submersible vehicles with exaggerated displays that feature strong flexion of the back (hunch), upturned snout, and deeply depressed pectoral fins (Figure 6–8). In this position the shark will exaggerate its normal lateral swimming movements. If this display is disregarded and the shark is pursued or more closely approached, a lightning-fast attack may result, with the shark slashing the intruder with its teeth before quickly fleeing. While it is not clear that such displays are territorial in nature, they are produced most often by single sharks patrolling isolated reef pinnacles and patches of coral. They clearly communicate a potential for aggression if the intruder continues to theaten the shark's individual space, if not its defended territory.

Learning. As sharks are considered asocial, so is their behavior written of as if it were stereotyped with little possibility for change. The idea is that you can't teach new tricks to a young shark, let alone to an old one. A new and more inquisitive breed of shark scientist,

DISPLAY   **NON-DISPLAY**

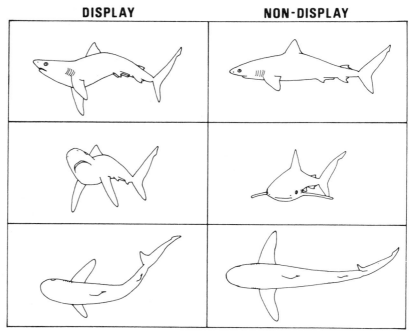

Figure 6–8. Threat display postures (left) and normal swimming (right) of the gray reef shark. (From Johnson and Nelson, 1973)

however, has demonstrated that sharks can undergo behavior modification—they can be taught. The first and most dramatic attempts to condition sharks were conducted at the Cape Haze Marine Laboratory in Florida. Contrary to the expectations of most behaviorists, it was found that adult lemon sharks could be trained to push a target (which rang a bell) with their snouts and then to swim to a particular location to receive food. Just as did Pavlov's dogs, these sharks came to associate the sound of the bell with the food reward. A couple of aspects of these pioneering experiments are noteworthy. First, the training success was achieved with sexually mature animals which, as animal trainers know, are more difficult to condition than are young ones. Secondly, the experiments with these sharks (and others subsequent to them) showed that they can be extraordinarily sensitive animals. Once accustomed to a training regimen, modifications made too swiftly can cause sharks to undergo radical changes in behavior that indicate obvious neurological disturbances.

These experiments show that elasmobranchs can be trained to learn seemingly inappropriate tasks. For example, at the Lerner Marine Laboratory on the island of Bimini in the Bahamas, large sting-

134

rays *(Dasyatis americana)* were routinely trained to swim up a ramp until they emerged halfway out of water to accept food from the hand of their keeper. Other experiments have shown that nurse sharks can also be instrumentally conditioned to press a target in order to receive food. Some workers have used this intellectual capacity of sharks to test their visual responses to light intensity, visual acuity, and color vision.

Unfortunately, because sharks are difficult to maintain satisfactorily in captive situations, they are not ideal subjects for the study of learning. Consequently, we know much more about the mental capabilities of goldfish than we do about sharks. The size and complexity of shark brains, the richness of their sensory capabilities, and the tantalizingly few shark training experiments all suggest, however, that goldfish are mental midgets when compared to elasmobranchs.

When the behavior of sharks is seen from this perspective, a clearer understanding and appreciation of it is gained. A shark, as seen by a trained observer familiar with its behavior, is not nearly as "unpredictable" as is popularly thought. Yet sharks are always capable of doing the unexpected, and they may give short notice of their intentions. An element of unpredictability does thus exist. We have seen that many elasmobranchs have large brains that provide behavioral options for them. Their unpredictability is thus a measure of their neurological complexity and the ability to explore these options. It is not an indication that they are insensate, vacuous beasts!

ADDITIONAL READING

Clark, E. "Maintenance of sharks in captivity, with a report on their instrumental conditioning." In *Sharks and Survival,* ed. P.W. Gilbert, 115–149. Boston: D.C. Heath and Company, 1963.

Demski, L.S. "Electrical stimulation of the shark brain." *American Zoologist,* 17 (1977), 487–500.

Graeber, R.C. "Behavioral studies correlated with central nervous system integration of vision in sharks." In *Sensory Biology of Sharks, Skates, and Rays,* ed. E.S. Hodgson and R.F. Mathewson, 195–225. Arlington, Virginia: Office of Naval Research, Department of the Navy, 1978.

Johnson, R.H., and D.R. Nelson. "Agonistic display in the gray reef shark, *Carcharhinus menisorrah,* and its relationship to attacks on man." *Copeia*, 1973, no. 1 (1973), 76–84. (Figure 6–8 is from this work.)

Klatzo, I. "Cellular morphology of the lemon shark brain." In *Sharks, Skates, and Rays*, ed. P.W. Gilbert, R.F. Mathewson, and D.P. Rall, 341–359. Baltimore: The Johns Hopkins Press, 1967.

Klimley, A.P. "Observations of courtship and copulation in the nurse shark, *Ginglymostoma cirratum*." *Copeia*, 1980, no. 4 (1980), 878–882.

Klimley, A.P. "Grouping behavior of the scalloped hammerhead." *Oceanus*, 24, no. 4 (1981), 65–71.

Klimley, A.P., and D.R. Nelson. "Schooling of the scalloped hammerhead shark, *Sphyrna lewini*, in the Gulf of California." *Fishery Bulletin*, 79, no. 2 (1981), 356–360.

Nelson, D.R. "Aggression in sharks: Is the gray reef shark different?" *Oceanus*, 24, no. 4 (1981), 45–55.

Northcutt, R.G. "Elasmobranch central nervous system organization and its possible evolutionary significance." *American Zoologist*, 17, 411–429. (Figure 6–5 is from this work.)

Northcutt, R.G. "Brain organization in the cartilaginous fishes." In *Sensory Biology of Sharks, Skates, and Rays*, ed. E.S. Hodgson and R.F. Mathewson, 117–193. Arlington, Virginia: Office of Naval Research, Department of the Navy, 1978.

Springer, S. "Social organization of shark populations." In *Sharks, Skates, and Rays*, ed. P.W. Gilbert, R.F. Mathewson and D.P. Rall, 149–174. Baltimore: The Johns Hopkins Press, 1967.

Tricas, T.C. "Courtship and mating-related behaviors in myliobatid rays." *Copeia*, 1980, no. 3 (1980), 553–556.

Tricas, T.C. "Diel behavior of the tiger shark, *Galeocerdo cuvier*, at French Frigate Shoals, Hawaiian Islands." *Copeia*, 1981, no. 4 (1981), 904–908.

7

Swimming and Body Form

The pelagic sharks encountered by fishermen, divers, boaters, and visitors to marine aquaria always impress people with the grace and smooth power of their movements. To watch, for example, a blue shark as it glides and wheels under clear offshore swells is to witness a sinuous beauty that compares with aerial artistry of shearwaters skimming above those same waves. Yet the even, almost languid, cruising pace maintained by a shark is deceptive. It belies an ability to accelerate rapidly and attack prey with incredible swiftness and ferocity.

I vividly remember one of the first sharks I encountered as a young boy. While fishing in the Atlantic Ocean off the coast of New Jersey, a dorsal fin was sighted, wagging slowly from side to side, signaling the lolling, leisurely pace of a shark just below the surface. When the shark saw one of the trolled baits skipping on the surface, its behavior changed dramatically. The fin stiffened, and with no further side-to-side motion, it sped directly at the bait. The shark struck in a sheet of white spray, missed, and was gone, leaving only the memory of an animal deceptive in its languor and amazing in its acceleration and agility. All my subsequent observations of elasmobranchs confirm that they are efficient, graceful animals that swim with an economy of effort and fluidity seldom seen in other fishes.

An evaluation of the swimming performance of sharks, skates, and rays should be prefaced by a few general considerations. The first of these is that elasmobranchs—unlike most bony fishes—lack all vestiges of a gas bladder, or lunglike diverticulum of the digestive tract, that could be used for buoyancy regulation. That the most generalized living bony fishes have such a bladder is but one suggestion of the evolutionary separation of Chondrichthyes, on one hand, and Osteichthyes on the other. The failure to have a gas bladder, the volume of which can be adjusted to regulate buoyancy, means that in order for elasmobranchs to position themselves in the water column, they must swim to create hydrodynamic lift. A few pelagic and deep-sea sharks such as the slow-moving whale and basking sharks are nearly neutrally buoyant due to the accumulation of low-density fats in their body tissues (particularly in the liver). Most sharks, however, sink when their forward motion ceases. They cannot passively hover, as can most bony fishes.

With a premium placed on motion, it is not surprising that sharks and rays have hydrodynamic specializations for swimming not found in most bony fishes. One of the principal adaptations involves the laws of water flow over solid objects. Part of the resistance to movement (drag) created by a body moving through a fluid is a function of the length of the body measured in the direction of movement. The longer the body, the smaller the drag, and thus the easier it is to move. This principle can be tested by holding your hand extended with the fingers pressed tightly together. Now submerge it in water and move it in the direction of the short axis (i.e., with the thumb as the leading edge). Then move the hand in the direction of the long axis—in the direction the fingertips are pointing. There is a perceptible difference in the drags encountered. It is easier to move in the direction of the long axis.

This hydrodynamic principle explains why many sharks have broad, long pectoral fins. These fins produce most of the lift required to overcome the basic negative buoyancy of sharks, skates, and rays. They do so with a minimum of drag because of their broad shapes. Early in their evolution, the batoids expanded the pectoral fins to the extent that the principal shape of the body became that of a disk. Most people correlate the flattened batoid shape with life on the bottom, but a disk moving through the water edge-flat is a hydrodynamically efficient shape. The success of the myliobatiform rays, which have many pelagic species, is testimony to this. Unfortunately, however, there have been few careful analyses of the swimming mechanisms or hydrodynamic performances of batoids. We know the most about the propulsive mechanisms and hydrodynamics of the cylindrical or torpedo shape of the basic shark form.

TURBULENCE

In order to swim efficiently, turbulence should be minimized in the flow of water over the swimming body. The most economical swimming performance would have completely laminar flow of water over the body. This would eliminate drag (pressure drag). Such a body would leave behind no turbulence—and hence no wake. To an extent, both rapidly swimming bony fishes (e.g., tunas) and sharks (e.g., lamniform sharks) are well designed hydrodynamically to re-

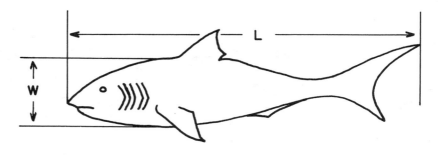

L/W = FINENESS RATIO

Figure 7–1. When the fineness ratio approaches 4.5, sharks become more efficient swimmers.

duce turbulence. A streamlined, torpedo-shaped body suffers drag proportional to its "fineness ratio," which is the ratio of length to maximum diameter. Turbulence and hence pressure drag is least when the body is about 4.5 times as long as it is in diameter. This approximates the fineness ratio found in the fast-swimming sharks (Figure 7–1).

Sharks also exploit another device to achieve hydrodynamic efficiency, one not utilized by most teleosts. The placoid scales of pelagic sharks form a uniform covering of small, closely spaced denticles. Skates and some rays, on the other hand, often have relatively few scales, which are large and spinous, and which serve a protective function (Figure 7–2). These large scales are sometimes separated by extensive areas of naked skin. Many rays have lost their scales almost completely, presenting a smooth, naked skin to the environment.

Shark dermal denticles have varied forms that are interesting and probably have hydrodynamic consequences. The denticles of

Figure 7–2. Placoid scales provide a spiny armament for this aptly named thorny skate.

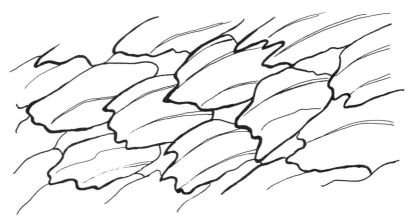

Figure 7-3. The placoid scales of actively swimming sharks are low, fluted, and loosely imbricated, as in this drawing of scales from a bigeye thresher.

Figure 7-4. Benthic, sluggish sharks often have nubbly, poorly streamlined scales like those of this Portuguese shark.

Figure 7–5. The fluted surfaces and the interstices beneath the mushroom-shaped scales of fast-swimming sharks absorb turbulence, reducing pressure drag.

sharks capable of efficient cruising speeds and fast bursts are often mushroom-shaped, with crowns grooved or fluted in the direction of the major body axis (Figure 7–3). The denticles do not overlap as tightly as the imbricated scales of bony fishes; and the interstices between them are continuous, with channels passing below the expanded crowns around the "stems" of the scales. In slower-moving, more sedentary sharks such as the bramble sharks, basking sharks, and the benthic carpet sharks, the placoid scales take different forms. In the nurse and carpet sharks and benthic squalomorphs, for instance, they are stout, round structures that give the skin a nubbly texture (Figure 7–4). Bramble sharks have scales that form enlarged spines and bucklers, similar to the defensive spines of skates. The slow-moving basking shark has a dense array of placoid scales, each with long, sharp spines, giving the skin an abrasive texture. The scales in these sharks, as well as those of most skates, are protective and defensive in function.

The degree of protection afforded by the low, streamlined scales of the faster-swimming sharks such as the lamnids and carcharhinids appears to be less. Their scales seem to serve a primary hydrodynamic function. The dermal denticles of pelagic sharks have a system of fluted surfaces and pores (the interstices between the scales) that communicate through the water-filled channels beneath the crowns (Figure 7–5). This sytem may damp out pressure differences created along the body surface by areas of turbulent water flow, significantly reducing drag and making the shark's swimming performance more efficient. This is particularly true at slow cruising speeds. The energy expenditure required to maintain a position in the water column is thus reduced, as is the energy required to search for prey.

The reduction of turbulence effected by streamlining and dermal denticle structure has yet another advantage. When sensitive

143

hydrophones are placed in a large aquarium in which bony fish are swimming, sloshing sounds of water turbulence created by the fish can be heard easily. But in the case of cruising sharks, no such swimming sounds are picked up. Apparently the reduced turbulence not only increases swimming efficiency, but also increases stealth, making the shark a quieter predator. The stomach contents of sharks like oceanic whitetips frequently include the remains of fast-swimming fishes such as tunas and billfishes. Possibly the "quiet mode" swimming of these sharks allows them to slip up undetected on loitering prey.

SWIMMING SPEEDS

The normal cruising velocity of bull sharks and sandbar sharks has been measured in a large (1.5 million liter) enclosed aquarium. The sharks (all about 2 meters in standard length—snout to base of tail) swam continuously at speeds of approximately 68 centimeters per second (62 to 72 centimeters per second). These velocities were close to the predicted speeds for fish of this size. Other direct measurements of shark cruising speeds include some for young sandbar sharks (less than 1 meter in length) made on tagged wild sharks. These showed that the sharks normally swam very slowly indeed. They spend most of their time moving with tidal currents, nearly drifting, changing direction to investigate possible sources of food. Long-term movements of tagged blue sharks in the Atlantic Ocean can be explained by passive drift with ocean currents alone. Sharks, it seems, are conservative in their energy expenditure for locomotion.

Seldom has the maximum swimming speed of a shark been measured. Calculations show that for a shortfin mako shark to leap 15 to 20 feet into the air (which they sometimes do when hooked), a velocity of 22 miles per hour (32.2 feet per second or 981 centimeters per second) is required—and this is for a shark impeded by the drag of a fishing line trailing from its mouth. A 6 feet, 6-inch blue shark was clocked at a velocity of 21.3 knots (24.5 miles per hour; 35.9 feet per second; 10.96 meters per second). There exists a dubious record of a small blue shark about 2 feet in length which was found to swim steadily against a current at 17.7 miles per hour (26 feet per second) and was reported to achieve 43 miles per hour in short bursts. Sharks are capable of far faster swimming velocities than their leisurely cruising paces suggest.

CAUDAL FIN

The swimming system of most pelagic sharks is distinctive for the shape of the tail or caudal fin. In these sharks the upper (epichordal) lobe of this fin is longer and more extensive than the lower (hypochordal) lobe. This asymmetric "heterocercal" caudal fin is quite different from the superficially symmetrical "homocercal" tail of most bony fishes. Some authors have suggested that heterocercal tails are "primitive" and therefore one more indicator of the presumed lowly status of elasmobranchs. A careful analysis of the form and function of the heterocercal tail of sharks shows this not to be the case.

As the tail of a shark sweeps from side to side, completing the lateral undulations of the trunk, its epichordal lobe is rotated so that its rear edge "leads" the rest of the lobe (Figure 7–6). The resulting hydrodynamic (epibatic) force acts to lift the tail. In one model of shark swimming, the hydrodynamic shapes of the pectoral fins and the flattened underside of the snout lift the forepart of the shark's body. Together, these fore and aft lifts overcome the underwater weight (negative buoyancy) of the fish and keep the shark from sinking—as long as it moves forward at a sufficient velocity.

This picture of shark swimming has been criticized on the grounds that as the shark swims faster, its tail would provide more and more lift, which must then be matched by more lift from the pectoral fins, or else the shark would dive to the bottom. The lift is produced by the pectoral fins increasing their angle of attack (similar

Figure 7–6. As the caudal fin of a sand tiger shark swings from left to right, the posterior edge of the fin (heavier line) becomes the leading edge. (From Thomson, 1976)

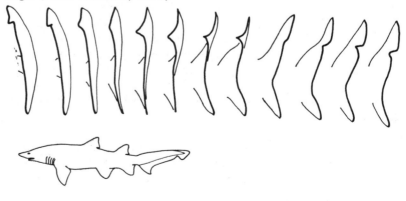

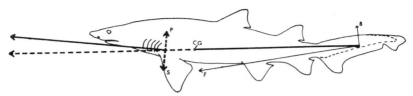

Figure 7–7. The balance of forces acting in a swimming shark. The line of net thrust from the tail is directed through the center of gravity (CG). The sinking effect (S) is offset by a lifting effect (P) from the planing action of the pectoral fins. (From Thomson, 1976)

to lowering the flaps on an airplane wing), thus increasing drag. It is not efficient to increase velocity and drag at the same time.

An alternative analysis shows that the ventral lobe of the caudal fin is important in resolving the problem presented by the caudal epibatic forces. Pelagic sharks generally have pronounced hypochordal caudal lobes. Benthic sharks such as the orectolobids and catsharks (Scyliorhinidae) lack them. As the caudal fin of a pelagic shark sweeps from side to side, it turns out that at least through part of the sweep, the trailing edge of the hypochordal lobe also leads, producing a downward-directed (hypobatic) force (Figure 7–6). When the opposing epibatic and hypobatic forces are resolved with the forward forces created by the tail, the resultant line of thrust passes through or near the center of balance of the shark (Figure 7–7). Increases of speed are thereby accompanied by adjustments of the hypochordal elements of the tail, not necessarily by changes of attack angle in the pectoral fins. The shark can swim forward faster without increasing unnecessary drag.

This view of shark locomotion also suggests that sharks are especially unstable in the vertical plane. That is, minor adjustments in the caudal fin and pectoral fin trim can allow them to move easily up and down in the water column. This hydrodynamic instability, plus the fact that they are unencumbered by gas-filled swim bladders that resist such movements, must be important to predators that can attack prey from below and above.

BUOYANCY

Most bony fish achieve neutral buoyancy through the use of swim bladders. They reduce the energy expenditure needed to maintain position in the water column. The swim bladder, however, extracts a price in vertical mobility and, possibly, in maximum size. Most of the bony fishes that grow to large body size (tunas, billfishes, ocean sunfish) have forsaken the swim bladder. A large fish requires a large swim bladder, and the regulation of one requires excreting and absorbing large quantities of gas.

Sharks, not having swim bladders, are vertically mobile, and many have evolved large body size. But sharks are not nearly as negatively buoyant as they might be, either. A 250-kilogram (air weight) bony fish with a ruptured swim bladder would weigh about 12.5 kilograms underwater. The same-sized shark weighs only about 3 kilograms—and this without a swim bladder. Where does the flotation come from? Most of the answer is in the large liver of the shark. Here low-density oils are stored so that the liver alone of the hypothetical 250-kilogram shark provides an upthrust of 5.2 kilograms. If the liver is removed the shark would weigh 8.2 kilograms underwater—still only two thirds of what the bladderless bony fish would weigh. So the liver is not the only factor. Another is the weight of the skeleton. Cartilage has about half the specific gravity of bone (1.1 to 2.0). Elasmobanchs derive a benefit from not having bony skeletons. The ultimate benefit is decreased underwater weight, which minimizes the swimming speed necessary to maintain position in the water column.

One persistent notion about sharks is that they must swim throughout their lives in order to oxygenate their blood and to maintain a vertical position. Actually, this is true for few species of elasmobranchs. With the exception of the mobulids and myliobatid rays, batoids spend most of their time resting on the bottom. The same is true for angel sharks and many galeomorphs, which also rest on the bottom (catsharks, carpet sharks, smoothhounds, hornsharks, and some requiem sharks—lemon sharks, for example). Other sharks—deep-sea dogfishes—achieve actual neutral buoyancy by means of oils (especially squalene) concentrated in their livers. Basking and whale sharks must achieve near-neutral buoyancy, for they swim extremely slowly for their lengths yet stay near the surface.

The sand tiger shark uses a unique technique for hanging motionless in the water column well above the bottom. Aquarium-held sand tigers are known to gulp air at the surface. This air is swallowed into the digestive tract, for bubbles of gas are sometimes emitted from the cloaca (Figure 7–8). The same specimens that gulp air can remain motionless well above the bottom. Neutral buoyancy has

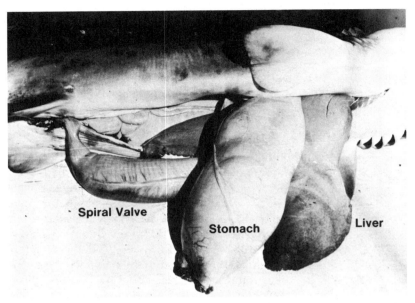

Figure 7–8. The liver of sharks can increase buoyancy due to stored fats and oils. In this sand tiger shark, air was swallowed, distending the stomach and producing additional buoyancy.

been seen in wild sand tigers in such diverse localities as South Africa and Australia, suggesting that this species regularly achieves neutral buoyancy by this technique.

Some requiem sharks rest motionless on the bottom under curious circumstances. These sharks are encountered by divers in certain underwater caves along the western coast of Mexico. Although otherwise healthy, the sharks are unresponsive to the presence of scuba divers. Many of the caves that harbor these sharks have freshwater springs that dilute the seawater and may have some correlation with this resting behavior. One hypothesis is that the sharks visit the caves to rid themselves of ectoparasites that might not endure the low-salinity water.

PECTORAL FINS

The few species of sharks that are probably obligate swimmers are those wide-ranging pelagic species associated with the upper level of the open ocean. The fast-swimming mackerel sharks (including the great white), the hammerheads (Sphrynidae), and pelagic requiem sharks like the blue shark and oceanic whitetip belong to this group. Many lamniform sharks have special metabolic adaptations to assist their swimming performance (Chapter 10), while the others maximize the hydrodynamic lifting surfaces of the pectoral fins and/or head. Blue sharks and oceanic whitetips, for example, have elongated pectoral fins that provide abundant planing surfaces for maximizing hydrodynamic lift at low cruising speeds. Indeed, both species spend large amounts of time virtually drifting with ocean currents. Hammerheads, of course, have the broad bow planes of the lateral ''hammer'' expansions of the head, which similarly provide substantial lift while swimming ahead. The hammerhead species with the broadest hammers (scalloped hammerhead, smooth hammerhead, great hammerhead) have proportionally the smallest pectoral fins, while species with smaller hammers (bonnethead) have the largest pectoral fins. The combined surface areas of the hammer and the pectoral fins, expressed as a ratio to body weight, are about the same in all species of hammerheads. This is an indication of the importance of the hydrodynamic function of this bizarre head form. Hammerheads, incidentally, appear to be among the densest (most negatively buoyant) of sharks.

In those sharks where hydrodynamic lift at low speeds is not as important, the pectoral fins are less expanded. This is true for fast swimmers such as mako sharks as well as for sharks like deep-sea squalomorphs, which are more nearly neutrally buoyant due to accumulated liver oils. Not requiring extensive anterior planing surfaces, which also steer the animals vertically, these fish rely more heavily on the hypochordal lobe of the caudal fin to make vertical adjustments. Consequently, in these sharks the hypochordal lobe is better developed, resulting in a more symmetrical tail than in other sharks (Figure 7–9).

Those sharks with reduced or absent lower caudal fin lobes, such as the catsharks and carpet sharks, swim in an eellike (anguilliform) manner. Wide-amplitude waves of muscular contraction pass backward along the body on alternate sides and continue through the length of the caudal fin. Sharks with pronounced lower caudal fin lobes cruise with a similar swimming mechanism. These sharks, however, are capable of more rapid acceleration and higher ''burst'' velocities. When swimming rapidly, these sharks adopt a different posture, which impresses the observer as being stiffer. The tail alone seems more propulsive and becomes the major driving force of the swimming mechanism. The fastest sharks, such as the mako and

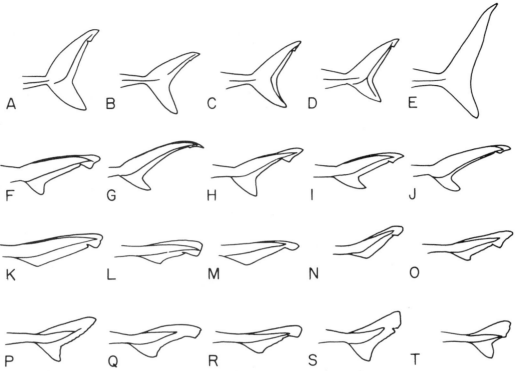

Figure 7–9. Examples of the caudal fin shapes of a number of elasmobranchs. (A) porbeagle; (B) shortfin mako; (C) white shark; (D) basking shark; (E) whale shark; (F) sand tiger shark; (G) tiger shark; (H) Atlantic sharpnose shark; (I) lemon shark; (J) silky shark; (K) nurse shark; (L) *Scyliorhinus boa*; (M) *Apristurus profundorum*; (N) false catshark; (O) smooth dogfish; (P) spiny dogfish; (Q) black dogfish; (R) *Etmopterus hillianus*; (S) Portuguese shark; (T) cookie-cutter shark. (From Thomson and Simanek, 1977)

white shark, never fail to give the impression of being stiff-bodied, even when swimming at cruising speeds.

Broad, streamlined fins are hydrodynamically efficient, in part because they have substantial length in the direction of movement. This is true for other parts of the shark as well. The heads of many sharks are frequently flattened dorsoventrally and are broad. This makes sideways movements of the head hydrodynamically efficient and helps the animal to make rapid turns of short radius. One impressive aspect of the quality of many sharks is that they are able to make 180-degree turns "on a dime"—actually within a distance of about one third of the body length.

150 Another part of the shark similarly streamlined for lateral movements is the caudal peduncle—the final region of the trunk just ahead of the caudal fin. The caudal peduncle makes substantial lateral excursions with each beat of the tail, and to that purpose is often broader than it is deep. The effect is to create a lateral "keel" on the caudal peduncle of many fast-swimming sharks. But even slower elasmobranchs can have substantial keels, especially sharks (like the tiger shark) that exaggerate lateral swings of the tail (Figure 7–10).

While the fins of sharks are stiff, broadly streamlined structures (unlike the ribbed and more flexible fins of most bony fishes), they do more than merely guide the shark in swimming. In the majority of batoids, for example, the pectoral fins are the main sources of propulsion—either through flapping motion (mobulid, myliobatid, and gymnurid rays) or through vertical sinusoidal undulations of the lateral margins of the fins. In certain skates and rays the pectoral fins also serve as adjuncts to feeding behavior; skates, for instance, may cradle or "basket" prey between their greatly depressed fins while they eat it.

The expanded pectoral fins provide abundant surface area for sensory organs. Pores of the ampullary electroreceptive system richly invest both the dorsal and ventral surfaces. The pectoral fins also allow the bottom-oriented batoids to blend in better with their environments. A partially buried skate or ray, with its dorsal surface darkened to match the substrate, is a cryptic animal, quite able to avoid detection by both potential predators and potential prey.

The expansion of the pectoral fins in most batoids was accompanied by reduction of their dorsal, caudal, and anal fins. These fins are retained in batoids such as the guitarfishes (Rhinobatidae) and sawfishes (Pristidae) where the pectoral expansion is not extreme. A few seemingly lethargic rays (the Atlantic torpedo is an example) have well-developed, symmetrical caudal fins with pronounced lateral keels (Figure 7–11).

Among the benthic batoids, the pelvic fins are not as reduced as the dorsal, anal, and caudal fins. In pelagic sharks pelvic fins function as stabilizers and antiroll devices. Yet their ubiquity in all sharks, skates, and rays—regardless of swimming ability—suggests that they may have other, more general functions. The pelvic fins lie on either side of the cloaca and, in male elasmobranchs, an obvious function is to provide the claspers (male intromittent organs—analogs of the mammalian penis), which are developed from the inner edges of these fins (see Chapter 8).

In most skates the posterior margins of the pelvic fins are deeply scalloped, producing leglike extensions of the outermost and

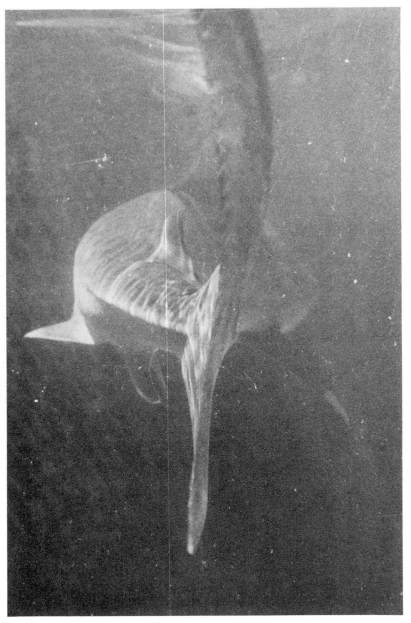

Figure 7–10. As a large tiger shark moves away from the camera, a prominent lateral keel on its caudal peduncle can be easily seen.

Figure 7–11. The Atlantic torpedo, an indolent ray, has a symmetrical caudal fin.

inner edges of the fins. Skates are known to use these extended fins as "legs" as they move slowly over the bottom. The principal function here is probably sensory rather than locomotor. Many rays have well-developed pelvic fins with broadly convex trailing edges. When the ray swims, these fins are confluent with the trailing edges of the pectoral disk and serve as trim tabs or ailerons, assisting in vertical steering and in making banked turns.

Even though shark fins appear to be stiff, immobile structures that cannot be folded back against the body, they are still capable of a surprising range of movement. Galeomorph sharks, for example, have thick levator muscles above and depressor muscles below the bases of their pectoral fins. In the faster-swimming sharks the trailing edges of the pectoral fins can be depressed almost 90 degrees to the direction of swimming to brake the animal's forward progress. This is seen during feeding (Chapter 4) when the shark attacks prey and then shakes its body around the fulcrum formed by these depressed fins.

A curious instance of pectoral fin mobililty occurs in young nurse sharks. Small specimens sometimes fold both pectoral fins under the forepart of the body, raising the head above the bottom as they rest motionless (Figure 7–12). From this position they lunge

153

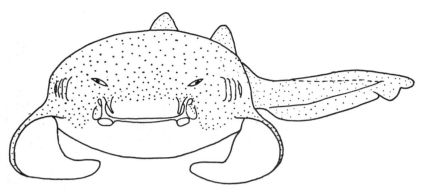

Figure 7-12. Front view of a young nurse shark propped up on its inwardly rolled pectoral fins. (From Moss, 1972)

forward, almost froglike, to pounce on the small crustaceans, worms, and mollusks that make up their diets. This behavior has not been reported for larger, mature specimens of this species.

ABDOMINAL PORES

Elasmobranchs have an anatomical feature not shared by other vertebrates except the lawless lampreys and hagfishes. Two openings connect the interior of the body cavity (coelom or peritoneal cavity) to the outside environment. These paired openings are known as abdominal pores. They are found in the cloaca, just behind and to each side of the rectal and urogenital openings (Figure 7-13).

The abdominal pores vary widely in their appearance and apparent importance among elasmobranchs. They can be slitlike structures that may, in fact, not be open at all, or pronounced nipplelike papillae which are capable of substantial dilation. The pores are most poorly developed (if at all) and are mere slits in bottom-dwelling sharks and rays such as the catsharks, angel sharks, nurse sharks, and stingrays (Figure 7-14). In the pelagic sharks and rays the pores are better developed with prominent papillae. This type of abdominal pore is found, for example, in the requiem, hammerhead, and lamnid sharks, as well as in the devil and manta rays. The papillae that guard the abdominal pores contain both sphincter muscles and erectile tissues which control the size of the orifice and thus the amount of fluid moving through them.

In lampreys and hagfish the function of the abdominal pore **154** (singular in these fishes) is clear. They lack systems of tubes or ducts

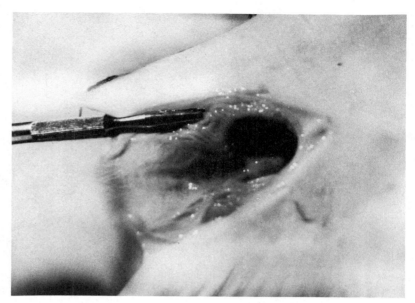

Figure 7–13. A probe demonstrates an abdominal pore of a
sand tiger shark.

to carry the eggs and sperm produced by the gonads to the outside.
The gametes are thus shed directly into the body cavity and make
their way outside via the abdominal (or more properly, genital) pore.

Elasmobranchs, however, have a well-developed reproductive
system that includes special ducts to guide the transport of gametes.
The abdominal pores of sharks, skates, and rays, therefore, have no
apparent reproductive function. As a matter of fact, there is presently no clear understanding of the purpose of these perforations. As
textbooks of vertebrate anatomy are wont to say, "The function of
the abdominal pores is obscure." Our improved understanding of
shark swimming behavior and the importance to it of good hydrodynamics may help, however, to understand them.

Several explanations have been advanced in the past to explain
the presence of these pores in elasmobranchs. They have, for example, been dismissed as vestigial structures, left over from the genital
pores of more primitive ancestors. This excuse for their well-developed presence is weak indeed. Another idea is that abdominal pores
allow coelomic fluid to escape from the shark, thereby ridding the
animal of waste products concentrated in this fluid. The chemical
composition of coelomic fluid, however, seems to contain no wastes

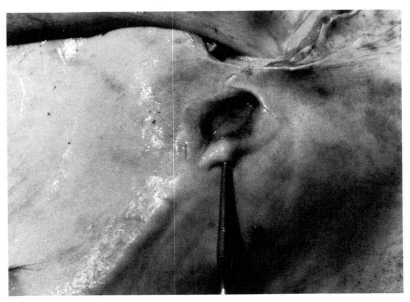

Figure 7–14. The slitlike abdominal pores of a benthic ray, the Atlantic torpedo.

that cannot be excreted by kidney and/or gill (Chapter 9). Moreover, this idea does not explain why benthic sharks and rays have less well-developed pores of a simpler design.

A third hypothesis about abdominal pores suggests that they help sharks adjust their volumes to pressure changes as they move through the water column. This idea takes into account the fact that active elasmobranchs that move vertically freely have the best-developed pores. However, because sharks lack swim bladders and because they are essentially incompressible, it is difficult to understand why a shark should have to adjust its volume with depth by releasing fluid from the coelom. Experiments, in fact, have failed to demonstrate the flow of fluid from the pores when sharks were placed under pressure in special chambers.

The new appreciation of the efficiency of shark swimming suggests a novel but simple hypothesis of abdominal pore function. Pelagic sharks are hydrodynamically "clean" and economical swimmers. They also are resourceful, opportunistic feeders (Chapter 4) that, when the occasion permits, eat large meals. One adaptation for this way of life is a large, capacious stomach. Viscera in the unfed shark have room for expansion in a large body cavity otherwise filled with coelomic fluid. There are at least two consequences when a shark eats a meal. First, the weight of the meal is added to that of the shark. Secondly, the girth of the animal is increased in the midsection. When we eat a large meal (which seldom amounts to more than 1 or 2 percent of our body weight), temporary discomfort can be relieved by letting out the belt a notch or two. In a shark (which can easily consume 10 percent of its body weight at a meal) the consequences may be more dramatic. First, the shark must generate more lift to carry the added weight. This can be accomplished by either swimming faster or by altering the line of thrust with adjustments in the posture of the caudal fin. At the same time the increased girth should alter the hydrodynamic shape of the shark, changing the fineness ratio and reducing its swimming efficiency.

It is possible that neither of these untoward consequences of feeding actually occurs. Instead, the shark, in good nautical tradition, might "blow its ballast" when eating by releasing coelomic fluid through its abdominal pores. This would allow the shark to offset part of the weight gained from the meal and also retain a constant hydrodynamic shape. Observations that support this idea include the above-mentioned correlation of swimming activity with pore development and the observation that sharks, including those that have recently eaten, seldom present a pot-bellied appearance—in contrast to predaceous teleosts with swim bladders. These hydrodynamic considerations, of course, would not apply to benthic, inactive elasmobranchs. This hypothesis does not predict that they should have well-developed abdominal pores—and they do not.

This brief survey of body form and swimming behavior among sharks reveals them to be diverse for such a small group of animals. In the evolution of this diversity, stealth seems to have been a major adaptive consideration. This is expressed both in the crypsis of the benthic batoid and in the hydrodynamic silence of the cruising galeomorph. Many of the anatomical features of shark body form are related to hydrodynamic efficiency, giving them economy of effort during what, for some species, is a constant search for control in the vertical plane, oxygen, and food. Such efficiency is important to predators that may go long periods without encountering prey.

The typical shark body form and constitution produce animals of great suppleness and agility, and make many of them exceedingly graceful swimmers. Yet beneath this flowing, leisurely beauty lies a capacity to transform abruptly into a rapid-swimming, violent, and ferocious hunter. It is this transformation, perhaps, that makes the shark the fascinating, spectacular, and successful predator that it is.

ADDITIONAL READING

Alexander, R.McN. "The lift produced by the heterocercal tails of Selachii." *J. exp. Biol.,* 43 (1965), 131–138.

Alexander, R.McN. *The Chordates,* 2nd ed. Cambridge and New York: Cambridge University Press, 1981.

Baldridge, H.D. "Sinking factors and average densities of Florida sharks as a function of liver buoyancy." *Copeia,* 1970 (1970), 744–754.

Baldridge, H.D. "Accumulation and function of liver oil in Florida sharks." *Copeia,* 1972 (1972), 306–325.

Bone, Q., and B.L. Roberts. "The density of elasmobranchs." *J. mar. Biol. Ass. U.K.,* 49 (1969), 913–938.

Clark, E. *The Lady and the Sharks.* New York: Harper and Row, 1969.

Corner, E.D.S., E.J. Denton, and G.R. Forster. "On the buoyancy of some deep-sea sharks." *Proc. R. Soc. Ser. B.,* 171 (1969), 415–429.

Medved, R.J., and J.A. Marshall. "Short-term movements of young sandbar sharks, *Carcharhinus plumbeus* (Pisces, Carcharhinidae)." *Bull. Mar. Sci.,* 33, no. 1 (1983), 87–93.

Moss S.A. "Nurse shark pectoral fins: An unusual use." *Amer. Midl. Nat.,* 88, no. 2 (1972), 496–497. (Figure 7–12 is from this work.)

Northcutt, R.G. "Elasmobranch central nervous system organization and its possible evolutionary significance." *American Zoologist,* 17, 411–429. (Figure 7–9 is from this work.)

Reif, W.-E., and A. Dinkelacker. "Hydrodynamics of the squamation in fast swimming sharks." *N. Jb. Geol. Palaont.,* 164 (1982), 184–187.

Thomson, K.S. "On the heterocercal tail in sharks." *Paleobiology,* 2, no. 1 (1976), 19–38. (Figures 7–6 and 7–7 are from this work.)

Thomson, K.S., and D.E. Simanek. "Body form and locomotion in sharks." *Amer. Zool.,* 17 (1977), 343–354.

Webb, P.W., and R.S. Keyes. "Swimming kinematics of sharks." *Fishery Bulletin* 80, no. 4 (1982), 803–812.

Weihs, D. "Body section variations in sharks—an adaptation for efficient swimming." *Copeia*, 1981, no. 1 (1981), 217–219.

Weihs, D., R.S. Keyes, and D.M. Stalls. "Voluntary swimming speeds of two species of large carcharhinid sharks." *Copeia*, 1981, no. 1 (1981), 219–222.

8

Reproduction

Sharks, like all other animals, reproduce their kind. What is unlikely about their reproductive biology, however, is that they are so sophisticated about it. Animals generally adopt one of two basic strategies for procreation. One is producing as many young as possible while investing little care in each. The ocean sunfish—a bony fish—may release as many as 30 millions eggs in a season. The chance of survival for each egg is slim, but a few will probably survive. When conditions are just right, many young could live, producing the phenomenon of "year classes" noted in important sport and commercial fishes such as striped bass, herring, and cod. Most invertebrates (there are lots of exceptions among the insects) and many bony fishes utilize this rather carefree approach to reproduction.

The alternative strategy is to give birth to a few young at one time, but to invest a lot of energy in each, either in terms of food energy (yolk) or parental care, or both. The epitome of this approach to genetic survival is found among birds with their large eggs, elaborate courtship, and intensive parental care; and in placental mammals where the developing young are sheltered and nourished within the uterus of the mother.

As mammals, we tend to regard our own pattern of reproduction as "advanced" and the alternate strategy as "primitive." It comes as something of a surprise, therefore, to find that some oviparous sharks lay a few large-yolked eggs like birds, while other elasmobranchs give birth to large, well-developed young just as do mammals. Some of these latter viviparous elasmobranchs even nourish their young by means of placentae completely analogous to the mammalian placentae which gave all of us our own start in life.

MALE REPRODUCTIVE SYSTEM

Internal fertilization is a key adaptation for energy-intensive reproduction. Rather than having eggs and sperm introduced separately

163

into an uncertain external environment, as do most bony fish, elasmobranch sperm are deposited within the reproductive tract of the female. This makes the fertilization of each of the few eggs more likely and provides the sperm with a carefully regulated environment. Among elasmobranchs the intromittant organs (analogous to the mammalian penis) are known as claspers. They are modified inner edges of the pelvic fins (Figure 8–1). From the fossil remains of claspers we know that internal fertilization is a very old process in sharks, for elasmobranchs had them hundreds of millions of years ago.

The internal anatomy of the male reproductive system includes the testes, which produce sperm, and a duct system to provide the fluid components of the semen, package the sperm, and conduct them to the outside. The two testes are suspended well forward in the body cavity (Figure 8–2). When sexual maturity occurs, the

Figure 8–1. Male elasmobranchs are distinguished by their intromittent organs—claspers. A male little skate has its left clasper flexed in position for mating.

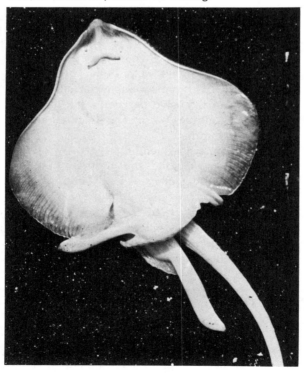

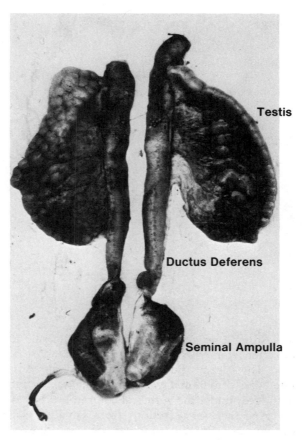

Testis

Ductus Deferens

Seminal Ampulla

Figure 8–2. The internal sexual organs of a
male skate.

sperm are produced in clumps that pass from each testis through
small ductules into highly convoluted tubes known as the epididymis. Each epididymis passes back underneath the vertebral column
in the upper wall of the body cavity. A viscous fluid is secreted in the
epididymis around the sperm to produce the semen, which
nourishes and activates the sperm. Although vertebrate sperm show
many variations on the basic tadpole shape, those of elasmobranchs
are among the most extreme. They are long, being close to 0.1 millimeter in length. The elongated heads, middle pieces, and tails are
twisted into helical or corkscrew shapes so that they revolve as they
swim (Figure 8–3). Indeed, these sperm move by twisting rather than

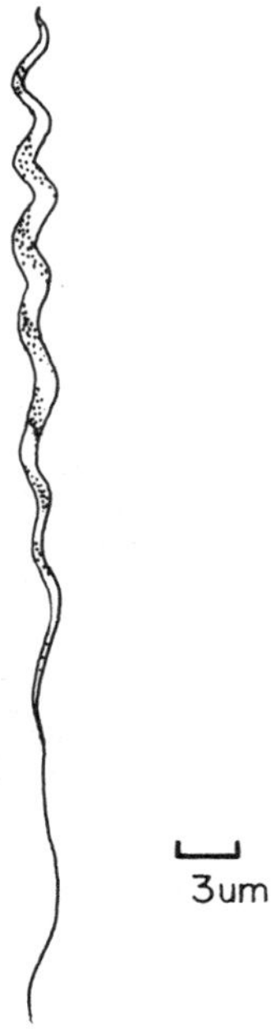

Figure 8-3. Diagram of the helical sperm of a blue shark.

3um

by lashing a flaggellumlike tail. They are said to be able to reverse direction merely by changing the direction of rotation.

The sperm and gathering semen move from the epididymis into a less convoluted, wider duct, the ductus deferens, which passes to the rear under the vertebral column. At its forward end the ductus deferens receives secretions from Leydig's gland—a gland that is continuous with the front part of the kidney. The fluids received from Leydig's gland add considerably to the volume of the semen. The ductus deferens widens as it passes under the kidney and expands into the seminal vesicles and seminal ampulla at the rearmost section of the body cavity.

Semen is stored in the seminal vesicles and seminal ampullae until needed. In large sharks, the volume of semen varies from a pint or so in tiger sharks to five or six gallons in a large male basking shark. In some sharks the ductus deferens is interrupted by a series of transverse membranes that force the semen through internal gates or pores. Here the semen is packaged into pelletlike spermatophores. From the seminal vesicles the semen flows through an orifice in the urogenital papilla into the cloaca. During copulation a clasper is flexed over this papilla to receive the semen and guide it into the female.

166

Claspers. The accessory sexual organs of male elasmobranchs are of two types. First there are the paired claspers, developed from the ventral fins; second are paired siphon sacs that lie under the skin in front of each clasper. The primary male sexual accessory organ, of course, is the clasper. Developed from the supporting cartilages of the inner edges of the pelvic fins, claspers were first named because early biologists thought they were used to clasp and hold the female during intercourse. Now we know that they are the organs of intromission, although controversy still remains about their exact use. The clasper is supported by expanded cartilages that elongate at sexual maturity and may become highly calcified. The soft tissue and skin of the clasper is not formed of erectile tissue. A deep semen-conducting groove passes along the upper and inner edge of the clasper. The entrance to this groove at the clasper base is known as the apopyle. The distant end of the groove near the clasper tip is called the hypopyle.

The clasper tip of many elasmobranchs is complex. It is capable of opening up like a flower, exposing cartilaginous hooks and spurs that dig into the walls of the female oviduct, anchoring the clasper during copulation (Figure 8–4). Copulatory wounds and scars

Figure 8–4. The clasper muscles of a male skate are electrically stimulated to demonstrate the position and opening of the clasper that occurs during mating.

are frequently found in the oviducts of female elasmobranchs. The claspers of skates and galeomorph sharks are large and well developed. Those of squalomorph sharks and stingrays are smaller and not as well armed.

During copulation, the clasper is flexed by muscles at its base through a 90-degree arc across the body axis so that the apopyle approximates the urogenital papilla. Although some early reports of copulation in elasmobranchs suggested that both claspers are inserted simultaneously into the female cloaca, the general consensus today is that only one clasper is inserted at a time.

Siphon Sacs. In squalomorph and galeomorph sharks the siphon sacs are hollow, muscle-bounded structures that can be large. In many sharks, for example, the siphon sacs extend forward from the pelvic fins to the level of the pectoral fins (Figure 8–5). In sharks such as the spiny dogfish they are not nearly as extensive. Filled with fluid, the capacity of a siphon sac is measured in gallons in a large shark. In addition to having an intrinsic musculature, the siphon sacs have glandular cells that are reported to secrete a product rich in 5-hydroxytryptamine (serotonin) into the lumen of the siphon sacs. Serotonin is a powerful stimulant for the contraction of the smooth muscle that lines the female reproductive tract.

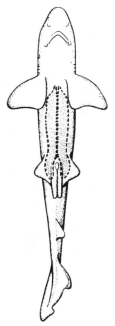

Figure 8–5. The position and extent of the siphon sacs in a male smooth dogfish. (From Gilbert and Heath, 1972)

SMOOTH DOGFISH

Most of the fluid contained in the siphon sacs of a shark preparing to mate is seawater that is pumped in from the outside. The exact mechanism by which this is accomplished is not completely clear. Some male sharks, however, have been seen to repeatedly flex their claspers, swinging one at a time forward in a horizontal arc across the midline of the body. When spiny dogfish seen to have done this were examined, the siphon sacs were partially filled with water. Other sharks are known to swim with a clasper fully flexed. Perhaps in this position seawater is "rammed" into the siphon sac through its single opening at the base of the clasper. At any rate, the siphon sacs operate by contracting during intromission. The mixture of seawater and glandular secretions is forced out of the sac and flows into the seminal groove of the clasper, washing the semen into the oviducts of the female. The serotonin presumably functions to stimulate waves of smooth-muscle contraction that assist the sperm in their journey through the female oviducts.

In batoids the siphon sacs are replaced by clasper glands. These are solid, glandular structures found at the base of each clasper (Figure 8–6). They do not fill with seawater, but secrete instead a copious

Figure 8–6. The location of the clasper gland and anatomy of the claspers in the round stingray. Cl. gl = clasper gland; Apop. = apopyle; Hypop. = hypopyle. Ventral view on the left; dorsal view on the right. (From LaMarca, 1964)

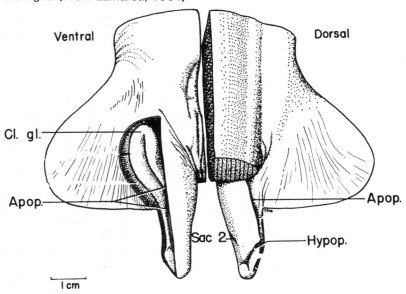

Ventral

Dorsal

Cl. gl.

Apop.

Apop.

Sac 2

Hypop.

1 cm

fluid containing protein and lipid-rich components. Several functions of the clasper gland have been suggested. These include providing a medium in which to transport and store sperm, lubrication to make the insertion of the clasper easier, and as a sealant to enclose the clasper groove so that the semen is not mixed with seawater. This last function is suggested by the fact that clasper gland secretions coagulate upon contact with seawater.

In addition to siphon sacs and claspers, some male elasmobranchs have additional secondary sexual characteristics. In species in which the male grasps the female with its mouth during copulation, the teeth frequently show sexual dimorphism. Thus in skates (*Raja*), rays (*Urolophus*), catsharks (Scyliorhinidae), and some squalomorph and galeomorph sharks, the teeth of the males are longer and narrower than those of the females. Male skates also have retractable placoid scales known as alar spines along the upper parts of the leading edges of the pectoral fins. These spines may be used to anchor the male to the female during copulation.

FEMALE REPRODUCTIVE SYSTEM

The ovaries are suspended from mesenteries well forward in the body cavity in a position analogous to that of the testes in the male. In elasmobranchs like smooth dogfish, hammerheads, sawsharks, and round stingrays only one ovary (usually the left) is developed and functional. Oviparous forms like the skates have both ovaries developed and functional (Figure 8–7). Within the ovary, germinal cells that develop into the functional eggs are nourished by follicle cells that supply the nutrients stored as yolk. The ova of most elasmobranchs reach heroic proportions, with diameters exceeding several centimeters. Indeed, it is said that the mature ovum of the whale shark is the largest example of a single cell known. The eggs of these great fish measure some 15 by 30 centimeters (6 by 12 inches). Those of the sawfish are not much smaller.

When their development is complete, the eggs burst from the ovary (ovulation) and enter the body cavity. Here they are moved to the entrance of the oviducts by tracts of beating cilia on cells that line the body cavity, liver, and mesenteries. The eggs enter the oviducts through a funnellike ostium, which lies near and in front of the ovaries. Many sharks have a single ostium that provides access to

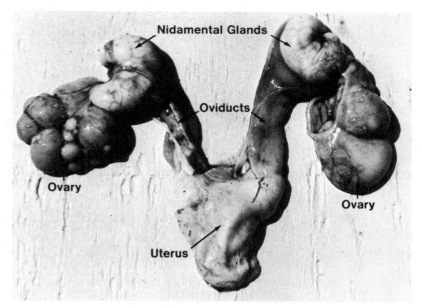

Nidamental Glands

Oviducts

Ovary

Ovary

Uterus

Figure 8–7. The reproductive organs of a female little skate.

both oviducts. Other elasmobranchs have two ostia—one connected to each oviduct.

The oviducts are straight, muscular tubes that pass back along the top of the body cavity on either side of and under the vertebral column. There is a swelling on each oviduct near its anterior end. This marks the nidamental (shell) gland (Figure 8–8). By the time the large yolky eggs reach the shell gland, they usually have been fertilized by sperm lurking in the upper end of the oviduct and shell gland itself. The shell gland secretes an albuminlike substance and then a tough collagenous membrane around the fertilized egg, investing it with both nutritive and protective layers. One function of the shell gland is to store sperm—perhaps for months or even years in some species. In a population of blue sharks studied off the southern New England coast of the United States, about 50 percent of the subadult females (ovaries not yet functional) had copulated and possessed sperm stored in their shell glands. Females of this species with nearly fully developed young in their uteri also were found to have sperm in their shell glands. Presumably these sperm survived from the initial mating and would be available to fertilize the next crop of eggs.

171

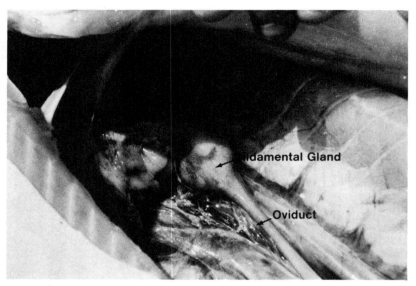

Figure 8–8. Nidamental (shell) gland of a female sand tiger shark. The liver and digestive tract have been removed.

Oviparity. Oviparous sharks—those that lay eggs—usually have a tough shell with a definite shape. The shells of skates are recognized as "mermaids' purses" by beachcombers (Figure 8–9). Some of the catsharks produce a similar egg, but with the four corners drawn out into longer, prehensile tendrils. The egg cases of hornsharks have an encircling helical flange wound around the otherwise ovoid egg. Those sharks that retain their embryos and give birth to live young (viviparous sharks) secrete a more fragile shell that is translucent amber in color (Figure 8–10). In some species—the spiny dogfish is an example—several eggs may be packaged in the same shell as a "candle." In these sharks the enshelled eggs continue to move down the oviduct until they reach an expanded region more richly supplied with blood vessels, the uterus. In oviparous sharks the eggs do not repose here long before they are deposited on the bottom of the ocean. Some species of skates—the little skate, for example—lay one egg every day or two through an extended period of egg laying; others such as the clearnose skate produce a pair of eggs a few minutes to a few hours apart, every four to six days.

Viviparity. Among the most diverse and spectacular adaptations of sharks are those associated with viviparity. Some species retain the

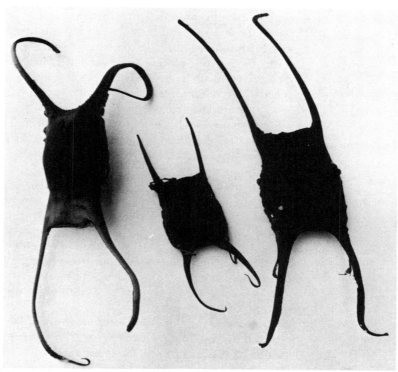

Figure 8–9. Egg cases from skates.

Figure 8–10. Egg and egg case from a viviparous shark, the smooth dogfish.

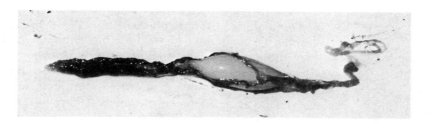

eggs in the uterus only until they hatch and then give birth. The nurse shark, for example, has been reported both to lay eggs and to give birth to live young. In the latter case the eggs hatch just prior to birth. In the former case the eggs hatch just after being laid. The nurse shark is incipiently viviparous and appears to have few if any special adaptations for nurturing the young before they are born.

A more specialized approach to viviparity is taken by squalomorph sharks such as the spiny dogfish. In this species, a few months after gestation begins, the single candle in each uterus ruptures, freeing an average of four to six embryos. These young sharks continue to receive all of their energy from nutrients stored in the original yolk of their eggs (Figure 3-5). The uterus, however, becomes highly vascular and may bring oxygen to the shark pups as well as remove accumulated waste products from them. The young sharks develop until the yolk is nearly used up. Birth then occurs after a gestation period that ranges from 18 to 24 months. This is probably the longest gestation period for any vertebrate, and is exceptional even among sharks. The slow development of these sharks is related, at least in part, to the cold water temperatures they prefer.

Aside from this non-nutritive form of viviparity (sometimes referred to as "ovoviviparity" or "aplacental viviparity"), other groups of elasmobranchs independently evolved at least three distinct modes of nourishing developing young. The first of these is found in several rays (stingrays, butterfly rays, devil rays, electric rays). Here the embryos deplete their stored yolk early in development. Indeed, some, like the butterfly rays, produce eggs measuring only a millimeter or so in diameter. Once the embryo has hatched from its fragile shell and consumed its initial yolk supply, it receives a nourishing secretion (uterine "milk") from the inner (endometrial) walls of the uterus. The uterus is highly modified for the production of uterine milk. The endometrium is thrown into a profusion of hairlike processes which enormously increase the surface area for secretion. These processes, known as trophonemata, proliferate and elongate as development proceeds (Figure 8-11). Most embryonic rays have exceptionally large spiracles, and it is through these openings that the uterine milk is imbibed and passed to the stomach for digestion and absorption. An extreme form of aplacental viviparity occurs in some rays (e.g., *Urolophus*) wherein groups of elongated trophonemata penetrate the spiracles and secrete uterine milk directly into the digestive tracts of the embryos.

The trophonemetal nourishment of ray embryos is an efficient

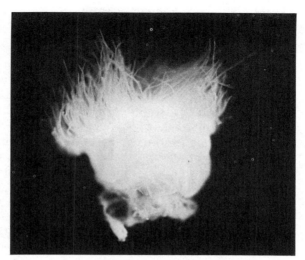

Figure 8–11. A block of tissue from the uterus of a roughtail stingray, showing the nutritive trophonemata.

means of viviparity. These elasmobranchs have shorter gestation periods than do other sharks. Ray embryos reach full term in only 2 to 4 months for many species. The usual gestation period is closer to 10 or 12 months for other kinds of viviparous elasmobranchs. Rays also have small litter sizes, ranging from 1 to fewer than 15 young.

Of the several groups of rays that practice trophonematal feeding of embryos, the electric rays (Torpedinidae, Narkidae) show the poorest anatomical and physiological specializations. The uterine linings in these fishes have the fewest trophonemata and the least-rich uterine milk. Analyses of full-term embryos show they actually contain less organic material than the eggs that produced them. On the other hand, stingrays, devil rays, and particularly the butterfly rays have the most extreme adaptations. Their trophonemata are numerous and long. The uterine milk contains much protein (23 percent) and fat (8 percent) and at birth, the embryos contain as much as 5000 percent more organic matter than had been present in the eggs at the beginning of development.

The rays we know as sawfishes are ovoviviparous in the mode of spiny dogfish. Their eggs, however, are great in size. They support the growth of just a few embryos at a time to a large size at birth.

Lamniform sharks are known to have a mode of embryonic nutrition completely unique among vertebrates. Sand tiger sharks, porbeagle sharks, thresher sharks, and mako sharks nourish their young by releasing successive crops of eggs from the ovaries throughout gestation. These eggs (which are small) pass to the uterus, where the developing young eat them and are thereby nourished. This form of embryonic nutrition is known as oophagy (egg eating) and is widespread among the lamniforms, including the white shark and perhaps even the basking shark.

The nutritive eggs of oophagous sharks are small (1 centimeter in diameter), but are prodigious in number. Usually only one embryo survives per uterus, it having consumed its potential competitors. It has been remarked that this is the ultimate solution to the problems posed by sibling rivalry! The few numbers of embryos produced are compensated for by their size and advanced developmental stage at birth. In the sand tiger shark, embryos as large as 105 centimeters long have been reported—fully half as long as the females that contained them! The intrauterine activity of the late-term young is extraordinary. They are voracious. At least one scientist was bitten by an embryo when he reached into the uterus of a recently caught sand tiger. It is likely that oophagy involves an unusual hormonal adaptation. Normally in vertebrates ovulation is inhibited by the hormonal profile of the pregnant female. That inhibition is clearly absent in the lamniform sharks.

A final adaptation by elasmobranchs for viviparity is found in the requiem and hammerhead sharks. In these animals, some time after the rupture of the fragile shell the embryo establishes a placental connection with the endometrium of the maternal uterus. The placenta formed is analogous to, although not exactly the same as, the mammalian type of placenta that at one point nourished each of us. The difference is that the embryonic membranes that help to form the shark placentae are derived from the yolk sac of the embryo rather than from the amnion and chorion as in mammals. Functionally, however, the shark placenta is equivalent to that found in mammals. In it, maternal blood and that of the fetus are able to exchange oxygen, nutrients, and waste products across the thinnest possible membranous barrier. The degree of intimacy that develops between the maternal and fetal components differs considerably from species to species. In some hammerheads special proliferations of tissue (appendiculae) develop from the umbilicus and suggest additional uptake of nutrients from the fluid of the uterine cavity. This fluid in the smooth dogfish is rich in organic nutrients that are incorporated into the fetus.

The distribution of placental viviparity is not uniform

throughout the Carcharhiniformes. Some species *(Mustelus laevis, M. antarcticus)* do not have placentae. The litter size may be large in some placental species. The blue shark can carry litters of up to 165 young, although 40 to 50 pups are more usual. Whaler sharks of the genus *Carcharhinus* have litters of a dozen or so embryos. The gestation period for most placental viviparous sharks appears to be between 9 and 12 months. Placentation occurs about 2 or 3 months after ovulation, when the embryos have consumed their yolk. Because the eggs are ovulated (and fertilized) sequentially at intervals of a day or so, there may be considerable variation in the developmental ages of shark pups in a given litter—particularly in large ones. It is not unusual to find embryos that have died during development and are in a state of decay among their normal siblings.

COURTSHIP AND MATING

Animals that practice internal fertilization generally have complicated courtship behaviors that produce the cooperation needed for successful intromission. In those vertebrates that show a lot of parental care of the young (as in birds and mammals), courtship behavior also serves to establish pair bonds that allow both parents to cooperate during brood rearing. The minimal parental care given by elasmobranchs to their young suggests that courtship in these fishes should not be as elaborate. Yet the fact of intromission requires cooperation between male and female of a kind that demands precopulatory foreplay. Unfortunately, however, observations of shark courtship and mating behavior have been rare. Most of what is known is inferred from a few ancedotal reports and a scanty amount of physical evidence.

Sharks are, with a few exceptions, not gaudy animals. Because of the plain, cryptic coloration of most sharks, and because their eyes are adapted for nocturnal activity, vision may not play a primary role in courtship. With the exception of the male claspers, there is little obvious external sexual dimorphism. It is predictable that with their nocturnal behavior patterns and acute senses of smell, sharks might rely on olfactory cues for sex discrimination and the identification of females near the ovulatory stage of the sexual cycles. In fact, on a couple of occasions, blacktip reef sharks were observed behaving as if the sense of smell was important in sexual matters. In the first instance a male shark turned accurately to follow a female that had passed by somewhat earlier but which was out of sight of the male. On other occasions the males of this species as well as of whitetip reef sharks oriented to the vents of swimming females as if attractants (pheromones) were being released. No other information exists on this aspect of shark sexual behavior. It remains a fertile field for future studies.

The use of teeth during courtship is important in several species of elasmobranchs. In pelagic galeomorph sharks nearly all of the mature, and many submature, females bear tooth wounds, or scars from earlier wounds, made by males during sexual advances. Males seldom carry such wounds, although interestingly, one hermaphrodite blue shark did. A curious feature of these wounds is that they are usually made by the upper teeth only. This suggests that the male slashes the female with its head high and mouth open. The strike must be made by depressing the head, without simultaneous jaw closure. The females that suffer such wounds usually receive them along the flanks, particularly on the rear half of the body (Figure 6–6).

Although courtship wounds can be severe, they heal quickly and with little risk of infection. The females of sharks like the blue shark have an adaptation to deal with these wounds. The skin of the female over the back and flanks is more than twice as thick as that from a male of the same size. Even though the tooth slashes may be deep, they seldom penetrate the thick dermis of the female.

Males of the scalloped hammerhead ram females from above with their blunt snouts. These encounters often leave scraped patches of damaged tissue on the backs of the females. Most females of this species carry the scars from these collisions, and their virtual absence from males suggests that this behavior is sexual in nature. While the meaning of these aggressive courting displays is not known, they may serve as releasing stimuli, producing copulatory responses in the females.

Judging from the absence of courtship scars in many species of sharks, it is probably true that most elasmobranchs are not nearly as "kinky" in their approach to sex. An early description of apparent courtship occurred in a pair of captive lemon sharks that swam at night in close parallel synchrony for at least one hour. So close together were the bodies of these sharks that intromission may have occurred while they were being observed. Other captive lemon sharks have also been seen to orient to each other in what might have been sexual foreplay. At the Lerner Marine Laboratory, on the island of Bimini in the Bahamas, male and female lemon sharks occasionally rested side by side on the bottom of their pen. So close together were these sharks that their pectoral fins overlapped one another.

Close following and synchronous swimming have been noted in batoids. In the roughtail stingray, for example, a male was observed from a research submarine in 80 meters (260 feet) of water to swim first behind and then closely above a larger female. Occasionally they settled to the bottom together, with the male biting the female's back. Copulation was not observed, but the behavior was obviously sexual in its intent.

Probably the best-known sequence of courting and mating behavior is that described for nurse sharks (Figure 8–12). They mate in captivity as well as in the clear shallow tropical waters of the Caribbean, where they are common. Courting pairs (and sometimes triplets) of nurse sharks show the synchronized parallel swimming described for lemon sharks, but usually with the male slightly behind the female, his snout at the level of her pectoral fin. The male sometimes slips farther back so that his snout is at the level of the female cloaca. After a bout of parallel swimming, both sharks will occasionally rest on the bottom side by side. The male is often noticeably darker in coloration than the female.

Occasionally the male grasps the hind edge of one of the female's pectoral fins. Several species of sharks, including hornsharks, catsharks, blue sharks, and whaler sharks, also bite the pectoral fin during courtship. In the nurse shark the pectoral-fin bite seems to serve as a stimulus for the female to turn in front of the male and roll over onto her back at right angles to his long axis. While on her back, the female is passive and rigid due to the tonic immobility reflex common to sharks and many other animals. While the female lies on her back the male nudges her with his head and moves her until she lies parallel to him. He may thrust his head under her back, lifting her off the bottom. After a period of nudging the male swims over the female and a single clasper is inserted. This may take from 10 to 30 seconds. The male then rolls over onto his back, nearly parallel to the female, revealing a clasper inserted for perhaps one third of its length, with both claspers swollen and pink, as if engorged with blood. After two or more minutes both sharks right themselves and swim away rapidly (Figure 8–12).

In smaller sharks such as hornsharks and catsharks, copulation is carried out with the female on her side and the male partially coiled transversely around her. When clearnose skates mate, the male holds the trailing edge of the female's pectoral fin in his mouth,

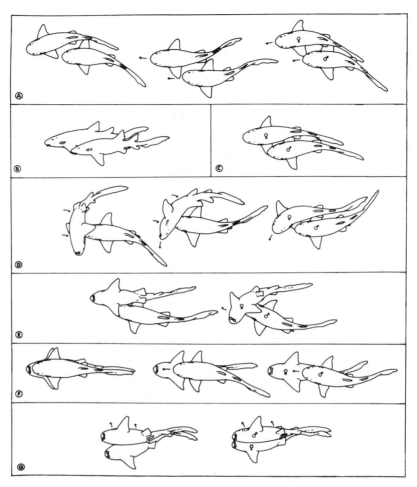

Figure 8–12. Courtship and mating behavior in the nurse shark. (A) parallel swimming; (B and C) pectoral fin biting; (D) the male pivots and rolls the female on her back; (E) the male nudges the upside-down female and (F) moves over her; (G) male rolls onto his back, exposing an inserted clasper. (From Klimley, 1980)

swings his tail and claspers beneath her tail, and inserts one clasper into her cloaca and reproductive tract. Copulation may continue in this position for as long as two hours. In all of these cases only a single clasper is inserted. Less reliable reports indicated both claspers are inserted simultaneously, although it is difficult to understand the mechanics of such a mating act.

180

EVOLUTION OF REPRODUCTIVE STRATEGIES

The modes of reproduction in modern elasmobranchs reveal tendencies toward the evolution of viviparity. These fishes arose from an ancestor that provided its young with nourishment in the form of large, yolky eggs and a tough outer shell to protect them. This ancestral state is retained today by skates, hornsharks, some orectolobiforms (including the whale shark), and the carcharhiniform catsharks. It apparently was but a short step to retain the eggs in the maternal uterus until they hatched, giving them further protection from the vicissitudes of the environment. This incipient, aplacental viviparity is seen today in some orectolobiform sharks, the sawfishes, and most squalomorph sharks, including the hexanchiforms, sawsharks, and spiny dogfishes. It also is the mode of reproduction in angel sharks and some batoids such as the guitarfishes. This most elementary form of viviparity must have evolved very early indeed, for even the sixgill sharks, including the frill shark, practice it.

As was noted earlier, from the simplest, aplacental form of viviparity at least three kinds of actively nutritive forms of viviparity evolved in elasmobranchs. These include oophagy in the lamniform sharks, uterine milk production in the myliobatiform rays, and placental viviparity in carcharhiniform sharks. There clearly must be adaptive advantages to the reproductive strategy of viviparty.

Several factors are important in this regard. The first is relative fecundity. Even the most fecund oviparous skates and sharks probably produce in the neighborhood of 100 or so eggs per year. Many produce fewer. This is low compared to the fecundity of most bony fishes. Aplacental viviparous sharks like the sixgill shark are equally fecund. Viviparity can evolve without sacrificing fecundity.

A second factor favoring the evolution of viviparity is the choice of habitat by elasmobranchs. Most oviparous forms are benthic and littoral (skates, orectoboforms, hornsharks, and catsharks), and because they are bottom dwellers, can easily deposit their eggs there. The whale shark is a notable exception to this generalization. The retention of embryos, and thus viviparity, would seem to be a decided advantage to the wide-ranging, pelagic, and migratory elasmobranchs, and indeed, these are the ones that show this reproductive mode.

Some biologists suggest that body size is related to reproductive mode, large forms being viviparous, small ones being oviparous—but lots of exceptions occur. Similarly, feeding ecology has been offered as a correlate with reproductive mode, but this is not well substantiated. It is probably an advantage to produce the largest newborn young possible. Larger body size allows faster movement and thus increased foraging efficiency and avoidance of predation. In general, viviparous elasmobranchs produce young that are much larger at birth than their oviparous peers are at hatching. Most oviparous elasmobranchs are less than 15 centimeters in length at hatching. The largest oviparous embryo—that of the whale shark—is about 35 centimeters long at hatching. This is not much larger than the birth size of even aplacental viviparous sharks of small size (such as the spiny dogfish). Most placental forms are considerably larger at birth, and the largest embryos (in excess of 100 centimeters) are found in the oophagous lamnoids.

Another suggestion to explain the advantages of viviparity relates to the osmoregulatory retention of urea in elasmobranchs (see Chapter 9). This argument holds that in viviparity the embryo is sheltered from an osmotically alien world until its own regulatory systems develop. This idea is not supported by measurements of urea production in embryos. Indeed, it also has been suggested that urea retention was, in the first instance, an adaptation to viviparity. Every coin has two sides, and more study is needed to know which side of this one is heads and which is tails.

Viviparity, as a form of parental care, increases the chances of survival for each embryo. Very early in the history of the group, elasmobranchs invested a lot of metabolic energy (yolk) rather than behavioral energy in the care of their young. That decision has been extended in several viviparous strategies to produce larger, well-developed young that are better able to care for themselves, lacking—as they do—concerned, doting parents.

In their modes of reproduction, the elasmobranchs present a range of adaptations probably unmatched by any other group of vertebrates of so few species. This, once again, makes them fertile ground for the inquiries of evolutionists, physiologists, and behaviorists. The rest of us, too, can marvel at the reproductive spectacles they have placed before us.

ADDITIONAL READING

Bigelow, H. B., and W.C. Schroeder. *Fishes of the Western North Atlantic*, Part 1, *Lancelets, cyclostomes and sharks*. New Haven: Sears Foundation for Marine Research, 1948.

Bigelow, H.B., and W.C. Schroeder. *Fishes of the Western North Atlantic*, Part 2, *Sawfishes, guitarfishes, skates and rays*. New Haven: Sears Foundation for Marine Research, 1953.

Chieffi, G. "The reproductive system of elasmobranchs: developmental and endocrinological aspects." pp. 553–580. In *Sharks, Skates, and Rays*, ed. P.W. Gilbert, R.F. Mathewson, and D.P. Rall. Baltimore: The Johns Hopkins University Press, 1967.

Francis, M.P., and J.T. Mace. "Reproductive biology of *Mustelus lenticulatus* from Kaikoura and Nelson." *New Zealand J. Mar. and Freshw. Res.*, 14, no. 3 (1980), 303–311.

Gilbert, P.W. "Patterns of shark reproduction." *Oceanus*, 24, no. 4 (1981), 30–39.

Gilbert, P.W., and G.W. Heath. "The clasper-siphon sac mechanism in *Squalus acanthias* and *Mustelus canis*." *Comp. Biochem. Physiol.*, 42A (1972), 97–119. (Figure 8–5 is reprinted with permission from this work by Pergamon Press, Ltd.)

LaMarca, M.J. "The functional anatomy of the clasper and clasper gland of the yellow stingray, *Urolophus jamaicensis* (Cuvier)." *J. Morph.*, 114, no. 2 (1964), 303–324. (Figure 8–6 is from this work.)

Klimley, A. P. "Observations of courtship and copulation in the nurse shark, *Ginglymostoma cirratum*." *Copeia*, 1980, no. 4 (1980), 878–882. (Figure 8–12 is from this work.)

Parsons, G.R. "The reproductive biology of the Atlantic sharpnose shark, *Rhizoprionodon terraenovae* (Richardson)." *Fishery Bulletin*, 81, no. 1 (1983), 61–73.

Pratt, H.L., Jr. "Reproduction in the blue shark, *Prionace glauca*." *Fishery Bulletin*, 77, no. 2 (1979), 445–470.

Reed, J.K., and R.G. Gilmore. "Inshore occurrence and nuptial behavior of the roughtail stingray, *Dasyatis centroura* (Dasyatidae), on the continental shelf, east central Florida." *Northeast Gulf Science*, 5, no. 1 (1981), 59–62.

Schlernitzauer, D.A., and P.W. Gilbert. "Placentation and associated aspects of gestation in the bonnethead shark, *Sphryna tiburo*." *J. Morph.*, 120 (1966), 219–231.

Stevens, J.D. "Observations on reproduction in the shortfin mako *Isurus oxyrinchus*." *Copeia*, 1983, no. 1 (1983), 126–130.

Wass, R.C. "Size, growth, and reproduction of the sandbar shark, *Carcharhinus milberti*, in Hawaii." *Pac. Sci.*, 27, no. 4 (1973), 305–318.

Wolfson, F.H. "Records of seven juveniles of the whale shark, *Rhiniodon typus.*" *Journal of Fish Biology*, 22 (1983), 647–655.

Wourms, J.P. "Reproduction and development in chondrichthyan fishes." *Amer. Zool.*, 17 (1977), 379–410.

9

Osmoregulation

An aquatic animal can be thought of as a bag of fluid swimming in its watery medium. Of course this living bag is elegantly subdivided into cells that are bathed by fluid (extracellular fluid or lymph), which in turn is separated from the outside environment by thin sheets of cellular tissue (epithelium). This epithelium, particularly at its extensive thinnest region—the gills—presents almost no barrier to the passage of water through it, and only slight resistance to certain other small molecules (some salts and small organic molecules such as alcohols, etc.). This bag is subject to some fundamental chemical rules about how molecules distribute themselves in solutions.

These rules are easy to understand if we know that molecules (solutes) dissolved in a solvent (water in biological systems) will move from regions of high concentration to regions of low concentration. A teaspoon of sugar crystals, dropped into a cup of hot tea, will dissolve and become evenly distributed throughout the cup—if given enough time—without stirring. The mixing process dependent on the random motion of the individual solute molecules is known as *diffusion.* Simultaneously, mixing is carried out by an analogous process known as osmosis. *Osmosis* can be thought of as mixing due to the random movements of the solvent (water) molecules. If there is a concentration difference (concentration gradient) of solvent, it will tend to be eliminated by osmosis. Water will "flow" from regions where it is in high concentration to regions of lower concentration.

With these rules in mind we can look more knowingly at a fish as it swims through the water. If a sample of its internal fluid (blood) is drawn off, we will find that it is a complex mixture of salts (sodium, chloride, potassium, calcium, sulfates, and others), large organic molecules (proteins, fatty acids), and some small ones (amino acids, simple sugar, urea, etc.). The total concentration of all these dissolved molecules will amount to about 1.5 percent of the fluid volume, with the remaining 98.5 percent made up of water. The water (solvent) concentration of this blood is thereby about 98.5 percent.

Physiologists prefer to think of these matters not in chemical concentrations, but rather in terms of their osmotic effect. It is easier to measure the total osmotic effect of the solutes in a biological fluid than to measure each molecular type separately and then sum them all up. The blood of a typical vertebrate might have an "osmotic concentration" of solutes of about 0.3 osmoles (300 milliosmoles). That is, it has the osmotic effect of about 0.3 moles (gram molecular weight) of a pure, nonionic substance dissolved in one liter of water.

Now consider the chemical makeup of the environment through which the fish swims. If it is a freshwater pond, there will be few molecules dissolved in the water, meaning that the solute concentration is virtually 0 percent and the water concentration is 100 percent. Two things will happen to the fish. First, water will move by osmosis from the pond into the fish. It will flow down the water-concentration gradient. The fish should swell. Secondly (and more slowly), salts will diffuse from the fish to the pond, reducing the solute concentration of the fish. This will happen unless the fish has the means to regulate these events. We know that goldfish and bass, or frogs and turtles for that matter, do not swell appreciably. Nor do they ordinarily show a net loss of salts. Freshwater fish, it turns out, "osmoregulate" by using several strategies. First, they have a somewhat lower osmotic concentration (about 250 milliosmoles) than do other forms. Next, they continually bail out the water that is osmotically invading their bodies. They do this by voiding a large quantity of urine. Finally, to replace the salts that are lost by diffusion from the gills and in the urine, they capture the relatively few salt molecules they do encounter in the water. This is done by special cells in the gills that spend energy to transport (active transport) these salt molecules (principally sodium and chloride) into the animal, against the salt-concentration gradient. These three strategies thus allow the freshwater bony fish to maintain a steady state in the face of severe osmotic constraints (Figure 9–1).

A reverse set of perils awaits the fish if it swims in the ocean. Oceanic water contains a host of dissolved salts (again, principally sodium and chloride) which add up to about 3.5 percent by volume (or about 1000 milliosmoles in osmotic concentration). The water concentration in the ocean is thus only about 96.5 percent. This means that the fish, having about 98.5 percent water inside, should lose water by osmosis to the sea and gain salts by diffusion. The fish should and will shrink, unless it too can regulate. Marine fish such as

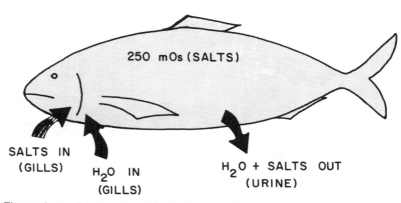

ENVIRONMENT – $\emptyset$ mOs

250 mOs (SALTS)

SALTS IN
(GILLS)

H₂O IN
(GILLS)

H₂O + SALTS OUT
(URINE)

Figure 9–1. Freshwater fish, being osmotically invaded by water (through the gills), bail water out as urine and absorb salts from the dilute environment through the gills.

tuna, flounders, and codfish, faced with this problem of osmotic water loss, regulate as follows. First, their internal osmotic concentration is higher (350 milliosmoles) than in freshwater fishes. Next, they cut down water loss by producing little urine. Indeed, some marine teleosts have secondarily lost the kidney structures (renal glomeruli) that allow for copious urine formation. Finally, to make up for the osmotic loss of water, the fish actively drinks seawater. The imbibed water *and* most of the salts are absorbed from the digestive tract. This strategy—which at first glance seems to be a loser—succeeds because the fish is able to excrete selectively the salts from its body. They are excreted not from the kidney, but through the gills in a reversal of roles played by the same cells by which freshwater fish actively absorb salts. There is an energy cost to excrete these salts. It is a price the fish pays to be able to osmoregulate in seawater (Figure 9–2).

All this brings us to elasmobranchs. Early in their evolutionary history, sharks happened upon a different method of dealing with the osmotic problems presented by their primary habitat, the ocean. It is a method not unique to sharks, for the coelacanth, *Latimeria chalumnae*, and a brackish water frog or two have also discovered it. If the body fluids of a typical marine elasmobranch are analyzed, the salt concentrations are only slightly higher than those of marine

189

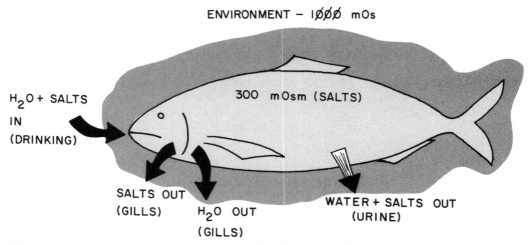

ENVIRONMENT – 1000 mOs

H₂O + SALTS
IN
(DRINKING)

300 mOsm (SALTS)

SALTS OUT
(GILLS)

H₂O OUT
(GILLS)

WATER + SALTS OUT
(URINE)

Figure 9–2. Marine fish lose water osmotically. Consequently, they drink seawater and excrete the salts through the gills. They lose some water and salts through a reduced urine flow.

bony fishes. When the osmotic concentrations are compared, however, there is a significant difference. Most elasmobranchs keep their internal osmotic concentrations slightly *above* that of seawater—1050 milliosmoles, for example, in water of about 1000 milliosmole osmotic concentration. How can this be, when the salt concentrations are well below that of seawater?

The answer is that sharks allow certain small organic molecules to build up to high concentrations in their blood and body fluids. There are two principal substances involved. The first of these is trimethylamine oxide, or TMAO for short. This substance is found in the fish and invertebrates that elasmobranchs eat (when reduced by decomposition, it has a characteristically strong "fishy" odor) and is retained (neither metabolized nor excreted) by the shark. Sharks can also synthesize TMAO in their tissues and build up concentrations of it in this way.

The second compound retained by sharks is more important and interesting. It is a nitrogen-containing molecule known as urea. Urea is most familiar as an important feedstock in industrial chemistry, where it is a basic component in the production of plastics and foam insulations. It is also used as a fertilizer for lawns and gardens. Urea is the principal organic molecule excreted by the kidneys of nearly all mammals, including ourselves. It is the most important nitrogenous waste product of mammals.

190

When proteins are metabolized or broken down by any animal, the atoms of nitrogen contained within these molecules pose a disposal problem. The nitrogen atoms are mainly found in the amino groups of the amino acids that make up proteins. The amino groups are essentially clipped off to produce ammonia. If ammonia can be gotten rid of easily, it forms the main nitrogenous waste product. The trouble is that ammonia is toxic to most animals, even in low concentrations, so a lot of water must be invested in excreting it in order to keep the ammonia concentrations acceptably low. Most aquatic animals can afford the necessary water, but terrestrial animals cannot. Consequently, land-dwelling animals have to do more work to get rid of their waste nitrogen. This is why mammals produce urea. They convert the amino groups to urea, which is less toxic than ammonia at equivalent concentrations. Therefore less water is lost when the urea is excreted.

UREA RETENTION

Elasmobranchs, like mammals, terrestrial amphibians, and a few other animals, convert their waste nitrogen to urea. But unlike mammals, their kidneys and gills retain it so that urea builds up to extraordinary concentrations in the cells and body fluids. Most marine elasmobranchs have osmotic concentrations of urea ranging from 350 to 650 milliosmoles per liter. Such concentrations in a human would quickly be fatal, for at these levels, urea is toxic to mammals. Sharks, however, have biochemical adaptations to withstand these concentrations—indeed, urea is necessary for normal cell function in sharks. The ultimate payoff, however, is that the retention of urea eliminates for the shark many of the osmotic problems faced by marine bony fish (Figure 9–3).

The elasmobranch, being slightly more osmotically concentrated (hyperosmotic) than the water in which it swims, is subjected to a modest osmotic influx of water. It handles this by excreting more urine than does the marine bony fish. Elasmobranch kidneys are conspicuous and well-developed organs that lie just above the posterior part of the body cavity (Figure 9–4). A more severe problem is posed by the diffusion of sodium and chloride into the animal from the sea. This salt load is handled in a unique way. At the hind end of the intestine on its dorsal side is a fingerlike structure that opens into the intestine near the cloaca. This is the rectal gland (Figure 9–5). For years it was an enigma to biologists. Only in 1960 did scientists find

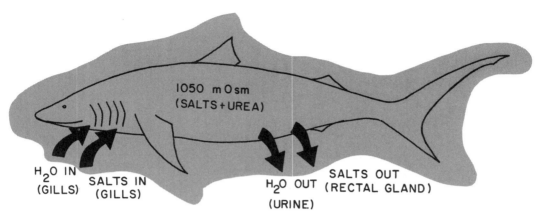

ENVIRONMENT – 1000 mOsm SALTS

1050 mOsm
(SALTS + UREA)

H₂O IN
(GILLS)   SALTS IN
            (GILLS)   H₂O OUT   SALTS OUT
                                       (RECTAL GLAND)
                            (URINE)

Figure 9-3. By retaining urea and TMAO, sharks have about the same osmotic concentration as seawater. They balance the moderate uptake of water and salts by urine and rectal gland secretions.

that the rectal gland secreted into the intestine a solution that is rich in sodium and chloride. The rectal gland is a salt-secreting gland that eliminates at least some of the salts accumulated from the sea by diffusion. More recent studies show that, as in bony fish, shark gills also assist in the elimination of unwanted salts and can compensate for rectal glands that have been surgically removed during experiments.

The elasmobranch pattern of osmoregulation is a metabolically efficient one when compared to that of marine bony fish. The diffusion salt load is almost equivalent to that experienced by bony fish, but the problems attendant to drinking seawater are nonexistent. A metabolic price must be paid by the liver to manufacture urea and by the kidneys to retain it, but this is probably not a high one.

Perhaps the retention of urea operates at cross purposes with the regulation of a gas-filled swim bladder. Bony fish secrete gas (often oxygen) into the swim bladder by suddenly and briefly adding solutes (usually lactic acid) to the blood in the capillaries that serve the swim bladder gas gland. This rise in solutes decreases the solubility of oxygen in the blood, and the gas bubbles out into the swim bladder. Because they already have such high blood-solute concentrations, elasmobranchs might not be able to fill a gas bladder by this mechanism.

192   The concentrations of urea and TMAO in the body fluids and

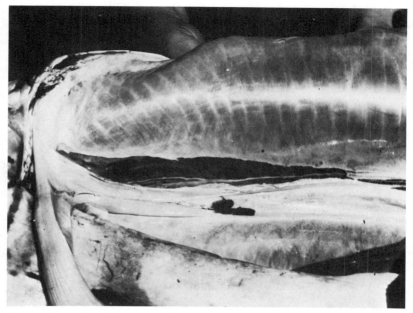

Figure 9–4. The kidneys of elasmobranchs lie above the hind end of the abdominal cavity.

tissues of elasmobranchs conspire to give them a characteristic odor that some people find offensive. Because sharks are often caught in warm climes where refrigeration is not available, they quickly deteriorate in quality. The fact that their tissues contain enzymes that break down urea into ammonia makes this problem even greater. It does not take long for a dead elasmobranch, lying in the hot sun, to become disgusting to the discerning nose!

A question often pondered by students of shark biology concerns the origin and original purpose of the urea-retention adaptation. Biologists suspect that the living bony fishes and cartilaginous fishes are derived from ancestors that lived in a freshwater habitat. The evidence for this comes from a common kidney plan that seems well adapted for life in a habitat with a high water concentration (hypoosmotic environment), and because all of these fishes have internal sodium and chloride concentrations well below those of the sea. Most marine invertebrates and the oceanic hagfishes (living remnants of the original vertebrates—the jawless fishes) have body fluids with sodium and chloride concentrations similar to those found in the ocean. Additionally, there are abundant fossil remains

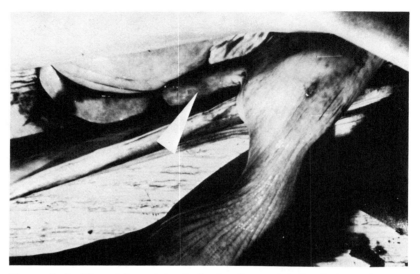

Figure 9–5. The white pointer indicates the rectal gland above the rectum of this sand tiger shark.

of elasmobranchs in deposits laid down in fresh water—or at least weakly saline water. Many of these fossils date from 250 million to 400 million years ago. When elasmobranchs and bony fishes entered (perhaps reentered) the marine habitat, they independently evolved their separate mechanisms for dealing with hyperosmotic environments.

The questions now asked include, "Is urea retention primarily an adaptation for dealing with hyperosmotic stress? Or did even freshwater elasmobranchs find an advantage to urea retention?" The latter notion has some support. Embryos that lie in confined quarters for long periods of time have to detoxify, store, and endure their own nitrogenous waste products. The outstanding example of this is found in reptiles and in the birds that are derived from them. Early in their evolutionary history reptiles developed large-yolked eggs confined within shells that would not dry out on land. The embryonic stage, rather than be poisoned by its own ammonia or urea production, developed the ability to convert its waste nitrogen into uric acid, a white, crystalline, nontoxic, nonsoluble substance that could be stored in the egg until hatching. Most adult reptiles and birds continue to excrete their nitrogen in this form—a fact to which practically every urban park statue is testimony!

194   Because modern elasmobranchs are derived from ancestors that produced large-yolked, shell-enclosed eggs (like those of living skates and hornsharks), similar advantages accrued to those embryos that could endure their own nitrogen (urea) pollution for the duration of gestation. Urea retention could thus have been primarily a physiological adaptation of the embryo to its environment, and only secondarily advantageous to the adult for coping with the marine environment.

While we can never know for sure how and why urea retention evolved, there are other lines of evidence to evaluate these notions. The first involves the aforementioned coelacanth, *Latimeria*. This fish (whose fossil ancestors are prominent in freshwater deposits) also retains urea as an apparent osmotic adaptation. But *Latimeria* also produces large-yolked eggs that are fertilized internally and are retained within the female until hatching. Again, the pressure to develop urea retention may have been placed on the embryo as an adaptation to the uterine environment rather than as one to the marine environment. The process of the adult form "capturing" or retaining a fundamentally embryonic adaptation is known technically as paedogenesis. There are many examples of this in biology, and elasmobranch urea retention may be yet another.

A further test of this idea can come from an examination of the osmoregulatory processes of elasmobranchs in fresh and brackish waters. Fortunately, there are sharks that adjust well to these low-salinity environments. Today their biology is becoming better known.

FRESHWATER ELASMOBRANCHS

Although a majority of elasmobranchs are confined to life in seawater, a few are able to venture into brackish water estuaries, and a few of these can penetrate upstream to completely fresh water. Also, there is a single family of rays, the Potamotrygonidae, that are confined to the fresh waters of tropical South America. The osmoregulatory mechanisms of these fishes can be instructive.

Coastal elasmobranchs, including some skates, smooth dogfish, scyliorhinids (*Poroderma*), bull sharks, and sandbar sharks, regularly move into estuaries to feed or to give birth to young. Experiments with the little skate, the clearnose skate, and the striped dogfish (*Poroderma*) show that these fish can survive reduced salinities down to about that of 50 percent seawater (400 to 500 milliosmole osmotic concentration), provided the dilution occurs gradually over a period of several days. The osmotic concentration of the blood comes to nearly that of the diluted environment. Moreover, the reduced blood osmolality is mainly due to loss of urea—the concentration of salts remains similar to that found in animals kept in 100 percent seawater. This ability to osmoregulate in more dilute environments is not impressive when compared with some other marine fishes. So even the osmotically adventuresome sharks must be classed as stenohaline (*steno* = narrow; *haline* = salinity) animals.

More impressive, however, are the osmoregulatory capacities of many of the stingrays, the sawfishes, and a few notorious galeoid sharks, including the bull shark. These animals are frequently captured or reported from pure fresh water, sometimes quite far from the sea. For example, bull sharks are known in the Amazon River system as far as 4,200 kilometers upstream from the mouth. Other major rivers and lakes from which these sharks are caught include Africa's Zambesi River, the Mekong River in Vietnam, and Lake Nicaragua in Central America. In the United States bull sharks penetrate the Mississippi River (to Alton, Illinois), the Atchafayla and Pascagoula Rivers, and the less saline portions of the Chesapeake Bay. Indeed, so many reports of bull sharks in fresh water exist that it is fair to expect their presence in virtually any tropical or subtropical river system in the world that has direct access to the sea.

Probably the best-studied population of bull sharks that enter fresh water is in Lake Nicaragua. For many years these sharks were considered to be landlocked, and were described as a distinctive species, *Carcharhinus nicaraguensis*. More recent work, including a tagging program, shows that the sharks are actually *C. leucas* and move freely between the Caribbean Sea and the lake through the San Juan river system. These sharks are capable of surviving for extended periods of time in fresh water, and records exist of individuals known to have lived from four to six years in this habitat. Reproduction, however, does not seem to occur in fresh water. The bull sharks, it is felt, return to at least brackish water for courtship and mating.

In the many tropical rivers that play host to bull sharks, sawfish also occur. In Central America, for instance, the largetooth sawfish is found in rivers that drain to the Pacific as well as those that drain to the Atlantic side of the isthmus. They are even more perfectly at home in fresh water than are the bull sharks, for they can reproduce, and thus complete the life cycle, in this environment.

The prevalence of bull sharks in the Lake Nicaragua–Rió San Juan system has allowed physiologists to make careful studies of their osmotic relationships across the entire range of salinities (from pure fresh water to full-strength seawater) in which they live. Specimens taken in 100 percent seawater conform in every way to the typical osmotic and ionic picture presented by other marine elasmobranchs. That is, the body fluids show total osmotic concentrations of about 1000 milliosmoles, or a little more than the seawater from which they were taken. About 40 percent of this osmotic concentration is due to conserved urea and TMAO.

In bull sharks caught in the lake, however, the concentration of solutes is about two thirds that of the marine values. The loss of solutes is due to a reduction by 20 percent of the marine values for sodium and chloride, and the loss of more than half of the urea. The sharks adapt to the freshwater existence by reducing the gradients that favor the osmotic uptake of water and the loss by diffusion of salts and urea to the environment.

Despite a reduced osmotic concentration in fresh water, these sharks still have more than twice the body fluid solutes of typical freshwater fishes. They must, therefore, experience an influx of water that is most likely dealt with by the kidneys. One early measurement of urine production by a sawfish in freshwater indicated a urine flow rate of 250 cubic centimeters per kilogram per day—a flow rate more than 20 times that of typical marine elasmobranchs (Figure 9-6).

When isolated living tissues of elasmobranchs are studied,

Figure 9-6. When in fresh water, marine elasmobranchs such as bull sharks have reduced urea, but still suffer the osmotic influx of water. This water is ultimately excreted by the kidneys and results in a high urine flow rate.

ENVIRONMENT — $\emptyset$ m Osm

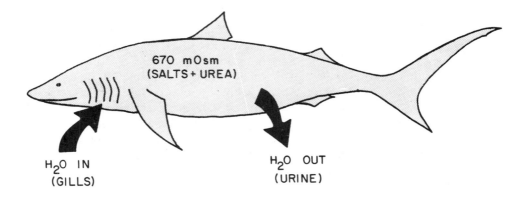

670 mOsm
(SALTS + UREA)

H$_2$O IN
(GILLS)

H$_2$O OUT
(URINE)

urea must be present in the solutions bathing them or the cells will not fuction properly. So completely are sharks adapted to urea that their cells cannot live without it. This is probably why euryhaline (*eury* = wide, *haline* = salinity) elasmobranchs like sawfish, stingrays, and bull sharks do not completely lose their urea after entering fresh water.

One group of elasmobranchs, however, has lost its dependence on urea and has also lost its ability to osmoregulate in the sea. This is the South American family of freshwater stingrays, the Potamotrygonidae. This group of closely related species occupies at least seven freshwater drainage systems on the South American continent. They range from the Atrato, Magdalena, Maracaibo, and Orinoco river systems in the north through the Amazon and Parana–Rió de la Plata systems in the central portion of South America. The rays grow to disc widths of three fourths of a meter and up to several kilograms in weight. While superficially similar to marine rays of the genera *Dasyatis* and *Urolophus,* they are distinctive in the anatomy of their pelvic girdles. An analysis of their distribution and the affinities of their helminth parasites suggests that they are derived from ancestors to the urolophid rays. The ancestors were marine and were likely trapped on the shallow western side of South America when the Andes mountan uplift occurred in the early to middle Cretaceous, perhaps 100 million years ago. By the close of the Cretaceous (70 million years ago), their isolation was complete and the freshening of their waters by runoff had been completed.

Today the Potamotrygonidae have an osmotic physiology distinctly different from all other elasmobranchs. Their blood osmolality measures less than 300 milliosmoles—a level similar to that of freshwater bony fishes and only half of the osmotic concentration of other freshwater-adapted elasmobranchs like the bull shark and sawfishes. Moreover, the body fluids of these rays have very low levels of urea—levels that measure only a milliosmole or less per liter (Figure 9–7). While these animals have rectal glands, they are reduced in size and apparently are not functional in the excretion of salts. Experimental attempts to adapt the potamotrygonids to oceanic salinities have failed, the upper limit of adaptation being about 50 percent seawater. At this salinity the body fluids of the rays are just about at osmotic equilibrium with the environment because of uptake of sodium and chloride. Under these conditions urea increases to levels as high as five milliosmoles per liter, but this is osmotically insignificant. While these rays have lost the ability to retain urea, they still have all of the enzymes necessary to make it.

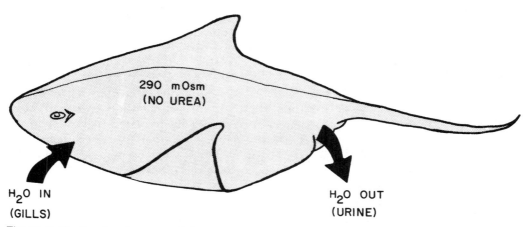

ENVIRONMENT — OmOsm

290 mOsm
(NO UREA)

H₂O IN
(GILLS)

H₂O OUT
(URINE)

Figure 9–7. Freshwater rays of the family Potamotrygonidae retain little urea and generally reduce their osmotic concentration. The osmotic uptake of water is lost in the urine, as in freshwater bony fish.

Although some have argued that the potamotrygonids represent an ancestral elasmobranch stock that has never moved out of fresh water, the evidence that they reinvaded this environment from a marine one is overwhelming.

Little is known about reproduction in the Potamotrygonidae, although it would be surprising if they were much different in this regard from their close urolophid relatives. Those stingrays nourish their young through uterine secretions that are absorbed by the digestive tracts of the embryos (Chapter 8).

A thorough understanding of the osmoregulatory capacities of embryonic sharks is critical to an evaluation of the idea that urea retention was first an adaptation to embryo confinement, and only secondarily to the osmoregulatory stress of the marine environment. Unfortunately, we do not know much about this aspect of elasmobranch biology. We know, however, that the body fluids of embryos of viviparous marine sharks are usually similar in chemical profile to that of the mother. This includes high urea levels. Embryos taken from pregnant bull sharks caught in brackish water also show great solute similarity to their mothers, although some have considerably more urea than the mother. Presumably this is because the mother buffers the fetus against rapid osmotic changes in the environment,

199

so that the fetus adjusts more slowly. The egg cases of skates are somewhat permeable to urea. The embryos of most elasmobranchs probably produce metabolic urea at an early stage.

Elasmobranch eggs (with only a few derived exceptions) are extremely large, being supplied with a great deal of yolk. The metabolism of this yolk by the embryo generates considerable nitrogenous waste which, if it cannot be expelled, must be endured. Most bony fishes, in contrast, produce small eggs without much yolk, and the young hatch quickly and enter a free-living larval stage. Teleosts excrete ammonia as their principal nitrogenous waste product. Those teleosts with the largest eggs generally have the highest requirements for continued water circulation around the eggs (generally fulfilled by stream environments or by parental mouth brooding) so that ammonia can be removed before it builds up to toxic concentrations.

We probably will never know if the pattern of urea retention seen in modern elasmobranchs was first an embryonic adaptation to life in an enclosed, large-yolked egg or as an osmotic adaptation to marine life. It is clear, however, that the latter function operates today. As such, it is an unusual but not unique osmoregulatory adaptation. It is one more example of a whole series of specialties that make sharks such biologically interesting animals.

ADDITIONAL READING

Forster, R.P. "Osmoregulatory role of the kidney in cartilaginous fishes (Chondrichthyes)." In *Sharks, Skates and Rays*, ed. P.W. Gilbert, R.F. Mathewson, and D.P. Rall, 187-195. Baltimore: Johns Hopkins Press, 1967.

Griffith, R.W., P.K.T. Pang, A.K. Srivastava, and G.E. Pickford. "Serum composition of freshwater stingrays (Potamotrygonidae) adapted to fresh and dilute seawater." *The Biological Bulletin*, 144 no. 2 (1973), 304-320.

Haywood, G.P. "Hypo-osmotic regulation coupled with reduced metabolic urea in the dogfish *Poroderma africanum*: An analysis of serum osmolarity, chloride and urea." *Marine Biology*, 23 (1973), 121-127.

Pang, P.K.T., R.W. Griffith, and J.W. Atz. "Osmoregulation in elasmobranchs." *American Zoologist*, 17 (1977), 365-377.

Smith, H.W. "The retention and physiological role of urea in the Elasmobranchii." *Biological Reviews,* 11 (1936), 49–82.

Smith, H.W. *From Fish to Philosopher.* Boston: Little, Brown & Co., 1953.

Thorson. T.B., C.M. Cowan, and D.E. Watson. *"Potamotrygon spp.:* Elasmobranchs with low urea content." *Science,* 158, no. 3799 (1967), 375–377.

Thorson, T.B., C.M. Cowan, and D.E. Watson. "Body fluid solutes of juveniles and adults of the euryhaline bull shark *Carcharhinus leucas* from freshwater and saline environments." *Physiological Zoology,* 46, no. 1 (1973), 29–42.

10

Metabolism

The discussions in preceding chapters suggest that sharks are economical swimmers that osmoregulate in metabolically efficient ways. In order to examine these ideas more carefully, we need to consider the metabolism of elasmobranchs—the intensities with which they burn as fuel the food they eat. Their metabolism can be compared with that of other fishes and animals, and by these comparisons teach us more about the efficiency of elasmobranch physiological systems. The first concept to cover in this quest is that of metabolic rate.

METABOLIC RATES

When a shark (or any other animal) eats a meal, it is consuming chemical energy in the form of the covalent bonds that hold atoms together as molecules. During the course of digestion, the food molecules are disentangled from one another, broken down into smaller ones, and most are absorbed through the intestinal walls, where they pass into the bloodstream of the shark. The absorptive process (known as assimilation) is usually not complete, and some of the food is thus lost in the feces. Although assimilation efficiencies have not been measured in sharks, we know that comparable bony fish absorb about 74 percent of the food energy they eat.

The assimilated molecules are delivered to the cells of the shark's body, where most are broken down, atom by atom, to release the energy contained in them. This energy can be used to build new molecules (growth) or to drive the chemical reactions by which we define life—muscle contraction (locomotion), active transport (osmoregulation, nerve cell function), manufacture of cellular secretions (hormones, neurotransmitters), and so forth. The transformations of energy, of course, are themselves not 100 percent efficient, so that heat and entropy are inescapable by-products. Moreover, the nature of the chemical (metabolic) reactions requires that oxygen be present to help dispose of the used-up atoms, and that carbon dioxide be given off as an additional waste product.

It is possible to estimate the overall metabolic process in a number of ways. For instance, the amount of food (or better, its caloric value) assimilated can be recorded over time. Other measures are the rate of weight loss in an unfed shark, the amount of heat given off, the amount of carbon dioxide produced, or the amount of oxygen consumed. In practice, this last measure is usually the method of choice when experimenting with fish. Metabolism is most often considered as a rate—the amount of oxygen consumed over a time interval. To adjust the metabolic rate for weight, these measurements are expressed as amount of oxygen consumed (mgO_2) per gram or kilogram of body weight per hour (mgO_2 $kg^{-1}hr^{-1}$).

The most meaningful metabolic rate measurements are made on animals during well-defined activity periods. For fishes, the two best-defined activity states are (a) resting, when the fish is quiescent and not under obvious stress; and (b) active, when the fish is forced to swim at its fastest sustainable swimming speed. The resting metabolic rate is known as the *standard* metabolic rate. It is usually the minimal rate of energy expenditure. When the standard rate is subtracted from the active rate, the difference represents the amount of energy a fish can mobilize and direct toward greater levels of activity. This is known as the metabolic *scope for activity.*

The accurate measurement of metabolic rates in fish is a time-consuming and meticulous business. Fish must be enclosed in special respirometers and held under carefully controlled conditions. For this reason, we know most about the metabolic rates of small, easily handled bony fish. Unfortunately, little is known about the metabolic performances of sharks. What is known, however, is tantalizing in its suggestion that elasmobranchs operate at a significantly different level from that of teleost fish.

Nearly all of the oxygen consumption studies performed on elasmobranchs have used specimens of catsharks and dogfish sharks about 2 kilograms or less in size. As body weight increases, the weight-specific metabolic rates decrease in vertebrates, so measurements on small sharks should produce higher metabolic rates than would be typical of larger animals. The most reliable experiments were performed on spiny dogfish that weighed just 2000 grams (2 kilograms). The resting metabolic rate recorded for these animals averaged 32.4 mgO^2 $kg^{-1}hr^{-1}$. This is only a third of the average resting metabolic rate for typical teleosts (90 $mgO_2kg^{-1}hr^{-1}$) of the same body size.

When these sharks were forced to swim maximally, their active metabolic rate averaged about 100 $mgO_2kg^{-1}hr^{-1}$. This is only three times the resting rate and indicates that these dogfish have a much lower scope for activity than do most teleosts. Many teleosts, for example, are capable of active metabolic rates of on the order of 1000 $mgO_2kg^{-1}hr^{-1}$—or metabolic scopes of about 10 times the resting rate.

The metabolic performance of these sharks can be put in a more meaningful perspective if the caloric equivalents of oxygen consumption are considered. For fishes, 1 milligram of oxygen consumed represents the production of 3.25 calories of energy by the metabolic system of the animal. The routine metabolic expenditure of the dogfish becomes about 3.9 kilocalories $kg^{-1}day^{-1}$, or a little less than 8 kilocalories per day for a 2 kilogram dogfish (a kilocalorie equals 1000 "small" calories, or 1 human dietary calorie). The typical prey of these sharks (herring) have a caloric content of about 1.3 kcal $gram^{-1}$ of flesh. This means that with a 74 percent assimilation efficiency, a 2-kilogram dogfish would have to eat only 8 grams (roughly one quarter ounce) of herring per day to satisfy its metabolic needs. Even if this value is doubled, it still is only about one quarter of the food required by a similar-sized salmon to support its routine metabolism.

Even though spiny dogfish seem to have metabolic rates lower than all but the most sluggish bony fish, they are active fishes. They aggregate and travel in schools segregated by sex. They catch and consume active prey (herring, salmon, squid). They are active when caught on hook and line, and are difficult to subdue when brought aboard fishing boats. The elasmobranch answers to the demand of physiological efficiency may be unique.

If the metabolic rates of small sharks are low, what about those of larger ones which, according to theory, should be yet lower? Oxygen consumption rates have not been measured in larger elasmobranchs. But there are a few records of weight loss and heat production in large sharks. In an experiment conducted at the Mote Marine Laboratory near Sarasota, Florida, single captive sandbar and lemon sharks were carefully weighed and then denied all food for a period of time. At the conclusion of the experiment the sharks were again weighed and samples of tissue were taken for chemical analyses. The intent of these experiments was to study the role of liver oils in the regulation of buoyancy in sharks (Chapter 7), but the data can be used for metabolic-rate "guesstimates" as well.

The male sandbar shark weighed 49.6 kilograms (109.1

pounds) at the beginning of the experiment. Fifty days later, it was found to have lost 11.5 kilograms (25.3 pounds), or 23.2 percent of its initial body weight. Of this amount, 2.8 kilograms (6.2 pounds) was due to oil metabolized from its liver. The remaining weight loss was presumably due to protein, carbohydrates, and fats metabolized from its tissue. The other shark, a female lemon shark, weighed 89.5 kilograms (196.9 pounds) initially. Eighty-four days after the start of the experiment, she had lost 18.3 kilograms (40.3 pounds), 3.5 kilograms (7.7 pounds) of which was liver oil. Both of these sharks were held in large outdoor pens where the water was about 29 °C in temperature.

If the total weight losses of these sharks are converted to caloric equivalents and then related to the appropriate oxygen consumption needed to support that metabolism, estimates of the routine oxygen consumption rates over the period of starvation can be made. For the sandbar shark this works out to 318 $mgO_2kg^{-1}hr^{-1}$, and 170 $mgO_2kg^{-1}hr^{-1}$ for the lemon shark. How does this compare to the metabolic-rate measurements made on much smaller animals at only 10 °C?

If the values for spiny dogfish are scaled for size and temperature, the expectation is that a 50-kilogram dogfish at 30 °C would have a routine metabolic rate of 78 $mgO_2kg^{-1}hr^{-1}$; or about one fourth that of the sandbar shark. A theoretical 90-kilogram dogfish at 30 °C would metabolize at a rate of 68 $mgO_2kg^{-1}hr^{-1}$. The lemon shark respired at about 2.5 times this rate. The question now posed is, Are the estimates of metabolism in these sharks way out of line, or do these animals have higher metabolic rates than the apparently less active dogfish?

A single record of a metabolic rate measurement for a small (2 kilogram) lemon shark exists. It was 210 $mgO_2 kg^{-1}hr^{-1}$, and is consistent with the rate calculated here for the larger lemon shark. Beyond this data point there is a metabolic-rate estimate made for the white shark in the feeding and telemetering experiment reported in Chapter 4. This animal, which was tagged with a radio transmitter relaying body temperature and environmental temperature, was followed for a period of 3.5 days. On the basis of its temperature changes, the heat production rate was estimated. Converted to units of oxygen consumption, the estimated metabolic rate was about 60 $mgO_2 kg^{-1}hr^{-1}$. This is about three times the rate expected for a dogfish scaled for size (1 ton) and temperature (20 °C). This estimate thus supports the suspicion that larger, more active sharks may have inherently higher metabolic rates than the smaller, more sluggish sharks for which, until recently, most elasmobranch metabolic rates were recorded.

If the metabolic performance of the white shark is compared with that of a salmon (a typical active bony fish) scaled for size and temperature, the white shark seems to have a little the better of it. The scaled salmon's standard metabolic rate is about 80 mgO$_2$ kg^{-1} hr^{-1} versus the shark's 60 mgO$_2$ kg^{-1} hr^{-1}. The value for the shark is from a swimming fish, whereas that for the salmon is extrapolated from resting fish. It may not be much of an exaggeration to suspect that the shark consumes about 40 to 50 percent less oxygen than an equivalent bony fish.

BODY TEMPERATURES

The metabolism of the white shark and many of its lamniform relatives is interesting, for these animals turn out to be capable of conserving the heat energy which most other fish dissipate to the environment. When heat is generated as an ultimate product of cellular metabolism, it quickly diffuses from the cells to the blood, where it is transported away from the muscle that generated it. Because heat diffuses many times faster than molecules such as oxygen or carbon dioxide, there is plenty of opportunity for the blood-borne heat to be lost to the water as the blood moves through the gills. Most sharks (and other fishes) have body temperatures about equal to that of their environment—even after bouts of strenuous muscular activity. The exceptions to this are found among the tunas and some of the lamnid sharks.

Porbeagle sharks, makos, the white shark, and the bigeye thresher have body muscle and visceral temperatures well above ambient—sometimes as much as 8 °C (14.4 °F) higher than the water in which they swim. The highest temperature gradients are shown by porbeagles and makos, with whites and threshers less able to maintain the highest thermal differentials. One striking feature of these warm-bodied fish is that only the body musculature and viscera are warm. The hearts and gills are at environmental temperatures. What is happening here? How do these sharks thermoregulate, and why do they do so?

The warm-bodied sharks differ substantially from all other elasmobranchs in terms of the pattern of blood supply to the swimming muscles and internal viscera. In other sharks the main blood

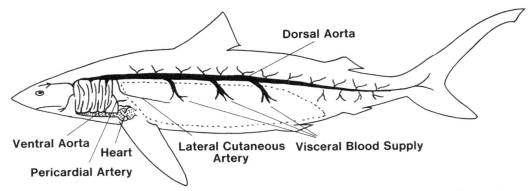

Figure 10-1. In most elasmobranchs, blood is pumped from the heart through the ventral aorta. It is then oxygenated in the gills and is distributed to the body and viscera from the dorsal aorta. The heart is supplied from a small pericardial artery.

supply to these organs is from the large dorsal aorta, which collects freshly oxygenated blood from the gills and transports it back through the center of the body, just under the vertebral column (Figure 10-1). The dorsal aorta provides paired segmental arteries that carry blood to the muscles from within, and major branches that drop down in the body cavity to serve the stomach, liver, intestine, and other internal organs.

In the lamnid sharks, however, the dorsal aorta is insignificant in size. Oxygenated arterial blood is brought to the muscles by large lateral cutaneous arteries that pass along the flanks of the animal just under the skin (Figure 10-2). At segmental intervals, arterial branches pass *inward* to the swimming muscles and penetrate a special organ, the rete mirable, as they go. The viscera likewise receive blood from a different source—greatly enlarged pericardial arteries. These large arteries, which are normally small in other sharks and serve only the heart cavity, pass back through the transverse septum at the head of the body cavity and enter another rete mirable before distributing oxygenated blood to the visceral organs (Figure 10-2).

The two retia found in these sharks operate as countercurrent heat exchangers. In them, small venules carry blood back toward the heart from metabolizing tissues and pass close to extremely small arteries bringing in the oxygenated blood. The two types of vessels carry blood in opposite directions. The arteries bring in cold blood from the gills, while the veins carry blood warmed through tissue metabolism. In the retia there is opportunity for the venous heat to diffuse to the arterial blood. Because of the countercurrent blood

210

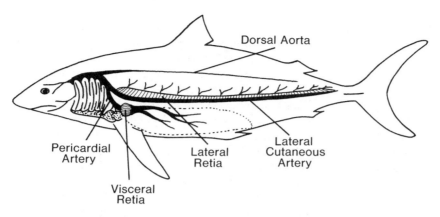

Figure 10–2. In lamniform sharks the dorsal aorta is reduced in size and importance. The body musculature is supplied with oxygenated blood from a large lateral cutaneous artery, the blood from which retains body heat in a special retia. The viscera receive blood from enlarged pericardial arteries, which pass through a visceral retia to retain metabolic heat.

flow, most of this heat is transferred, and it cycles back to the muscles or visceral organs that produced it in the first place. With this system the shark retains a substantial percentage of its metabolic heat and is thereby able to maintain muscle and visceral temperatures well above the ambient. Many of the tuna fishes, although quite distantly related to the lamnid sharks, have developed a similar (but not the same) system of vascular retia which do exactly the same job. Both of these groups of warm-bodied fishes are wide-ranging inhabitants of the open oceans of the world. Both are known for their ability to swim exceptionally fast and powerfully. The technique of maintaining a high body temperature is an adaptation to that lifestyle.

It is a principle of physiological chemistry that a 10-degree rise in temperature will increase the rate of chemical reactions (and physiological processes) by two to three times. In theory, by having its body warm, a shark should be able to contract its muscles faster, providing more power from a given muscle mass. The result should be a shark capable of swimming faster. The elevated visceral temperatures of these sharks (which are highest in the spiral valve) should speed up the rate of digestion and assimilation of foodstuffs, and thereby make more food available per day for the increased metabolic needs of the animal.

211   In addition to digestion and muscle contraction, the developmental processes of embryos held in warm uteri should also increase. Unfortunately, we know so little about gestation periods in lamnids that they cannot be compared with those of other sharks.

The warm-bodied sharks tend to be widely distributed species. The salmon shark and porbeagle are found in the cooler waters of the North Pacific and North Atlantic oceans respectively. Shortfin makos are found in warm oceans, but seasonally penetrate temperate-zone waters where they encounter cool environmental temperatures. The white shark is well known for its distribution in colder waters of southern Australia, the Gulf of Maine in the Atlantic, and in cool upwellings off the coast of California. Bigeye threshers are often taken in deep water at cool temperatures. Telemetering experiments have shown that makos and white sharks make vertical descents from warm surface waters through the thermocline to colder depths. No doubt the heat-retaining retia of these sharks free them from being captives of isotherms and allow them to range across the breadth and depths of the ocean.

GROWTH RATES

After a shark has eaten its fill and its immediate metabolic needs are cared for, excess energy can be stored in fats or oils (usually in the liver), or it can be used to support growth. The rates at which shark grow are important because they indicate how elasmobranchs exploit their environments and provide measures of comparison between species and other taxonomic groups.

The problem of determining how fast elasmobranchs grow is not a trivial one. For one thing, it is usually impossible to catch enough individuals of all growth stages at one time and place. Without such a sample, significant errors are introduced into the growth analysis. A further problem is that hard tissues of sharks are not as useful for age determination as are the scales of many bony fishes. Because of their size, scarce numbers, and low fishing pressure, tag and recapture experiments often return little good growth data. Finally, because most elasmobranchs are difficult to maintain in captivity, growth data on aquarium-held individuals are scanty.

Over the years, however, some growth-rate evidence has accumulated for a few species of elasmobranchs. Several approaches have been utilized toward this end. Under appropriate conditions, the vertebrae of some elasmobranchs can be stained with silver nitrate or other solutions to visualize concentric rings of alternating

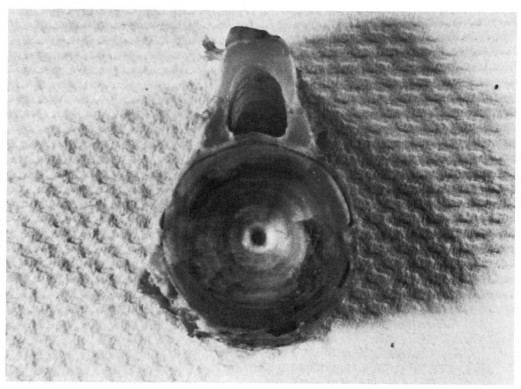

Figure 10–3. Growth rings in vertebrae can be visualized after silver nitrate staining, as in this blue shark vertebra, which shows five rings.

dense and less-dense areas of calcification (Figure 10–3). These rings are annual—that is, only one dense ring is laid down per year—in some species of skates (including *Raja clavata*). A few sharks (makos, basking sharks) produce two rings per year. By correlating the number of vertebral rings with the lengths or weights of the sharks, a relationship between size and age can be constructed. In addition to vertebrae, the fin spines of some squalid sharks also have what appear to be annual rings (although that assumption has been challenged). The use of fin-spine rings was used to provide growth estimates for the spiny dogfish.

Another means of aging sharks beginning to bear fruit is a long-term tagging experiment coordinated by biologists at the Narragansett (Rhode Island) laboratory of the U.S. National Marine Fisheries Service. This program, which has tagged over 49,000 sharks of more than 30 species since the early 1960s, retrieves about 3 percent of the tagged sharks. Although the information on growth is often imprecise (due to the difficulty of gathering accurate before-and-after measurements), some useful data have been obtained. There have also been some important tagging studies of discrete populations of commercially important (and small-sized) species such as spiny dogfish and Australian school sharks.

Shark growth rates have been estimated from a variety of less-direct techniques. These include length-frequency measurements from large samples and projections made from the study of the incremental growth of teeth. A few anecdotal reports of growth in captive sharks also exist. The results of these studies present a mixed bag. Some elasmobranchs grow rapidly, while others show much slower growth rates. The results of some of these studies of different groups of sharks are summarized here.

Squalomorph Sharks. The spiny dogfish is the most studied of all sharks. Its economic importance, particularly in Europe, and its large populations in both the North Atlantic and North Pacific facilitate its study. Fin-spine analyses and tagging experiments conclude that this shark, which grows to a maximum length of only 3 to 5 feet (1 to 1.5 meters), is a slowly growing shark. Its life span may be beyond 30 years, with females reaching maturity as 12-year-olds or later. Males mature somewhat earlier, at 9 years of age.

Spiny dogfish are residents of cold boreal and north temperate seas. The temperatures that they prefer (usually less than 13 °C) are not conducive to rapid growth or high metabolic rates. Even so, bony fish cohorts like cod, haddock, and herring grow and mature much faster than do these sharks. The low metabolic rates of this species as well as its exceptionally long gestation period (up to two years) are consistent with the picture of a long-lived, slow-growing animal. It is not known whether this pattern of growth is typical of other cold-water elasmobranchs. If squalomorph sharks such as the Greenland shark and the sixgill shark grow as slowly, they must live to very old ages indeed, for they both reach large size.

Batoidea—the Skates and Rays. Because they are small, often abundant fishes, several species of skates have been the objects of growth-rate studies. These investigations show that larger species of skates live longer than smaller species. The little skate, for example, lives to 8 years and matures at between 3 and 4 years. The thornback skate lives to at least 14 years of age and matures at about 7 years. Tagging studies indicate that another skate, *Raja montagui* of the northeast Atlantic, reaches at least 18 years of age. As in other elasmobranchs, female skates grow to be larger and live longer than males. Similar growth relationships are seen in the white spotted stingaree from New Zealand. This fish, which grows to a length similar to that of the little skate (50 centimeters), lives to 8 years for males and 10 years for females. Growth is reasonably constant throughout life.

The growth of a different batoid, the largetooth sawfish, was studied in the Lake Nicaragua–Rió San Juan system of Central America. These fish, which reach lengths of almost 4 meters for males and 4.5 meters for females, have life spans of about 30 years. They grow rapidly (30 to 40 centimeters per year) for their first 3 years, then slow thereafter to a steady growth rate of 3 or 4 centimeters per year.

The weight of the evidence for batoids suggests that, like the spiny dogfish, they grow more slowly and live to older ages than do comparable teleosts. This pattern holds for the galeomorph sharks as well, although there are some exceptions.

Galeomorpha—Hornsharks, Carpet Sharks, Requiem and Hammerhead Sharks. The small hornsharks of the genus *Heterodontus* are inactive residents of rock and reef habitats in the Indo-Pacific. *H. portjacksoni* of Australia is another slow-growing, long-lived fish. After hatching from their curiously flanged eggs following about 12 months of development, these sharks grow at about 5 to 6 centimeters (2 inches) per year until they reach sexual maturity. The age of sexual maturity is 8 to 10 years for males and 11 to 14 years for females. After maturity, hornsharks continue to grow at about 3 centimeters (1 inch) per year. They could live a total of about 25 years.

Almost no information is available on the age and growth of nurse and carpet sharks (Orectolobiformes). These sharks are sluggish in their behavior. Some, like the nurse shark, grow to large size. The closely related whale shark is, of course, the most massive of all fishes. Everything about their biology is consistent with the picture of slow growth, producing old ages in the largest species.

Among the requiem sharks (Carcharhiniformes), the Australian school shark was studied intensively in the late 1940s because of the commercial fishery that developed around it (Chapter 2). An extensive tagging program was initiated then and has been carried on since using internal tags (metal tags slipped into the body cavity and recovered when the fish are commercially processed). This shark is most common in the cool waters off Tasmania, South Austrialia, and the southwest coast of western Australia. Large specimens are about 1.5 meters (5 feet) in length. They reach maturity at 10 to 15 years of age and may attain a maximum age of about 40 years. Their growth rates are described as "remarkably slow."

The sandbar shark is a widely distributed shark found in the Atlantic, Pacific, and Indian oceans. They contributed heavily to a shark fishery in the 1940s in the southeastern United States. Studies of this species at that time suggested that they grow rapidly, reaching maturity (about 5 feet) in only two years. Direct observations of the growth of sandbar sharks held in captivity in Hawaii, and fed regularly, confirmed rapid growth. At the rates these young sharks grew, maturity could have been expected in three years. Tagged sandbar sharks, however, do not bear out these estimates. A single mature male tagged and recaptured after 595 days of liberty near Hawaii was found to have grown not at all! An immature male sandbar shark, tagged on the middle Atlantic coast of North America and recaptured 15.2 years later, was found to have grown only 49 centimeters in that time. This averages only 3.3 centimeters (1.3 inches) of growth per year. The shark was probably 20 years old by the time it was caught the second time—and it was still immature!

The results of tagging studies suggest that this treatment may adversely affect sharks and inhibit their growth. Not a few tagged and recovered sharks have been found to have diminished in size during the tagged period. A captive tagged group of young lemon sharks was held with others that were not tagged. The untagged sharks grew 8 percent faster.

The population of bull sharks that enter fresh water in the Rió San Juan–Lake Nicaragua system of Central America were studied by tag returns and by analysis of growth rings in the vertebrae. The results indicate a life span of about 16 years for females and 12 years for males. Growth is rapid for 2 years (16 to 18 centimeters per year) and slows to 9 to 10 centimeters per year after maturity.

The age and growth of the blue shark was estimated from studies of vertebral rings and length frequencies in the eastern North Atlantic segment of the population. Both estimates show blue sharks growing to 3 meters total length (10 feet) in about 10 years. This puts maturity at about 5 years and suggests that this species grows to large size rather quickly.

Other sharks that reach maturity rapidly are the smoothhounds of the genus *Mustelus*. These small sharks grow to lengths that may range from about 0.9 meter (3 feet) for the smallest *(M. gri-seus)* to about 1.9 meters (6 feet) in the largest *(M. mediterraneus).* Projecting the growth rate from knowledge of the gestation period and the size of the newborn results in estimates of ages at maturity of 1.3 years in *M. manazo* to a maximum of 4 years in *M. lenticulatus.* Most of the seven *Mustelus* species that have been studied appear to mature in about 2 years. They thus reach maturity faster than do many other small sharks.

Shark growth rates have been estimated from analyses of their tooth replacement rates. By measuring the size increment of successive replacement teeth and correlating tooth size with body length, it is possible to estimate growth rate if the tooth replacement rate is known. Growth rates estimated for smooth dogfish and lemon sharks made by this technique are faster than those predicted by tagging studies, direct observation of captive sharks, or embryonic growth projections.

Some other galeomorph sharks for which growth estimates exist are the scalloped hammerhead, the bigeye thresher, and the whitetip reef shark. The hammerhead measurements were made on newborn pups held in captivity and fed to satiation. They grew at an initial rate of about 4 to 5 centimeters per month, or 50 centimeters per year. Adults of this species range from 2.5 meters (8 feet) and might mature as 5-year-olds. The bigeye thresher is a rarely caught and wide-ranging pelagic species found around the world in warm and temperate seas. Estimation of its growth by gestation-period projection suggests that this shark approaches maturity at about 4 years and reaches its maximum size (4 meters) after only 10 to 12 years. It seems to be a fast-growing shark.

The whitetip reef shark is widely distributed throughout the tropical waters of the Indian and Pacific oceans. It grows to 5 or 6 feet (2 meters) in length and is a sluggish shark that may retire to "home" caves in the reef after foraging. Tagged and captive reef whitetips are reported to grow about 1.5 centimeters (about 0.5 inch) per month as newborns and about 2.5 centimeters (1 inch) per year as adults. Maturity may be reached after 5 to 8 years, and they may live to ages of at least 25 years.

When the fragmentary data on aging and growth of elasmobranchs are reviewed, a number of generalizations can be made. Most are slow-growing species with long life spans. Males grow faster and reach maturity faster at smaller sizes than do females. Several experiences with captive sharks indicate that growth rates are affected by the intensity of feeding. Better-fed sharks grow faster. Evidence exists that tagging significantly slows the growth rate of sharks. This last observation casts doubt upon what otherwise would seem to be the best estimates of shark growth. It also leads to the conclusion that no technique of age and growth determination currently in use can provide unchallenged results. A basic and useful aspect of the life history of virtually every species of elasmobranch thus remains mysterious. This is unfortunate, because age and growth data are critical to a complete analysis of the population dynamics of sharks.

The slowness to reach maturity for many species, combined with their low reproductive potential (Chapter 8), presents a picture of slow population growth with little capacity to recover quickly from sudden depletion of stocks. The consequence of this life-history strategy for shark fisheries was presented in Chapter 2. Slow growth plus long lifetime are appropriate adaptations for animals that are near the apex of the food pyramid and which have few enemies. Competition for scarce food resources should produce stable populations with relatively few far-flung individuals. To understand better the relations sharks have with other components of their ecosystems we will, in the last chapter, examine their predators, the parasites of sharks, and their other symbionts.

ADDITIONAL READING

Brett, J.R., and J.M. Blackburn. "Metabolic rate and energy expenditure of the spiny dogfish, *Squalus acanthias.*" *J. Fish. Res. Bd. Canada*, 35 (1978), 816–821.

Carey, F.G., J.W. Kanwisher, O. Brazier, G. Gabrielson, J.G. Casey, and H.L. Pratt, Jr. "Temperature and activities of a white shark, *Carcharodon carcharias.*" *Copeia*, 1982, no. 2 (1982), 254–260.

Carey, F.G., and J.M. Teal. "Mako and porbeagle: warm-bodied sharks." *Comp. Biochem. Physiol.*, 28 (1969), 199–204.

Carey, F.G., J.M. Teal, and J.W. Kanwisher. "The visceral temperatures of mackerel sharks (Lamnidae)." *Physiol. Zool.*, 54, no. 3 (1981), 334–344.

Clarke, T.A. "The ecology of the scalloped hammerhead shark, *Sphyrna, lewini*, in Hawaii." *Pac. Sci.*, 25, no. 2 (1971), 133–144.

Edwards, R.R.C. "Aspects of the population dynamics and ecology of the white-spotted stingaree, *Urolophus paucimaculatus* Dixon, in Port Phillip Bay, Victoria." *Aust. J. Mar. Freshwater Res.*, 31 (1980), 459–467.

Francis, M.P. "Von Bertalanffy growth rates in species of *Mustelus* (Elasmobranchii: Triakidae)." *Copeia*, 1981, no. 1 (1981), 189–192.

Grant, C.J., R.L. Sandland, and A.M. Olsen. "Estimation of growth, mortality and yield per recruit of the Australian school shark, *Galeorhinus australis* (Macleay), from tag recoveries." *Aust. J. Mar. Freshwater Res.*, 30 (1979), 625–637.

Gruber, S.H. "Lemon sharks: supply-side economists of the sea." *Oceanus*, 24, no. 4 (1981), 56–64.

Gruber, S.H., and L.J.V. Compagno. "The taxonomic status and biology of the bigeye thresher, *Alopias superciliosus*." *Fish. Bull.*, 79, no. 4 (1981), 617–640.

Holden, M.J. "The growth rates of *Raja brachyura*, *R. clavata*, and *R. montagui* as determined from tagging data." *J. Cons. int. Explor. Mer.*, 34, no. 2 (1972), 161–168.

Holden, M.J., and M.R. Vince. "Age validation studies on the centra of *Raja clavata* using tetracycline." *J. Cons. int. Explor. Mer.*, 35, no. 1 (1973), 13–17.

McLaughlin, R.H., and A.K. Gower. "Life history and underwater studies of a heterodont shark." *Ecol. Monogr.*, 41, no. 4 (1971), 271–289.

Moss, S.A. "Tooth replacement and body growth rates in the smooth dogfish, *Mustelus canis* (Mitchill)." *Copeia*, 1972, no. 4 (1972), 808–811.

Randall, J.E. "Contribution to the biology of the whitetip reef shark (*Triaenodon obesus*)." *Pac. Sci.*, 31, no. 2 (1977), 143–164.

Richards, S.W., D. Merriman, and L.H. Calhoun. "Studies on the marine resources of southern New England. IX. The biology of the little skate, *Raja erinacea* (Mitchill)." *Bull. Bingham Oceanogr. Coll.*, 18, no. 3 (1963), 5–67.

Stevens, J.D. "Vertebral rings as a means of age determination in the blue shark (*Prionace glauca* L.)." *J. Mar. Biol. Assoc. U.K.*, 55 (1975), 657–665.

Thorson, T.B. "Life history implications of a tagging study of the largetooth sawfish, *Pristis perotteti*, in the Lake Nicaragua–Rió San Juan system." *Env. Biol. Fish.*, 7, no. 3 (1982), 207–228.

Thorson, T.B., and E.J. Lacey, Jr., "Age, growth rate and longevity of *Carcharhinus leucas* estimated from tagging and vertebral rings." *Copeia*, 1982, no. 1 (1982), 110–116.

Wass, R.C. "Size, growth, reproduction of the sandbar shark, *Carcharhinus milberti*, in Hawaii." *Pac. Sci.*, 27, no. 4 (1973), 305–318.

11

Friends and Enemies of Sharks

In its broadest sense, symbiosis means "living together." The types of symbiotic relationships between organisms are several. When one participant benefits and the other is not affected the interaction is *commensalism*. When both individuals benefit from the association, the relationship is described as *mutualism*. However, if one party benefits at the expense of the other, *parasitism* is the result. The individual with which the commensal, mutualist, or parasite interacts is called the host. Commensalism, mutualism, and parasitism are thus symbiotic relationships, and examples of all three are found among elasmobranchs and their various "hangers-on."

COMMENSALISM

The most widespread and best-known examples of commensalism involving elasmobranchs are the interactions of pelagic sharks and rays and the pilot fishes that often accompany them. These teleost fish, which include several species, commonly swim in front of the snout or pectoral fins of sharks—and sometimes just above or below the pelagic mobulid and myliobatid rays. Pilot fishes most often are of the jack family (Carangidae), including the pilotfish, *Naucrates ductor*, the rainbow runner, several species of amberjacks and pompanos. Young cobia are known to accompany cownose rays.

Because the smaller, younger sizes of these fish adopt what seem to be precarious positions just in front of the mouths of large sharks, a considerable folklore has grown up about them. Stories exist, for instance, of pilot fish purposefully leading sharks to prey so that the pilot fish may feast on the scraps. In return, these scenarios suggest, the shark refrains from eating its benefactor, the pilot fish. Although divers have reported pilot fish leaving sharks and excitedly swimming around potential prey, experiments do not indicate a clear intent on the part of the teleosts to direct the sharks. Nor do the sharks benignly spare the lives of the pilot fish.

223   A more parsimonious explanation of piloting involves the mechanisms by which these fishes orient to objects in their environments. All of these are schooling fishes. A basic feature of the schooling response is the optomotor reflex. This is an orientation to a moving brightness contrast (edge) in the environment. Obligatory schooling fishes, like most carangids, are attracted to a moving black-white interface and swim in a constant relationship to it. In an aquarium fitted with a rotating drum painted with black and white vertical bars, such a fish will swim until it is exhausted.

Pilot fishes encountering a shark in the featureless pelagic realm probably relate to it as a moving contrast edge, swimming in orientation to its snout or fins. The fish is more likely an automaton than a pilot, captive through its optomotor response to the moving shark. In their smaller sizes, pilot fishes seem to gain a hydrodynamic advantage at certain positions relative to the shark, and seem to jockey for rides on the "bow" wave, much as porpoises do with ships. The optomotor response and the hydrodynamic lift work together to make the fish virtually uncatchable by the shark. Sharks, not being the most stupid of animals, quickly habituate to the presence of the fish.

Divers occasionally report large schools of fishes such as rainbow runners accompanying sharks and clustering around them. Occasionally these small fish jostle and even attack the hind ends of the sharks. Whether or not this behavior represents attempts to pick ectoparasites from the shark is not clear. The usual relationship of the pilot fish to the shark appears to be a commensal one, however, with the teleost gaining an orientation to an object in the environment, an occasional meal from the shark's leavings, and perhaps protection from its predators. The shark probably gains very little, if anything, from the association.

MUTUALISM

There are at least two clear examples of mutualism that involve elasmobranchs. The first, and least well documented, is the relationship of small reef fishes, known as "cleaners," to certain sharks. Captive sharks, held in large, semi-natural tanks, approach reefs where the territories of cleaners such as small wrasses occur. Lemon sharks and nurse sharks cease swimming and rest on the bottom while being inspected by the wrasses. These fish search the shark, picking off and eating parasitic copepods lodged on the shark's skin. So cooperative are the sharks that they will open their mouths and cease ventilation movements for as long as two minutes while the wrasses enter the mouth to pick parasites from the oropharyngeal and gill cavities. Bull sharks, which seldom stop swimming, slow down when cleaner wrasses approach to make brief feeding forays over their bodies.

The extent of cleaner relationships between small fishes and sharks is not known. Many teleosts avail themselves of cleaners to get rid of ectoparasites. This may be a widespread and common practice among the less pelagic sharks as well. The relationship is clearly a mutual one: The shark gains by having some of its parasites removed and the cleaner gains by getting a meal.

A more widespread and better-known mutualistic relationship with sharks involves the diskfishes of the family Echeneidae. These distinctive fishes, known popularly as sharksuckers or remoras, have dorsal fins bizarrely modified into louvered suction cups by which they can attach to any broad, reasonably smooth surface like a sea turtle, large fish, boat bottom, or shark (Figure 11–1).

The diskfishes—there are eight species worldwide—are closely related to the carangids and cobias that so often accompany sharks

Figure 11–1. The back of a remora, showing the louvered suction cups used to attach the fish to its elasmobranch hosts.

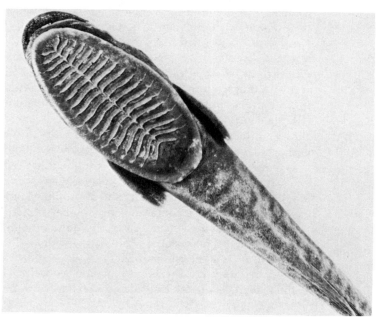

as pilot fish. Each species is most often found with a specific host. Thus the remora, *Remora remora*, is usually found with sharks, while the whalesucker, *Remorina australis*, nearly always associates with cetaceans. Of the diskfish species, only three are commonly found with elasmobranchs. In addition to the remora, these include *Echeneis naucrates*, the sharksucker, and *Remorina albescens*, the white suckerfish. This last species usually accompanies the devil rays (Mobulidae).

The degree of independence from its elasmobranch host varies with each species. The remora and white suckerfish are seldom encountered alone. They have stumpy bodies and reduced fins and are usually recovered from the mouths and gill chambers of their hosts, which are the more pelagic and oceanic elasmobranchs. The sharksucker, on the other hand, is a good swimmer and is often observed swimming by itself.

The sharksucker is the largest—up to 3 feet—of the diskfishes. It is an associate of inshore and coastal sharks such as lemon, nurse, and bull sharks. Contrary to popular belief, the sharksucker does not spend most of its time firmly attached by its sucker to its host. Rather, these fish often plane in the "bow waves" raised by the shark's pectoral fins and body as it cruises through the water. Close underwater observation of captive sharks shows that these sharksuckers apply their dorsal suckers when the sharks abruptly change direction or slow down. When sharks rest on the bottom, the sharksuckers make inspection forays over the shark's body or venture some distance away from their hosts. Sharksuckers freely move from one shark to another. Native fishermen in the Bahamas are aware that the appearance of a sharksucker swimming close to their boat and attempting to attach to it usually heralds the presence of a large shark.

What is the nature of this association? What benefit, if any, does the shark derive from tolerating these hitchhikers? The answer is in the diets of the diskfishes. Prominent in their stomach contents are the parasitic copepods that generally infest the skin, mouths, and gills of sharks. In the stomachs of a sample of remoras, for example, 70 percent of those containing any food at all had parasitic copepods in them, including species normally found only in the mouth and gill tissues of the host shark. The sharksucker is less, but still significantly, dependent on ectoparasites—16 percent of stomachs having food included copepods or parasitic isopods. The diskfishes earn their keep. Their relationships with sharks are mutual.

PARASITISM

Like nearly all other organisms on earth, elasmobranchs are host to a variety of parasites that either feed directly on their tissues and body fluids or on nutrients in their digestive tracts. Most elasmobranch parasites are either crustaceans (copepods, isopods) or flatworms (flukes, tapeworms), although leeches, blood-borne protozoa, and nematodes are also known.

Ectoparasites. Ectoparasites of the body surface, including mouth and gills, are mostly copepods (sea lice) (Figure 11–2). Well over 200 species of them infect elasmobranch hosts. Some of these sea lice are similar to their nonparasitic relatives, which are important elements in the zooplankton of the world's oceans. Others have adapted to parasitism so completely that the adults little resemble their free-living peers. In many of the highly modified forms, sexual dimorphism is extreme, with males being smaller, serving almost as appendages of the robust females.

Figure 11–2. A group of parasitic copepods (*Dinemoura producta*) clustered on a section of basking shark skin.

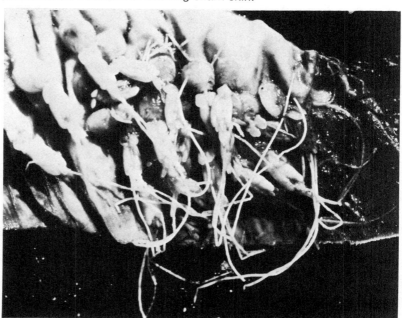

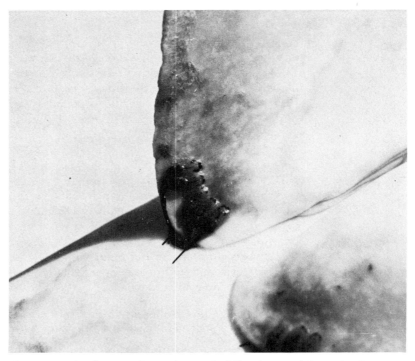

Figure 11–3. Copepods on the ventral fin of a sand tiger shark.

The copepods, which are adapted to a life of riding the body surface, are streamlined, with broad cephalic and thoracic plates. They feed on the epidermal and dermal tissues of the host, gradually eroding the skin around their attachment sites. These ectoparasites sometimes select distinctive attachment locations, particularly on the fins and around the cloaca (Figure 11–3). At least one species, *Ommatokoita elongata*, is a bioluminescent form that attaches to the corneas of Greenland shark eyes. It has been suggested that these copepods, glowing in the dark oceanic depths, act as fishing lures, attracting prey to the lethargic sharks. If this is true, this particular association is more mutualistic than parasitic.

In one genus of copepods, *Pandarus*, the males and females select different sites of attachment. Male *Pandarus* are found scattered over the body surface of the shark, while the females cluster on the fins. Parasitic copepods found in the stomachs of *Remora remora* include *Pandarus* males but seldom the females. This suggests that the remoras do not forage on the fins for ectoparasites.

The abundance and diversity of copepods resident on the skin of sharks is much greater than that found on the less well-armored body surface of batoids. Only 25 percent of the copepod species found in association with elasmobranchs are recorded from skates and rays. The smaller, more closely spaced placoid scales of the sharks seem to provide a more favorable environment than the more naked batoid skin. Nurse sharks, smooth dogfish, and lemon sharks, which often rest on the bottom, host fewer copepods than more pelagic, constant-swimming species such as the hammerheads, blue sharks, and silky sharks. The more sedentary sharks may be better groomed by reef cleaner fishes.

Most of the batoid-infecting copepods prefer to attach themselves in the mouth and especially in the gills. Copepods that infest gills are greatly modified and can damage these delicate host tissues. *Nemesis lamna*, a copepod parasitic on the gills of the shortfin mako, locates itself near the vessels that carry oxygenated blood away from the gill capillaries and conspicuously changes the appearance of the gill filaments. It causes tissue proliferation, particularly of mucous cells in the gill epithelium, and fibrosis in the connective tissue layer beneath. Heavy infestations of these parasites could make the gills of these sharks less efficient in their job of gas exchange.

Although the most abundant, copepods are by no means the only ectoparasites of sharks. Batoids, for example, host a number of monogenetic trematodes on the surfaces of their skins, mouths, branchial cavities, and cloacas. The monogenea constitute a widespread group of flatworms characterized by two ventral suckers and a life cycle involving only one host. Leeches (Annelida: Hirudinea) also infect the body surfaces, especially the cloacal region and the claspers, of many sharks and rays. Some of them can grow to several inches in length.

One special elasmobranch ectoparasite is the planarian flatworm, *Micropharanyx parasitica*. This animal is a turbellarian, representing a group of flatworms generally not parasitic. It is found on the body surface of a skate, *Raja radiata*. Its life history and behavior suggest how the parasitic Trematoda (flukes) and Cestoda (tapeworms) could have evolved from the Turbellaria.

Endoparasites. Urea retention has apparently made difficult the invasion of the interior of the body of elasmobranchs by parasites. Relatively few monogenetic or digenetic trematodes have made that leap. Although few kinds of internal parasites (some blood-dwelling protozoans, nematodes, aspidogastrea, and digenea) have found elasmobranchs to their liking, the tapeworms (Platyhelminthes: Cestoda) are a different story. Five orders of tapeworms represented by over 400 species have been found in the digestive tracts (almost always the spiral valves, Figure 4–13) of more than 150 species of elasmobranchs. Among elasmobranch parasites, their numbers and species diversity exceed that of the copepods. Generally speaking, larger sharks harbor larger tapeworms in their spiral valves, although tapeworms longer than 20 centimeters occur in fewer numbers. Smaller tapeworms can be very numerous indeed, with several thousand infesting a single intestine.

The abundance and species diversity of elasmobranch tapeworms are functions of ocean depth and latitude. Sharks and rays living in shallow tropical waters harbor more tapeworms of more species than do those from colder and deeper waters. The reasons for this are not completely understood, but there may be a greater abundance and diversity of intermediate hosts in warm coastal waters.

Many tapeworms have complicated life cycles. Eggs released from the adults hatch in the environment, and the larval stages infect intermediate hosts such as crustaceans (usually free-living copepods), mollusks, or annelids. In most tapeworms a subsequent larval stage develops when the infected invertebrate is eaten by a small teleost fish. Eventually the final intermediate host (the small fish) is eaten by an elasmobranch, and the hitchhiking tapeworm larvae within are released by digestive action within the spiral valve, where they grow to maturity.

Tapeworms have specific primary and intermediate hosts. Elasmobranchs that live in regions of high species richness (tropics), and which have diverse diets, are exposed to more species of tapeworms. The host specificity of tapeworms means that an elasmobranch carries with it natural "tags" in the form of its cestode parasites. If the distribution of a tapeworm's intermediate host(s) are known, its presence in the spiral valve of a shark can provide information about the shark's prior whereabouts. At our stage of understanding, however, we know woefully little about the life cycles of most elasmobranch tapeworms. Greater knowledge of these matters can help our understanding of elasmobranch distributions and movements.

The adult cestode attaches to the inner walls of the host's spiral valve by means of an elaborate, often spiny scolex or head (Figure 11–4). When many tapeworms crowd the intestine, they may release

Figure 11–4. The head or scolex of a tapeworm (*Thysanocephalum crispum*) taken from the spiral valve of a tiger shark.

from their attachment sites to wander about, seeking less crowded conditions. Reproductive segments also may detach prematurely and wander through the valve under these conditions. The distribution of tapeworm species varies within the spiral valve. Some are found only in specific areas (cranial or caudal regions of the valve), while others are more evenly distributed through it.

Since so many tapeworms can infest an individual shark, the host must suffer considerably. The irritation created by several thousand scoleces embedded in the intestine is considerable, and much loss of digested nutrients must be experienced by the shark. But even heavily parasitized elasmobranchs usually are in good condition, so the debilitating effects of parasites on them are difficult to measure. Of interest is the occasional shark that is without parasites of any type. What this means in terms of parasite immunity or rejection and shark food selection is not clear.

231

ELASMOBRANCHS AS PREY

Although many, if not most, elasmobranchs are at the top of their food webs, with almost no natural enemies, some occasionally end up in the stomachs of other predators. The list of their enemies—excluding other elasmobranchs—is not long. There is a record of an 8-foot shark (probably a basking shark) in the stomach of a 52-foot sperm whale taken near the Azores. A small blacktip reef shark was found in the stomach of a grouper speared in the Pacific. A California sea lion was seen eating the entrails of a still-living 1.5-meter shark. Stories, largely undocumented, abound of porpoises battering sharks to death. Actually, porpoise meat is a frequent item found in shark stomachs. In shark–porpoise encounters in marine aquaria, the sharks generally win. Nonetheless a female porpoise, with friends, and defending her young, could probably give a shark a difficult time. No doubt as well, a pack of killer whales could destroy and consume practically any elasmobranch that swims.

The real enemies of elasmobranchs are other sharks. In particular, the stingrays are heavily preyed upon by galeoid sharks, especially the hammerheads, bull sharks, and blacktip sharks. Hammerheads not infrequently are found with the spines of many stingrays embedded in their mouths and jaws—the remains of batoid banquets (Figure 4–10). Stingrays are also frequently seen with segments missing from their tails and bites taken from their pectoral fins—presumably due to shark attacks.

This penchant for a stingray diet is interesting in a couple of ways. First, not all hammerheads or bull sharks carry stingray spines. Individual sharks must therefore learn to seek rays as food. Second, stingrays seem unlikely candidates for shark predation because they are inconspicuous on the bottom and are not hesitant to use their defensive, venomous spines. Apparently, however, they are both vulnerable and toothsome.

In view of the frequency with which stingrays are attacked by sharks, it is surprising to observe that skates (Rajidae) are eaten much less often. Both groups of batoids are cryptic, spending long periods partially buried in the silt and sand of the bottom. Both have some sort of defensive armament—the stingrays with their venomous and potentially lethal tail spines, the skates with enlarged placoid scales that make them rough and spiny to touch. It would appear that the stingrays have the better armament. But the occurrence of

skates in the stomachs of sharks, while not unknown, is rare. Skates are as ubiquitous and abundant as stingrays—and even more numerous in temperate waters. What conceivable advantage could skates have?

Of course skates are more completely armored than stingrays, having enlarged placoid scales arranged as thorns, shields, and bucklers (Figure 7–2). Also, skates tend to be less "meaty" than the stingrays, and perhaps are less appetizing for that reason. Another difference between skates and rays is the presence in the former of special electric organs in their tails.

Electric organs. Although the electric organs of the electric rays (Torpediniformes) have been well studied, those of skates are less so. The ray electric organs consist of modified muscle cells from the branchial (gill) region (Figure 11–5). There broad cells (electroplaques) are stacked into piles 500 *(Narcine)* to 1000 *(Torpedo)* cells deep. Many hundreds of these stacks are aligned together, presenting as much as 500 square centimeters of surface area on the back of the ray. Only one surface (the ventral one) of each electroplaque is innervated. When the nerves give the command, each electroplaque fires (depolarizes), creating a flow of sodium and potassium ions. Because of the number of electroplaques piled on top of each other (wired in series), and the number of stacks next to each other (wired in parallel), the nearly simultaneous depolarization of all the electroplaques produces amperages capable of stunning prey or predator. The electric organs of skates, however, have a different organization and less clear-cut functional properties.

The electroplaques of skates are small disk- or cup-shaped cells that are less regularly oriented to each other than are the electroplaques of the rays. They are organized axially, running in columns anterio-posteriorly, and parallel to the vertebral column in the tail region of the trunk (Figure 11–6). As electric generation cells, they have some unusual properties that are not well understood by physiologists.

The electric discharge in the skate is also distinctly different from that of other electric fishes, either elasmobranch or teleost. The discharge has a slow time course, rising and falling in intensity over an interval measured in seconds rather than the rapid discharge that occurs in milliseconds in other fishes. The absolute magnitude of this discharge is also unique. Teleost fishes that use self-generated electric fields for navigation and orientation produce very weak voltages, while the defensive or offensive organs of the rays, electric eels, and catfish can produce discharges measured as tens or even hun-

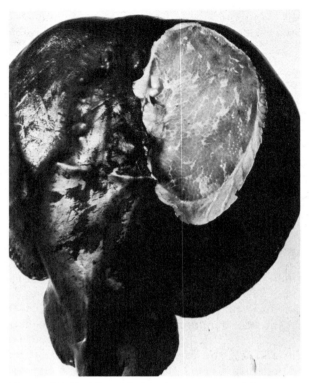

Figure 11–5. The skin has been removed from this Atlantic torpedo to show the extent of the electric organ on its right side. Columns of electroplaques can be seen.

dreds of volts. Rajid electric organs, however, produce discharges intermediate in intensity, measuring from a few millivolts to a volt or two. These discharge characteristics are an enigma. Of what use could these curious (and often overlooked) electric organs be?

With navigation and defense ruled out, communication remains a possibility. Perhaps the discharges of the skate electric organs serve as releasers for mating behavior (although sexual dimorphism in the organs or their discharges have not been reported). Another, and novel, suggestion is that these organs may be useful in warding off attacks by predatory elasmobranchs, particularly those that rely heavily on their electrosensory apparatuses when feeding.

Sharks are good at locating prey buried in sand, using just their ability to sense the weak electric fields given off by the buried prey

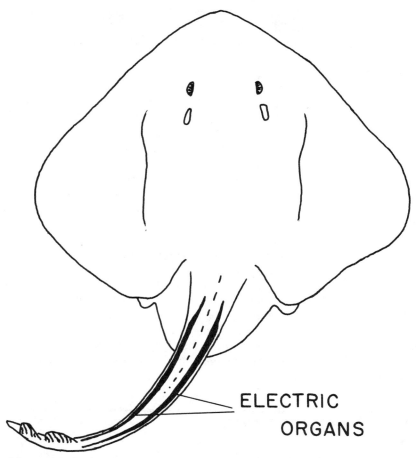

ELECTRIC
ORGANS

Figure 11–6. Location of the caudal electric organs of skates.

(Chapter 5). Perhaps buried skates, when threatened by a predatory shark zeroing in on their normal electric fields, discharge their electric organs and present a suddenly altered electric "picture" to the predator. Even the weak discharge of the skate electric organ produces voltages capable of saturating and jamming the extraordinary electrosensitive ampullary system of the marauding shark. Or the pattern of discharge could present a sudden and unexpected electric field array that could startle the shark and cause it to abandon its attack.

235   This scenario is, of course, armchair speculation. No evidence exists to support it, but it suggests a function for the skate electric organ while providing an explanation for the rarity of skate consumption by sharks. Above all, it highlights how little we understand about the relationships of elasmobranchs with the rest of their natural living world.

If stingrays are desirable as shark food, are other elasmobranchs palatable? Certainly the smaller galeomorphs, including the newborn young, are fair game for certain sharks. Bull sharks, in particular, are known for the frequency with which the remains of other sharks appear in their stomachs. Large sharks hooked on set lines are frequently attacked and mutilated by their peers.

The relationships sharks have with their predators, their symbionts, and their prey are complex, and our knowledge of these relationships is fragmentary at best. Indeed, our understanding of most aspects of shark biology—although much improved in the past 20 years—leaves a great deal of room for future study. People will continue to be fascinated by these fishes, for they will continue to evoke a sense of drama and mystery in the onlooker. Scientists will continue to probe their biology, for sharks will continue to provide marvelous examples of morphological, physiological, and behavioral processes. In the next 20 years we will know much more about them. But the elasmobranch fishes will continue to amaze us, for if we have learned anything about them, it is that as our knowledge of sharks deepens, it exposes ever more elegant levels of biological adaptation.

ADDITIONAL READING

Bennett, M.L.V. "Electric organs." In *Fish Physiology*, vol. 5, ed. W.S. Hoar and D.J. Randall, 347–491. New York: Academic Press, 1971.

Benz, G.W. "Tissue proliferations associated with *Nemesis lamna* Risso, 1826 (Copepoda: Eudactylinidae) infestations on the gill filaments of shortfin makos (*Isurus oxyrinchus* Rafinesque)." *J. Fish Diseases*, 1980, no. 3 (1980), 443–446.

Campbell, R.A. "Parasitism in the deep sea." In *The Sea*, vol. 8, ed. G.T. Rowe, 245–288. New York: John Wiley & Sons, 1983.

Cressey, R.F. "Caligoid copepods parasitic on sharks of the Indian Ocean." *Proceeding of the U.S. National Mus.*, 121 (1967), 1–21.

Cressey, R.F., and E.A. Lachner. "The parasitic copepod diet and life history of diskfishes (Echeneidae)." *Copeia,* 1970, no. 2 (1970), 310–318.

Grundfest, H.A. "Comparative physiology of electric organs of elasmobranch fishes." In *Sharks, Skates, and Rays,* ed. P.W. Gilbert, R.F. Mathewson, and D.P. Rall, 399–432. Baltimore: The Johns Hopkins Press, 1967.

Keyes, R.S. "Sharks: An unusual example of cleaning symbiosis." *Copeia,* 1982, no. 1 (1982), 225–227.

Smith, J.W., and J.V. Merriner. "Association of cobia, *Rachycentron canadum,* with cownose ray, *Rhinoptera bonasus.'' Estuaries,* 5, no. 3 (1982), 240–242.

Yamaguti, S. *Parasitic Copepoda and Branchiura of Fishes.* New York: Interscience Publishers, 1963.

Appendix

COMMON AND SCIENTIFIC NAMES

Atlantic Angel Shark	*Squatina dumerili*
Atlantic Manta	*Manta birostris*
Atlantic Sharpnose Shark	*Rhizoprionodon terraenovae*
Atlantic Torpedo	*Torpedo nobiliana*
Australian School Shark	*Galeorhinus australis*
Barndoor Skate	*Raja laevis*
Basking Shark	*Cetorhinus maximus*
Bigeye Thresher Shark	*Alopias superciliosus*
Black Dogfish	*Centroscyllium fabricii*
Black Whaler	*Carcharhinus obscurus*
Blacktip Shark	*Carcharhinus limbatus*
Blacktip Reef Shark	*Carcharhinus melanopterus*
Blue Shark	*Prionace glauca*
Bonnethead	*Sphyrna tiburo*
Bramble Shark	*Echinorhinus brucus*
Bull Shark	*Carcharhinus leucas*
Bullnose Ray	*Myliobatis freminvillei*
Butterfly Rays	*Gymnura* species
Carpet Sharks	sharks of the family Orectolobidae
Catsharks	sharks of the family Scyliorhinidae
Chimaera	*Hydrolagus collei*
Clearnose Skate	*Raja eglanteria*
Cookie-cutter Shark	*Isistius brasiliensis*
Cownosed Ray	*Rhinoptera bonasus*

239

Dusky Shark	*Carcharhinus obscurus*
Eagle Ray	*Aetobatus narinari*
False Catshark	*Pseudotriakis microdon*
Frill Shark	*Chlamydoselachus anguineus*
Galapagos Shark	*Carcharhinus galapagensis*
Ganges River Shark	*(Carcharhinus?) gangeticus*
Goblin Shark	*Mitsukurina owstoni*
Gray Reef Shark	*Carcharhinus amblyrhynchos*
Gray Smoothhound	*Mustelus californicus*
Great Hammerhead	*Sphyrna mokarran*
Greenland Shark	*Somniosus microcephalus*
Horn Shark	*Heterodontus francisci*
Largetooth Sawfish	*Pristis perotteti*
Leopard Shark	*Triakis semifasciata*
Lemon Shark	*Negaprion brevirostris*
Little Skate	*Raja erinacea*
Longfinned Mako	*Isurus paucus*
Mackerel Sharks	sharks of the family Lamnidae
Megamouth	*Megachasma pelagios*
Night Shark	*Carcharhinus signatus*
Nurse Shark	*Ginglymostoma cirratum*
Oceanic Whitetip Shark	*Carcharhinus longimanus*
Pacific Electric Ray	*Torpedo californica*
Pacific Lemon Shark	*Negaprion acutidens*
Pacific Manta	*Manta hamiltoni*
Pacific Sleeper Shark	*Somniosus pacificus*
Porbeagle	*Lamna nasus*
Port Jackson Shark	*Heterodontus portjacksoni*
Portuguese Shark	*Centroscymnus coelolepis*
Ragged-tooth Shark	*Odontaspis ferox*
Requiem Sharks	sharks of the family Carcharhinidae
Roughtail Stingray	*Dasyatis centroura*
Round Stingray	*Urolophus halleri*

Salmon Shark	*Lamna ditropis*
Sandbar Shark	*Carcharhinus plumbeus*
Sand Tiger Shark	*Odontaspis taurus*
Sawsharks	sharks of the family Pristiophoridae
Scalloped Hammerhead	*Sphyrna lewini*
Sevengill Shark	*Notorhynchus maculatus*
Shortfin Mako	*Isurus oxyrinchus*
Shovelnose Guitarfish	*Rhinobatos productus*
Silky Shark	*Carcharhinus falciformis*
Sixgill Shark	*Hexanchus griseus*
Smooth Dogfish	*Mustelus canis*
Smooth Hammerhead	*Sphyrna zygaena*
Soupfin Shark	*Galeorhinus zyopterus*
Southern Stingray	*Dasyatis americana*
Spinner Shark	*Carcharhinus brevipinna*
Spiny Dogfish	*Squalus acanthias*
Spiny Butterfly Ray	*Gymnura altavela*
Spotted Dogfish	*Scyliorhinus canicula*
Swell Shark	*Cephaloscyllium ventriosum*
Thornback	*Platyrhinoidis triseriata*
Thornback Skate	*Raja clavata*
Thorny Skate	*Raja radiata*
Tiger Shark	*Galeocerdo cuvier*
Whale Shark	*Rhiniodon typus*
Whaler Sharks	sharks of the genus *Carcharhinus*
White Shark	*Carcharodon carcharias*
White Spotted Stingaree	*Urolophus paucimaculatus*
Whitetip Reef Shark	*Triaenodon obesus*
Winter Skate	*Raja ocellata*
Wobbegongs	sharks of the genus *Orectolobus*
Yellow Stingray	*Urolophus jamaicensis*